WITHOUT HINDSIGHT

WITHOUT HINDSIGHT

A HISTORY OF THE PROGRESS TRUST

1943–2005

RICHARD RITCHIE

First published in Great Britain in 2018 by OS Publishing

Edited, designed and produced by Tandem Publishing
http://tandempublishing.yolasite.com/

ISBN: 978-1-5272-2809-2

10 9 8 7 6 5 4 3 2 1

A CIP catalogue record for this book is available from the British Library.

Printed and bound in Great Britain by CPI Group (UK) Ltd, Croydon CR0 4YY.

Contents

Acknowledgements

The first debt of gratitude should, on the Progress Trust's behalf, be given to Bridget Lakin for keeping and preserving all the PT's minute books and extant documents at her house in the Isle of Wight. Without them, this history could never have been written. Her personal experience of the Progress Trust was invaluable and surpassed all others.

The PT archives are now kept and maintained in the Conservative Party Archive in the Bodleian Library, University of Oxford and I am grateful to Mr Jeremy McIlwaine for all his advice and assistance in this connection.

I am indebted to Lord Lexden, Official Historian of the Conservative Party, for his advice and encouragement in writing this history. Any errors therein contained would be absent were he the author.

Finally, my thanks to Sam Carter for all his editorial advice and assistance. This is the third book we have worked on together, and his generous involvement on all three has been indispensable.

Any factual errors or omissions are my responsibility alone. I decided at an early stage to quote extensively from the PT's minutes verbatim, even when they may have contained errors of name or fact. I attempted to correct the most obvious of them, but some have probably slipped through the net. And if Members of the Trust who are still alive do not recognise some of the views attributed to them, I hope they will appreciate that anything recorded in this history is not offered as an infallible record of their opinions, but as a small addition to the history of the Conservative Party as a whole. Nothing should be held against them.

INTRODUCTION

The Progress Trust (PT) exerted influence within the Parliamentary Conservative Party for over fifty years. But the purpose of writing this history is not to exaggerate this influence or its political importance – considerable though it was at times. It is more to fulfil an obligation. For over twenty years, I was the Trust's Research Officer. This involved writing each week, when Parliament was sitting, an Ebury Research Note – so called because the PT had once been based in London's Ebury Street – intended for discussion at the Trust's weekly meeting. These discussions never leaked to the press, and the Trust's MPs were therefore free to speak without restraint. My reward was to introduce the subject, and hear their conclusions which were frequently reported to the Chief Whip. It provided me with unusual and privileged access to a senior group of Conservative MPs whose opinions mattered, even though few of them were in a position to influence policy directly. I felt at the time that, one day, this untapped archive of Tory backbench opinion, expressed privately and without the benefit of hindsight, would deserve a more permanent record. After the Trust ceased to exist and its files (which had been read by nobody other than the Trust's secretary and previous Chairmen) came into my possession, I was able to write the history which I had always thought the PT, and Conservative Party, deserved.

Anyone looking through old guides to the House of Commons will be struck by how unfamiliar are most of the names. Members of Parliament who were respected and well known in their day can quickly be forgotten – even those who reached the Cabinet. And yet, many of them were once influential and some were even famous. If that is true of MPs in general, it is especially true of Conservative Members of Parliament who belonged to the PT. It was formed in 1943 with four basic purposes: to encourage closer links between industry and Parliament; to increase Parliament's general understanding of industrial matters; to assist Conservative Members of Parliament in their scrutiny of legislation; and to champion free enterprise, although interpretations of what this meant in practice could lead to disagreement. As the years went by, the PT's interests widened, and at its peak its opinion was sought and its influence was exercised across a wide political field.

The PT was also a dining club. Since 1945, there have been a number of influential Conservative dining clubs, but the PT was different. For a start, 'dining' was not its primary purpose, even though few Parliamentary dining clubs existed for so long or possessed such ample financial resources. Discussing politics over dinner with Cabinet or Shadow Cabinet Ministers was an adjunct, especially in its early days, to the much more important task of policy formulation and research. When the PT was formed, it operated from its own substantial premises in Great College Street, and employed permanent staff. Its mission was to halt the socialist advance and provide a research facility for its members. Even after its research capability was cut back for financial reasons, the PT continued to operate in a distinct way.

An MP would be invited to become a member by the PT's Chairman, after soundings were taken amongst existing members. For a large part of its life, until Parliament and the Conservative Party changed, membership of the PT was much sought-after by those aware of its existence. No MP could apply for membership; it was by invitation only, and any candidate could be 'blackballed' by an existing member. Most shades of Conservative opinion were embraced, provided they were of no threat to the existence of a Conservative Government. The two unpardonable offences were disloyalty to the Conservative Party and unauthorised leaks to the press.

The PT was unattracted by dogma, and could simplistically be described as loyalist, traditional and conservative with a small 'c'. It was not in existence to champion radical reform, yet its role on occasions was contentious – never more so than in the aftermath of the Suez crisis when the PT was accused of undermining Rab Butler's chances of becoming Prime Minister. This was one of the rare occasions when proceedings of the Trust attracted the interest of the press. Sometimes, the PT was branded as 'right-wing'. More accurately, it favoured a strand of Toryism which was uncomplicated, evolutionary and patriotic. No existing or past member of the Government could be a member of the PT. But many PT members over the years joined the Government, and two – Sir Alec Douglas-Home and David Cameron – became Prime Minister. Later, the rules were relaxed and former Ministers were allowed to rejoin the Trust once their Government careers were over; but this was because by this stage the demise of independent, 'old-school' MPs, often with private means, had led to a shortage of suitable recruits. (It was not until 1986 that the first female member of the PT, Virginia Bottomley, was elected.)

Originally, the lack of ministerial experience within the PT was due more to lack of ambition than ability. Even as Conservative MPs became more full-time and professional, there was until 1997 a sufficient number of Conservative backbenchers to provide the Trust with suitable members. How this came about was explained by Sir Paul Bryan, a former Chairman of the PT, in a conversation with the author.

He believed that so long as an MP considered the privilege of belonging to the House of Commons as sufficient, he or she would be content and fulfilled as a mere backbencher. The problems arose, in his view, when this was not enough, and ambition for ministerial office intervened. Few members of the PT were in danger of falling into this trap – although in its latter years the PT was also keen to recruit 'high-flyers' from the younger MPs.

Those in the PT destined to remain backbenchers were not deprived of influence. On the contrary, many were office holders of other important Conservative Backbench Committees – in particular the 1922 Committee – and thus able to command a hearing at all levels of the Conservative Party. When the PT was at its most influential during the 1950s and 1960s, some 50 per cent of the officers of the 1922 Committee and over 60 per cent of its Executive Committee were also members of the Progress Trust – indeed between the years of 1943 and 2005, six of the thirteen MPs who chaired the 1922 Committee were also members of the Progress Trust.

Historians debate whether history repeats itself. True or not, the PT's history illustrates how past political battles are frequently refought by future generations. In economic areas especially, the minutes of PT meetings leave the reader with a constant sense of déjà vu. The economic and industrial debates, for example, which dominated so much of Mrs Thatcher's period as Prime Minister were often a replay of the economic arguments within the Conservative Party immediately following the Second World War. The extent to which the 'Butskellite' consensus should govern economic policy was a question overhanging the PT's discussions throughout its existence. In particular, the problems experienced by Mrs Thatcher with her own colleagues in introducing her economic reforms – especially during her first term as Prime Minister – are more easily understood when seen from the perspective of a cautious and conventional Progress Trust. Their general mood at the time was unhelpful to Mrs Thatcher. The PT was never a hotbed of 'Thatcherism'.

How and when a significant political issue was first identified and regarded by politicians of a past generation is always of interest, and the PT's history provides many such examples. Take immigration. The PT's minutes record the first time the word 'coloured' is mentioned in a discussion; how the transition from Empire to Commonwealth merged with the need to control immigration and define British citizenship; and the moment when it dawned upon the Trust's MPs that the control of immigration had also become an issue of European competence.

Europe is another constant theme. The Conservative Party's disagreements over Britain's membership of the Common Market when it was first proposed – and which have grown in intensity ever since – are played out in the PT's deliberations. It is possible to chart the progress of this issue as witnessed by senior Conservative Members of Parliament, most of whom were supporters of the concept of a Common Market but who had increasing difficulty in reconciling this with its eventual political implications.

The issues of Europe and immigration are so important and relevant today that they have been given separate chapters in this history – with, some may think, an undue emphasis upon the influence of Enoch Powell. As his archivist, I am open to the accusation of partiality. There is, however, an objective justification for the attention paid to his views in this history. For ten to fifteen years he was a crucial and divisive figure in the Conservative Party who challenged its philosophy, its record in Government, and caused almost unparalleled turmoil over immigration and Europe. How any Conservative reacted to Powell during this period was almost a litmus test of their Conservatism.

Other issues which were considered important at the time now feel as if they belonged to a different world. For example, the PT was strongly opposed in 1964 to the repeal of Resale Price Maintenance. The Trust considered calling for Edward Heath's resignation over the matter, and believed it was a major contributor to the Conservative Party's election defeat of 1964. Yet today, few would know what the initials RPM even stood for. It is strange to think that an obscure policy to protect small shopkeepers by maintaining prices above a minimum level – because that was the purpose of Resale Price Maintenance – was once regarded as sacrosanct by a section of the Conservative Party.

The PT could sometimes be naïve, and their predictions disproved by events. On other occasions, the Government would have been well advised to have heeded their warnings and advice. Although the PT might sometimes have been guilty of defending class interests, its deepest antipathy was to class warfare and its fondest wish was for national unity.

Generally, the PT was not in business to come up with original thoughts. Its strength was based on its common sense and a sound judgement of character. Members of the PT knew what was going on in the constituencies; their contacts with the outside world were superior to most in the Conservative Party; and the fact that they were loyalists meant that any disagreement they expressed was taken seriously by a Conservative Government. Their very discretion gave them a right to be heard.

In this history, the views attributed to individual members are those recorded in the PT's minutes or in Hansard. The latter cannot be contested; the former might be. The minutes were approved by the Chairman, but never read out formally at meetings; and while mention is often made of an 'agreed' position, no vote was taken at meetings, and different views were often expressed. Nevertheless, on the major issues, PT members were normally of like mind. Despite the informality of the meetings, and the lack of process, their conclusions were seldom disputed and the Chairman was always trusted to speak on behalf of members.

Some of the discussions recorded in this history are of greater importance than others, if only because some meetings were much better attended. PT members could be forgiven for having better things to do than discuss an obscure topic chosen by their researchers. But their political antennae were well tuned, and it was rare for an important development to be missed. This explains why only on certain occasions does this account record the names of those attending meetings. Even if a meeting was poorly attended, the views expressed on most topics were likely to be shared by those who were absent. During the Trust's early years, this impression of unity is strengthened by constant reference in the minutes to a member's military rank. Many of the original PT members had distinguished war records, and for them their military service was probably more important than their involvement in politics. Even for those who came after, a shared sense of patriotism put into perspective any internal disagreement.

Finally, the history of the PT makes sense only in the context of the Conservative Party's history as a whole. And yet, this is not a history of the Conservative Party. It is an account of how a representative group of senior Conservative

MPs viewed the prospects, personalities or policies of their Party and Government at certain crucial moments and without the benefit of hindsight. The PT was concerned with the 'bread and butter' of politics. The fact that it no longer exists should not blind us to the reality that, during the life of any Parliament, there are members of the House of Commons unknown to the general public and destined to be forgotten by history who, during their time, kept the show on the road. They deserve acknowledgement and respect.

1

THE PROGRESS TRUST'S FORMATION

"Our policy is everything for the war and, after the war is won, fair, free review under normal political conditions." (Winston Churchill)

"The Progress Trust: Oh, they've got money." (Enoch Powell)

On Tuesday 30th March 1943, the House of Commons met at its usual wartime hour of 11am in order to save fuel. The Prime Minister, Winston Churchill, was present to respond to a question concerning the right of members of the armed forces to appear on the electoral register for a pending by-election. Churchill gave a very short and dismissive reply which went down badly in the House. The day's main debate concerned India, preceded by oral questions which covered subjects mostly pertaining to the war – including "Boiler Suits and Overalls", parachute pay, the Home Guard, and military bands. Later that afternoon, at 4.30pm, the Progress Trust (PT) held its first Council meeting in a room at the House of Commons.

An unremarkable fact in itself, save as a reminder that even when fighting a world war domestic political considerations were never far from mind. Wartime Members of Parliament may have spoken, when entitled, "in military uniform", but they didn't just talk about the war – they also discussed the minutiae of politics, and the policies which would follow once the war finally ended. Nobody knew in 1943 when precisely this would be, or for how long a General Election would therefore be delayed. Had it not been for the war, the country should have gone to the polls by November 1940 at the latest. But although hostilities were to continue for more than two years, by 1943 both sides of the political divide were preparing for the resumption of normal politics – although some were preparing more energetically than others. Winston Churchill said in the House of Commons "Our policy is everything for the war and, after the war is won, fair, free review under normal political conditions" (Hansard, 6th April 1943 c. 491). Unfortunately, this was not how everyone in the Labour Party saw it. In the words of the Progress Trust's first and full-time Research Officer, Harold (Harry) Fells:

> The Progress Trust was founded in 1943 at a time when the Conservative Party and Central Office were obeying, to the full, the spirit of the political wartime truce between the Parties but when the Labour Party, particularly through the speeches and writings of Mr Herbert Morrison, was breaking it. (Memo dated 1st July 1955)

The founding members of the PT respected this truce, but knew that it placed the Conservative Party at a disadvantage. They sensed in 1943 that not all was well for their side, and that the tide of public opinion was moving against them. It was to combat this trend that the PT was originally formed, and their plan of action was to 'educate' and influence both their Conservative colleagues in Parliament, and political opinion more generally.

The first members of the PT Council – all senior Conservative Members of Parliament – were:

Sir Alexander Galloway Erskine-Hill, MP, Chairman
Lieut. Comm. Rupert Brabner, DSO, MP
Mr Henry Brooke, MP
Captain Edward Charles Cobb, DSO, MP
Col. Harold Paton Mitchell, MP
Mr Spencer Summers, MP
Sir Douglas Thomson, Bart., MP
Mr Henry Urmston Willink, MC, KC, MP

And their first action on 30th March was to appoint the following additional members:

Commander Thomas Galbraith, MP
Major E. G. R. Lloyd, MP
Mr Kenneth Pickthorn, MP
Mr G. I. Woodham-Smith[*]

At subsequent meetings, further appointments to the Council were made and a full list is contained in Appendix I. In addition, three Trustees were appointed:

George Francis Baron Milne of Salonika & Rubislaw, GCB,
     GCMG
William George Baron Tyrrell of Avon
Lieutenant-Colonel The Hon. Arthur Murray, CMG, DSO

The Trust's Chairman and moving spirit was Alex Erskine-Hill[†] who, at this time, was also Chairman of the 1922

---

[*] G. I. Woodham-Smith of Messrs. Richards, Butler & Co., solicitors, Cunard House, 88 Leadenhall St, EC.

[†] Sir Alexander Erskine-Hill (1894–1947) was the Member of Parliament for Edinburgh North between 1935 and 1945, when he lost his seat in the

Committee. This automatically gave him influence in the highest circles of the Conservative Party. Many of his successors would also combine membership of the PT with senior office in this most important forum of Conservative backbench opinion.

The objects of the PT were encapsulated in a Trust Deed, executed on 26th March 1943:

OBJECTS

1. The objects of The Progress Trust are to promote the advancement of education and in particular political and sociological education and to promote the study of –

(a) economic and industrial conditions with a view to the fostering of industrial and agricultural prosperity and the avoidance of unemployment.

(b) the contribution of individual effort to National Prosperity, individual liberty and the welfare of the British people.

(c) the machinery of Government best adapted to further and safeguard democratic principles.

(d) the history of the development of constitutional principles and their contribution to the improvement of social conditions.

(e) the relationship between Science and the State.

(f) civics and the theory of Government.

(g) the welfare of the British Empire.

(h) the factors affecting the formation of public opinion including the influence of the Press, the theatre, the cinemas and broadcasting.

(i) the inter-relation of social progress in the United Kingdom with conditions in the post-war World.

Labour landslide. He was a Scottish Unionist having formerly been a Liberal of the free-market, unionist persuasion. He became Chairman of the 1922 Committee in December 1940.

and to promote and encourage informed discussion on all or any of the above subjects.

The emphasis here was upon education and well-informed debate. In a later document (June 1948) it was stated:

> As will be seen from the Objects of the Trust, its principal function is educational. This function it proposes to implement in two ways:
> (a) By informed speeches in the House of Commons, and
> (b) By speeches and lectures in the Country: the publication of pamphlets and books: and by articles and letters in the Press.
> Education of Members of Parliament is no less necessary than education of the Public. It is essential that when Members speak in the House they should be accurate, well informed, and have a thorough understanding of their subject...

Long before they became fashionable in the 1960s, words such as "sociological" and "civics" were surely included to demonstrate a modernist and academically detached approach to the evolving political debate. But stating the mission in such pseudo-scientific terms was a distraction from the main political objective of influencing political thought in a Conservative direction, and of counteracting the missionary zeal of the PT's socialist opponents.

Neither could clever words disguise the PT's social origins. Sir Peter Hordern,* Chairman of the PT between 1987 and 1994, described their background in a note for new members as follows:

---

* Sir Peter Hordern (b. 1929) was the Member of Parliament for Horsham from 1964–1997. He was Chairman of the PT between and 1987 and 1994.

They were the knights of the shires, often landed gentry, who came to Westminster from their estates out of a sense of duty and service. They were the ultra-loyal core of the Conservative Party, somewhat resistant to change, many of them with distinguished war records.

This patrician element became less important over time, but it was always evident. As Sir Peter himself explained to Michael Howard in November 1992 when inviting him to address the PT over dinner as Leader of the Conservative Party:

> You may know that the PT is the senior backbench dining club, in terms of longevity and quality! It was formerly the dining club of the Knights of the Shires, but there not being enough of us to go round, we now have PPSs and old sweats like me. We are right at the centre of the Party, drawing our membership from all wings. We would like to think we act as a steadying force, and rather better briefed than most.

As mentioned by Sir Peter, the PT was also a dining club, and was described in one of its early historical notes, perhaps inaccurately, as "the oldest Conservative Parliamentary dining club." Certainly, the regular dinners held by the PT were an important part of its existence and gave members the chance to discuss politics informally with leading members of the Conservative Party. But unlike many of the dining clubs which were to follow, the PT began life as a policy and research organisation at the service of its members and for the promotion of ideas further afield. Indeed, in its early days, the PT sought to fulfil the same function as the Conservative Research Department which had been shut down in 1940 and with all of its furniture placed in storage.* The dinners were part of the process but not the PT's main rationale, and this was true for most of its existence.

This is one reason why the PT's first requirement in 1943 was to acquire suitable premises and staff – not a light undertaking in wartime. Apart from the very first meetings which were held in the House of Commons, their first lodging was an office in Victoria Street, comprising three large rooms and a small additional one. But this was merely a stopgap until the acquisition of new premises at 16 Great College Street in July was finalised. This was problematical because "The Ministry of Parks and Planning ... have an eye on these premises and may requisition them." Once this threat was removed, the property became the PT's main home for the next six years and satisfied the requirements which the PT Council had set for themselves, i.e.:

a) Within the Division area
b) Available on a lease of 7, 14 or 21 years at our option
c) With a good size boardroom
d) With accommodation not only for offices, but for a resident housekeeper and a couple of emergency bedrooms.

It was a fine eighteenth-century house, but the Trust was never again to occupy such grand premises, once it became too expensive to maintain.

Not that they were considered extravagant at the time, fully according with the advice of Kenneth Pickthorn† "that

---

* Tory Policy-Making: The Conservative Research Department 1929–2009, ed. Alistair Cooke.

† Sir Kenneth Pickthorn (1892–1975) was the Member of Parliament for Cambridge University 1935–1950 and then, on the abolition of university

there should be a modest start in accommodation". The main requirement was that the premises should be in close proximity to the House of Commons "despite the fact that after the war, when motor transport is again freely available, it will be possible to be some further distance from the House and yet get to it for Division." Erskine-Hill was insistent that the PT premises (including its library) "should be open at all times throughout the day" and for the purpose of providing "busy Members with accommodation for dictating to their secretaries and also for the provision after the war of lunch or dinner if other urgent occasions arose".

Early PT documents make very little reference to the war. In so far as it impinged at all, it was to cause inconvenience and frustration. The impact of war damage, the difficulties in effecting repairs and of equipping adequately the office – such as the purchase of one Remington and two Underwood typewriters at a cost of £116-9s-3d on 19th May 1943 – were the constant problems of the day. The office manager, Mrs Hornsby, reminded the Business Committee "of the difficulty of obtaining furniture (whether standard office equipment or otherwise)". Dealings with the British Window Cleaning Company, Miss Fine's Employment Agency, and arguments over the Commercial Two-Part Tariff submitted by Central London Electricity Ltd were some of the mundane matters demanding attention. Another example of bureaucratic control was the requirement to apply formally to the electricity company for permission to place an electric fire in any room "where there might be some other form of heating available" – such were the wartime regulations of London

---

constituencies, the Carlton Division of Nottinghamshire 1950–1966.
He was an academic and was Parliamentary Secretary to the Ministry of Education 1951–1954.

which Conservatives suspected socialists of wishing to continue and duplicate in peacetime.

The premises also possessed a basement which, it was decided, "should be made suitable for living quarters and that, subject to a satisfactory reference from his present employers, Mr Redknap and his wife should be engaged as housekeepers at a wage of £2 per week each, with free lighting and heating". In July 1943, it was estimated that "When we move to Gt. College Street it would appear that with the present staff the expenses will run to between £5,500 and £6,000 p.a." This would be equivalent to some £200,000 p.a. today – a considerable sum for a political organisation with no history, setting out in wartime.

No reference to actual hostilities appears in the PT records until 30th June 1944 when Thomas Galbraith* mentioned "doodle bugs still coming over". A few days earlier, the Business Committee minutes record that "The question of paying Perrot [the new caretaker] for fire-watching was raised and after discussion it was remitted to the Secretary to inform him that as this was his home the Trust did not feel obliged to pay him anything." In the same meeting it was mentioned that another member of staff, Mrs Woodhouse, "had been bombed out and had moved from London" so that it would be necessary to replace her.

When I first became associated with the Trust and mentioned this to Enoch Powell,† his immediate response was

---

* Thomas Dunlop Galbraith, later Lord Strathclyde (1891–1985), was the Member of Parliament for Glasgow Pollock 1940–1955 and was Chairman of both the PT's Political Committee (1945–1951) and Council (1955–1982).

† Enoch Powell (1912–1998) was the Member of Parliament for Wolverhampton South West between 1950 and 1974, and South Down

"Oh, they've got money." Raising money was always a necessity. By the end of July 1943, financial contributions to the Trust totalled £19,000 – the sum of £5,000 to be retained by Trustees against their liabilities in respect of 16 Great College Street – and by November this had increased to some £24,000. Not long after, in March 1944, a memorandum stated that "Our immediate objects should be to create a fund of £100,000 and in addition an annual promised subscription list of at least £12,000 per annum either by seven-year guaranteed or by definite promises. This is a minimum for the Trust to be effective." The Trust aspired to build up a capital fund of over £4 million in today's money and a guaranteed income of over £500,000 per annum. Money was made available from the Trustee Account towards the costs and activities of the PT.

These very early beginnings of the PT were described by Thomas Galbraith, later Lord Strathclyde, in a letter to Sir Paul Bryan[*] (17th February 1980), who was at the time Chairman of the PT's Council. This letter sets out, more conversationally, the process of the PT's formation described above:

> I was invited to join the Political Committee early in 1943, when Erskine-Hill, then the Chairman of the 1922 Committee, was the Chairman. At that time the members of the Council were very distinguished people representing those who had financed us.

---

between 1974 and 1992. For a period, he was perhaps the most famous and controversial politician of his generation. For a very brief period he was also a member of the PT. (See Chapter 5).

[*] Sir Paul Bryan (1913–2004) was the Member of Parliament for Howden between 1955 and 1983, and subsequently Boothferry 1983–1987.

At that time the PT occupied a little office in Victoria Street, with one Political Assistant and a couple of typists. As money came in from people in Industry, it moved to 16 Great College Street. The staff grew with our move. There were three well paid people versed in Politics, Economics, etc. and with connections with Industry and the Press. '16' was opened with a party to which the Press, etc. were invited.

The Chairman had a Secretary, as a PA. I was appointed Treasurer and provided with a Secretary. There was a Cashier and there were four Typists plus a Caretaker who also kept the house clean and tidy – assisted by her husband and daughter.

The PT very quickly established itself, though it never advertised itself – unlike another Group which came into being a little later called 'Young Conservatives'* or something of that kind, whose leading figures were Peter Thorneycroft, Quintin Hogg, David Eccles, etc.. Perhaps they were too clever or ambitious but it didn't last long.

No record exists of exactly who financed the PT at its inception, but by October 1943 the Business Committee was discussing "who might be approached in reference to further finance". A "satisfactory meeting" between Erskine-Hill, Galbraith and Major Lloyd and "a group of influential businessmen in Glasgow" is referred to at around this time.†
Others approached included Sir Harry McGowan of ICI, Sir Robert Sinclair of the Imperial Tobacco Company and Sir Richard Ferry of the Aircraft Industry. These approaches are indicative of the industrial support which the PT was

---

* This must be a reference to the Tory Reform Committee – see Chapter 2.

† These were: Messrs. T. H. Coates, Crawford Hogarth, Henry Lithgow and Sir George Mitchell, all proposed by the General Manager of the Union Bank.

keen to encourage. Sometimes financial assistance was forthcoming from MPs themselves such as Sir Archibald Southby* who in return was allowed "the use of one of the spare rooms on terms to be communicated to him by the Chairman". In April 1945, the PT was insistent that the list of subscribers need not and should not be divulged to the Inspector of Taxes.

By early 1944, the Trust employed three principal members of staff, namely the already mentioned Mr Fells, the PT's Research Officer; Mr Chaloner who attended the House every day to monitor its proceedings and act as the PT's public relations officer; and Mrs Boschen who served as secretary to the Council and Committees, keeping very discreet (and sparse) minutes of their proceedings. She also acted as i/c of the PT office as a whole, which comprised an additional seven clerical posts, including a librarian (Miss Lyall). Fells was paid an annual salary of £1,100 which, net after tax, left him with £744 and, as he said, no scope for saving. Nevertheless, £1,100 p.a. was equivalent to nearly £50,000 p.a. today. Fells had previously been a journalist with *The Times of India*. Although Bridget Lakin – who would become the Trust's most loyal, indispensable and longest-serving member of staff – had a good relationship with him, she described him as "a very difficult man" and "very insecure".

PT Members of Parliament were scrupulous over their expenses. On 16th September 1943, Erskine-Hill explained in a letter to Galbraith how he intended to ensure that he was not "in a better position financially than I was before the Progress Trust was formed". Thus, he paid for part of his secretary's salary at the PT out of his own pocket because she

---

* Sir Archibald Southby (1886–1969), formerly an officer in the Royal Navy, was Conservative MP for Epsom 1928–1947.

helped him with some of his constituency work. In addition, so long as he was "the loser rather than the gainer", he would not charge for PT telephone calls at home even though these exceeded his personal telephone calls from the PT office; and "with regard to luncheons and dinners undertaken with outsiders, the test must be whether the object of the luncheon or dinner is mainly in the interest of the Progress Trust." Later in the year, any planned lunch or dinner required the approval of the Business Committee before going ahead.

These were distinct from the PT's club dinners, the first of which took place at the Dorchester Hotel on 1st June 1943 where, in Galbraith's words, "one of our supporters had a suite which he put at our disposal." According to Galbraith, "We had dinners every month or so with the Party Leaders." In the files, however, these were not listed until 1947 when R. A. (Rab) Butler accepted the first of many invitations. As early as September 1943 "The Business Committee considered that the attention of the Council should be drawn to the entertainment bill, and particularly to the consumption of wine." As the war continued, the need for frugality increased and on 8th November the Business Committee "agreed that in the future, except on special occasions and at the discretion of Mr Erskine-Hill and Commander Galbraith, beer only should be served at PT dinners. The before-dinner drinks will be charged to members as heretofore."

At its inception, the two most important decision-making bodies of the Trust were the Council and the Business Committee – although it wouldn't be long before the Political Committee replaced both as the most visible and active part of the Trust. In the early years, there was a strict adherence to process and accountability. The Council consisted of fifteen members, nine of whom should be MPs. Its primary duty was to decide the political objectives and messages in accordance with the terms of the Trust Deed. As late as 1960, it was reaffirmed that the Council "… as a body are solely responsible for the PT. They delegate various matters to the Business and Political Committees but nevertheless the Council carries full responsibility for all decisions taken" (23rd November 1960). This would have included nominations for membership, and anything said to the Conservative Party's leadership of a political nature. The Trustees were there to provide independent oversight and scrutiny, while the Business Committee was expected to help raise money, oversee day-to-day expenditure and all matters relating to staff.

As the Trust's membership expanded, however, it was to the Political Committee where most matters were referred in practice and which became the focal point for discussing the political situation and for making representations. Although the Council's overall accountability was never formally removed, its political function was delegated entirely to the Political Committee. So long as the Trust had a significant establishment to maintain, the Business Committee also fulfilled an important function. By the 1970s, however, the Chairman of the Political Committee was responsible for everything, merely reporting to the Council twice or three times a year. Moreover, from 1982 the Chairman of the Council and Political Committee was the self-same person, ending all pretence of non-executive accountability. From this moment, the Political Committee was answerable only to itself, choosing its own members and making representations on its own behalf.

It is understandable why the rules of governance became lax. In the early years of the Trust, its ambitions were wide and the demands of the Trust Deed required the Council and

Trustees to provide external supervision and accountability. There were plenty of volunteers willing to give time and energy to the new undertaking. But as both time and volunteers became scarce, the Trust operated within the confines of the House of Commons and its energies became more concentrated upon Parliamentary proceedings.

At its birth, however, there was no limit to the PT's ambitions and its hopes of preparing the Conservative Party for the resumption of peacetime office once the war was won. By the end of 1943, the PT had been successfully established as a functioning, well-resourced political undertaking, capable of carrying out research, publishing pamphlets and other political material, and servicing the daily requirements of its individual MPs. As knowledge of its existence seeped out, PT membership became a sought-after privilege amongst Conservative MPs eligible and desirous of joining. Membership conferred status, and influence within the Conservative Parliamentary Party. Within a mere two years of its formation, the PT was firmly established on the political map.

2

EARLY POLITICAL OBJECTIVES

"The British point of view should be stressed and it must be pointed out that it is not wicked for our Government to think in terms of defending the legitimate interests of its own people, and that this island can only be defended by defending the Empire." (September 1943)

"Rule by regulation and bureaucratic control and interference, however necessary in war time, should NOT continue in Peace." (May 1944)

The PT's first task was to establish its Committees and modus operandi and, secondly, to articulate more clearly its core beliefs – although its existence and objectives were not announced to the press until 15ᵗʰ October 1943.

The first task was more straightforward than the second. As mentioned in the previous chapter, one of the Trust's objectives was to increase the knowledge not only of its own members, but of Conservative MPs in general, in order to enhance their performance in Parliamentary debates. The PT's Committee and research work was largely directed towards this purpose.

But in propounding its core beliefs, the PT's objective was more party-political – to fight what it feared was an inexorable, nationwide drift towards socialism with no respect for the commercial and economic realities of post-war reconstruction. In this regard, it was sometimes easier to itemise policies which the PT opposed, rather than those it advocated.

Partly, this is because the PT never at any time favoured a doctrinaire approach. To the PT's critics this could, on occasions, be interpreted as lack of principle and backbone – especially during the Thatcher years. But fundamentally, it amounted to a suspicion of any Conservative who might allow his principles to bring down, or make less likely, a Conservative Government. Electoral defeat was always the outcome to be avoided. The PT never subscribed to the theory that, in order to perfect policies, a period in Opposition might prove beneficial.

Moreover, the PT was a broad church and if a particular policy was considered internally divisive it was left alone. When, for example, disagreement arose in April 1943 over famine relief in Europe, the Chairman ruled "that where such cleavage of opinion was evident on any particular question, it should not be pursued in the first place as a subject on behalf of the Council." The problem did not frequently arise: on major issues of principle, a consensus was normally achieved without difficulty. Nevertheless, the Chairman's ruling remained in force throughout the PT's existence.

But while there might be differences of opinion over tactics or which areas to prioritise, the PT was united in its conviction that the Labour Party was more zealous and effective than Conservatives in preparing for post-war politics. Indeed, on 23rd March 1944 one of the PT's members, Wing Commander Archibald James,* read a letter to the Political Committee which he had sent three years earlier to twenty-two Conservative MPs serving abroad "urging them to return to their Parliamentary duties". In other words, in 1941 a former soldier judged it to be as necessary for his

---

* Wing Commander Sir Archibald James was the Unionist MP for Wellingborough, 1931–45. He had served in the First World War.

fellow officers to fight socialism in the House of Commons as to fight fascism on the battlefield. The PT followed his example by sending a similar letter "not only to those serving abroad but to all Conservative members with official positions in this country which kept them from attending the House of Commons".

A related anxiety was the failure of the Conservative message to reach the armed forces. In January 1944 they and the auxiliary services were singled out by the PT as "the most important groups to be influenced and that serious efforts should be made to put the Conservative point of view before them". This required the PT's message to be clear and unambiguous. An unpublished statement of its core beliefs was agreed at a meeting of the PT Council held over two days on September 8th and 9th 1943. As the minutes of the meeting record:

> The Council agreed to expound the following arguments:
> (a) That peace and the maintenance of peace can be controlled only though commitments proportional to our power, and power is not only influence but actual force or the actual force possessed by Allied Governments on whom our Government can rely. The British point of view should be stressed and it must be pointed out that it is not wicked for our Government to think in terms of defending the legitimate interests of its own people, and that this island can only be defended by defending the Empire. These facts have been made all the clearer by the demonstration of what we have been through in this war. Having painted the picture of the British point of view it should be followed through by pointing out that we should not adopt foreign ideas (i.e. Russian) and in this way attack the Socialists and in particular the Communists.
> (b) The Council will advocate freedom from state control and

unnecessary planning as soon as possible, this involves a direct attack on Socialism.

(c) To urge that the standard of living can only be raised by increasing the productivity of our population and in particular by getting a fair share of foreign trade and transport.

The belief that "this island can only be defended by defending the Empire" was fundamental for most Conservatives of this generation, and to this extent domestic, defence and foreign considerations were inseparable. While the PT's main concern was domestic policy, Churchill's prosecution of the war did not escape scrutiny. An important member of the PT during this period was Kenneth Pickthorn who was the Member of Parliament for Cambridge University and was amongst those most suspicious of any attempted accommodation with socialist beliefs. His son, Henry Pickthorn, emphasised in a private conversation the significant degree of pre-war suspicion in which Churchill was held by many in the PT, including by his father. It was a suspicion which, as is well documented, persisted in certain sections of the Conservative Party throughout the war, and affected their judgement of Churchill's handling of both foreign and domestic affairs. Examples of the former recorded in the PT minutes include Churchill's treatment of King Peter of Yugoslavia and the accommodation made with Tito; and the failure to satisfy "Polish concerns over possible Frontier re-adjustments in Eastern Europe at the end of the War" as well as the eventual conclusions of Yalta in February 1945.

However, while PT members individually may have had reservations on the conduct of the war, it was not the Trust's priority to pass judgement in this sphere unless it also had domestic political impact, or when the welfare of those fighting was concerned. For example, in the first Parliamentary Resolution ever handed in to the Vote Office by PT MPs on 3rd June 1943, they affirmed:

> That this House is of the opinion that in the event of any member of the Fighting Forces being invalided, disabled or dying on service, the illness, disability or death shall be deemed to be attributable to military service unless the contrary is proved, and the person concerned or his dependant shall forthwith become entitled to such pensions as are payable on death or disability directly attributable to enemy action.

But while the PT had a natural affinity for the armed forces, it had a more detached understanding of the sort of peace for which this generation was fighting. The PT's basic position was captured in its proposed resolution to the annual meeting of the Conservative and Unionist Associations in May 1944:

> That as it is contrary to the National tradition, to the well established principles of Conservative policy, and a serious danger not only to the rights and liberties of the individual but also to family life, rule by regulation and bureaucratic control and interference, however necessary in war time, should NOT continue in Peace.

As time would show, this uncompromising statement was not necessarily shared by all Conservatives, let alone the country as a whole. State planning was in vogue, and many of the future Labour Government's policies were originally devised by Churchill's coalition Government, including Conservative Ministers. Sir William Beveridge, a member of the Liberal Party, was under intense PT scrutiny. He had been appointed in 1941 to head an inquiry into Social Insurance and Allied Services which reported in November 1942 and met with the Government's response in a White Paper published in 1944. While the Conservative Party may have shown less enthusiasm than Labour at Beveridge's proposals, they were far from being dismissed entirely. This alarmed certain members of the PT such as Pickthorn, and as early as 1943 there were intimations of the 'wet' versus 'dry' debate that dominated political discussion in the 'Thatcherite' years.

One of the earliest manifestations of this divide was the formation of another group of Conservative MPs at around this time called the Tory Reform Committee (TRC), mentioned in Lord Strathclyde's letter quoted above. The TRC was a group of Conservative MPs who in today's parlance would have been described as 'modernisers' and on the 'left' of the Party – although then, as now, such labels were simplistic. Its members included Viscount Hinchingbrooke,* Hugh Molson,† Peter Thorneycroft,‡ and Christopher York.§ The

---

* Viscount Hinchingbrooke, formerly Victor Montagu, was elected an MP in 1941 and remained in the House until 1962, when his father, the Earl of Sandwich, died. Described as a radical backbencher at the start of his career, he ended up on the far 'right' of the Conservative Party.

† Hugh Molson was Conservative MP from 1931–35 (Doncaster), and then again 1939–61 for High Peak. He was a barrister, served in the armed forces 1939–42, and held ministerial office between the years 1951–59.

‡ Peter Thorneycroft was an MP almost continuously from 1938–66 (for Stafford, then Monmouth). He was the Chancellor of the Exchequer who, along with the whole of the Treasury Team, resigned in 1958 over public expenditure. He returned to the front-line of politics in 1975 when Margaret Thatcher appointed him Chairman of the Party, a post which he held until 1981.

§ Major Christopher York was the Conservative MP for Ripon (1939–50)

PT was from the outset suspicious of the TRC, and extracted from the Conservative Chief Whip an assurance that "he would take steps to deal with the matter" (23rd March 1944) and warn new MPs "not to join any new group until they had an opportunity to settle down".* On the other hand, at a meeting of the Political Committee of 20th April 1944 they decided "that no action should, for the time being, be taken about forming a group within the Party to counter the Tory Reform Committee".

This refutes the idea held by some that the Progress Trust was itself originally formed to counter the influence of the TRC. In a publication *Clear Blue Water? The Conservative Party and The Welfare State since 1940* (Policy Press, University of Bristol 2015) Robert Page sheds further light upon the nature of the TRC but is mistaken in assuming that the PT was formed at a later date:

> The progressive voice was strengthened by the formation of the Tory Reform Committee in March 1943 … The group sought to encourage the Conservative leadership to disassociate itself from economically liberal influences within the party and to press ahead with social reform. The group, which eventually attracted around forty members, produced a manifesto – *Forward by the right* (Tory Reform Committee, 1943) – as well as articles for the party's monthly journal *Onlooker*, pamphlets and short works including *Full speed ahead! Essays in Tory reform* and *One year's work*. The group was supportive of

---

and Harrogate (1950–54).

* The Conservative Chief Whip at this time was James Stuart (the office of Chief Whip in the wartime coalition Government was held jointly between Conservative and Labour, whose Chief Whip at this period was William Whiteley).

Keynesian demand management techniques and the pursuit of full employment. It explored a wide range of topics in its publications including 'aviation, agriculture, coal, education, housing, land use war pensions and workmen's compensation' (Dorey, 2011, p. 74). One of its greatest 'coups' was to secure a government defeat by just one vote on an amendment brought by Thelma Cazalet-Keir in March 1944, on the question of equal pay for women teachers. This prompted the government to turn this issue into a vote of confidence, which led to a tactical retreat by the 'rebels' and the reversal of the original decision. According to Ball (2013), the group's 'lack of practical experience, blithe confidence, self-absorbed cliquishness, desire for the limelight, open ambition, and the loose attitude to loyalty which often seemed to accompany it, did not render them attractive to the main body of older and staider backbenchers' (p. 351). Indeed, a number of those with strong free market and individualistic sentiments, such as Sir Spencer Summers, Alexander Erskine-Hill and Ralph Assheton,* were so concerned by what they perceived that they set up a counter-organisation, the Progress Trust, in November 1943 to promote their anti-collectivist version of Conservatism.

Robin Harris, in *The Conservatives: A History* (Bantam Press, 2011) is similarly mistaken in his chronology, although not in his analysis when stating that the "Tory Reform Committee did not reflect majority Party opinion. The Progress Trust, set up in November 1944 to combat what Tories considered 'back-door socialism', probably has a better claim to do so."

The mistake over dates is not the only reason for dismissing the suggestion that the PT was created to resist the ideas of

---

* This is incorrect. Ralph Assheton did not become a member of the PT until 1951.

the TRC. As the minutes reveal, the PT would hardly have discussed the possibility of forming a new counter group to the TRC if it had been formed itself for this specific purpose.

Furthermore, while the TRC may have been more outspoken and less well behaved than the PT – so much so that its activities were closed down by Butler on Churchill's instructions at the end of the war – the views of either group were not always as far apart as both Page and Harris assume. Hinchingbrooke, for example, who was a founding member of TRC, became an important member of the PT only four years later in 1947. Lord Hailsham, in his memoirs, adds to the confusion:

> When I got home, I found that my views were already shared by a group of youngish MPs mostly returned from the forces who were meeting regularly for a dinner at a little restaurant in Charing Cross Road. They included Peter Thorneycroft, Viscount Hinchingbrooke (as he was then), Hugh Linstead, Alfred Beit and Norman Bower. This small group was the nucleus of the Tory Reform Committee which thereafter played a considerable part in the public debate on post war social policy and, with the aid of a Conservative Fund called the Progress Trust, later published a series of political pamphlets which I believe had a considerable and beneficial effect on Conservative thinking at the time.[*]

Hailsham was not a founding member of the Tory Reform Committee, and was surely mistaken in believing it received financial support from the Progress Trust. But he was correct in assuming that the PT and TRC had certain beliefs in common. Collectivist thinking about national insurance,

---

[*] *A Sparrow's Flight*, memoirs of Lord Hailsham, Collins 1990.

national health, land values and planning was shared by many younger Conservative MPs, irrespective of their wing of the party. Even the PT considered in 1943 the case for a basic price for land, calculated upon its agricultural value. Indeed, where countryside matters were concerned, the PT was always ready to champion the interests of the farmer and landowner over the consumer. During this period, only a few PT members would have harboured 'libertarian' sympathies (despite authorising, at a cost of 10/6d, the purchase of Hayek's *The Road To Serfdom* as one of the PT's first library acquisitions). The bias of most was towards a patrician approach with only a modest inclination to challenge fundamentally Beveridge's philosophy. They all believed in free enterprise and opposed nationalisation. But they were far from asserting there was no need for state intervention in the economy.

This is no surprise, given the political background of the original PT members. As already mentioned its Chairman, Alexander Erskine-Hill, had originally been a Liberal, albeit of the free-market variety.* Of other founding members, Henry Willink† was no outright opponent of Beveridge, having shared responsibility for the 1944 White Paper on Social Insurance and Allied Services mentioned above. He was one of three members of the PT's 'Beveridge and Health' Sub-Committee, established in June 1943, and he convened the PT's 'Youth & Education' Sub-Committee which was

---

* By and large, the PT was anxious to keep its distance from the National Liberals (most of whom were Conservatives under a different label), to the extent, in May 1944, of telling Fells from not to have any 'accommodation' with them, and denying them the use of PT premises.

† Sir Henry Willink (1894–1973) was the Member of Parliament for Croydon North from 1940–1948.

established at the same time. But within months of the PT's formation, Willink was obliged to resign from the Trust on his appointment as Minister of Health in November 1943, an office which he occupied until the defeat of Churchill's interim Conservative Government in 1945. As Nye Bevan's predecessor, Willink is a reminder of the major part played by Conservatives in the introduction of a National Health Service. He rejoined the PT after the Conservative defeat, but left Parliament in 1948. Henry Brooke,* who had been a prominent supporter of Neville Chamberlain before the war and was another founding member of the PT, was also sympathetic to Beveridge's approach. On the other hand Captain Cobb, who became Leo Amery's Parliamentary Private Secretary, had been one of Chamberlain's fiercest critics and Rupert Brabner was still a serving member of the armed forces. This combination of fighting men, appeasers and reformers demonstrates the breadth of the PT membership at its inception, but also explains why there was little appetite for radical disagreement with contemporary proposals to reform health, education and social security.

Despite the importance of Beveridge's proposals, and their implications for a welfare state, the PT's focus was on developing closer links between industry and Parliament. This necessitated an eye for detail, which the PT's Research Department was expected to provide. For example, at its very first meeting on 1ˢᵗ April 1943, the Political Committee concerned itself with the need for "specialisation on the finest types of manufactures", given that "the present war time telescoping of industries and standardised output must in some

---

* Henry Brooke (1903–1984), was the Member of Parliament for Lewisham West from 1938–1945 and subsequently Hampstead (1950–1966). His highest office was as Home Secretary (1962–1964).

ways be detrimental to the maintenance of a pool of skilled craftsmanship and design, etc." This was dry stuff, hardly calculated to capture the headlines.

The Trust's early priorities can also be discerned from the Committees which were established, and the questions they pursued. Examples of the former included ad-hoc Committees to study Emergency Powers; the Education Bill; and the "present coal situation". Permanent Committees covered Imperial Affairs; Foreign Affairs; Industry and State Control; Housing and Uthwatt,* Scott† and Barlow‡ Reports; Workmen's Compensation and Comprehensive Medical Service; and Agriculture.

Also raised were so-called "minor questions" pertaining more to daily politics such as:

- why the Minister of Information (Brendan Bracken) had "waited for two years and until he was in the USA before releasing the information regarding Hess";
- why Mr Bevin had announced the demobilisation scheme "at the TUC meeting" and not previously to the House of Commons;
- unease over AMGOT's [Allied Military Government of Occupied Territories] operations in Sicily and their implications for a "preliminary attack on the Emergency Powers Act" (whose provisions had to be renewed annually);
- taking up "the matter of drafting youths for the coal mines";
- encouragement of "any member who is interested" to speak

---

* The Uthwatt Report of 1942 led to the modern planning system.

† The Scott Report of 1942 on Land Utilisation in Rural Areas.

‡ The Barlow Report on the urban concentration of population and industry had been produced in 1940, but it was not until 1942 that its conclusions became the basis of policy towards the new town movement.

in the debate on the call up of women over 45;
- implications of the closing down of factories in Scotland, including "the enforced migration of female workers from Scotland".

On one occasion (March 1945), the PT raised the sensitive subject of "the responsibility of American soldiers for the support of their illegitimate children". Reginald Manningham-Buller* "noted that the American authorities were offering lump sums which fell far below the weekly rate legally enforceable in this country".

Issues which were more 'party-political' in character included:

Electioneering technique and propaganda of Nazi Party in early elections, and comparison with those of the left-wing movement Common Wealth†
  Left-wing history books and teaching in LCC schools
  Material to counter Fabian pamphlets

These are all revealing of the political atmosphere of this

---

* Sir Reginald Manningham-Buller (1905–1980) was the Member of Parliament for Daventry and then Northamptonshire South between 1943 and 1962 when he was appointed Lord Chancellor (1962–64).

† Common Wealth had been founded in July 1942 and opposed the electoral pact between the main parties, sponsoring independent candidates in by-elections. In 1944, it published a booklet entitled 'Fellowship or Morality?' and its electoral success during (but not after) the war was an early indication of the move to the 'left', which resulted in Labour's massive majority in 1945. On 19th April 1944, Fells was actually instructed to obtain a professional opinion on whether or not this booklet infringed the laws of libel and copyright.

period. Some will be encouraged that, even in wartime, MPs were jealous of their Parliamentary privileges and on guard against any attempt by Ministers to escape Parliamentary scrutiny. The criticism of Bevin for informing the Trades Union Congress of his demobilisation scheme in advance of the House of Commons is a case in point, and which has many parallels today.

But underlying everything was the failure of the Conservative message to get through to the electorate. Even though its existence had yet to be announced to the press, part of the PT's purpose was to address the public at large. And so, in September 1943 the PT's Publications Committee was charged with preparing "the script for a broadcast of about 2,000 words which could perhaps be delivered by a humble person (i.e. taxi driver) to put up the British point of view."

Perhaps it is unsurprising that this desire to communicate with the public led to criticism of the BBC. The PT distrusted the BBC's performance, not only in its coverage of the war, but more especially in how it presented the political choices facing the country in the aftermath of war. Many of these complaints sound familiar to us today. As early as April 1943, for example, Pickthorn had sought assurances that the BBC "would not indulge in pre-boosting (or, in modern parlance, 'spinning') of future Reports in the way they had done over the Beveridge Report" and which, in his opinion, was a clear example of the BBC's desire to influence post-war politics in a 'left-wing' direction. There was anger that *The Listener* "which is an official organ of the BBC" always took the opportunity to highlight "books critical of Britain and British Policy" and of employing left-wing intellectuals (such as the writer Konni Zilliacus* who "has for years been

---

* Konni Zilliacus was, at this time, working for the Ministry of

engaged in criticism of the Government"). When Professor Hilton of Cambridge University died, who was a regular BBC contributor and whose opinions were disliked by his Member of Parliament, Pickthorn was anxious that he should be replaced "by someone outside politics".

The biggest concern of all centred upon the BBC's coverage of Russia. Many Conservative MPs felt that the Corporation, as explained internally by the BBC's Director of Talks, George Barnes, was "… selling sunshine about Russia". To be fair, the BBC was also under attack from 'the left' for not paying "tribute to Russian qualities" (BBC internal memo dated 29.11.1944). But it was mostly Tory MPs who were suspicious of the BBC's political bias. Its coverage of Poland, with its constant references to Poland's "former border" and the implication that the war's original objectives were super-seded, particularly irritated the PT. Pickthorn went so far as calling for BBC broadcasts to Europe to be vetted, especially when in January 1944 J. B. Priestley was given a new BBC responsibility for overseas broadcasts.

Concerns over unmerited sympathy towards Russian intentions were not restricted to the BBC. It extended to the Government. In March 1945, three members of the PT – Sir Archibald Southby, Mr Manningham-Buller and Lord Dunglass – arranged to see Mr Eden "regarding the reports received about the treatment of British prisoners by the Russians". After the meeting, they reported it had been "as satisfactory as could be expected".

Information, but subsequently was elected a Labour MP in 1945, only to be expelled from the Labour Party in 1949 for his alleged support of Communism and Russia (although he strenuously denied that he was a Communist). He was re-elected in 1955 and remained a Labour MP until his death in 1967.

In the meantime, the research activities of the PT accelerated in pace and intensity both in respect of daily Parliamentary business and in preparing for the election campaign itself. Just before the 1945 General Election, on 30th June, a half-yearly report on the PT's activities was prepared which summarised both the structure and scope of the PT in the final months of the war. The Council at this time met monthly, "while the various committees of the Trust met frequently until the beginning of April when it was decided that the Business Committee should take charge of all activities and concentrate on preparing for the Election". The summary continued:

> Members of Parliament associated with the Trust have been extremely busy with the heavy volume of legislation presented in the first half of 1945 and the [PT's] Research Department has assisted on more than 220 occasions with material for questions or debates. Members were particularly occupied with:
> the Income Tax Bill and the Budget;
> the Requisitoned Land and War Works Bill *from the point of view of the rights of the citizen*;
> the Distribution of Industry Bill *with a view to presenting any discouragement of industrial development*;
> the Wages Council Bill *from the point of view of obtaining a reasonable limit of time to the virtual freezing of wage rates*;
> the urgency of the Housing programme; and
> Service matters.

The italicised words underline the direction in which the PT wished to shape this legislation, and again implies concern that Churchill's coalition Government was too easily tempted down the paths of state regulation and intervention. In this same summary, it stated that "Close attention is being given to the increasing number of attacks on private enterprise in electricity distribution so that Members of Parliament can be kept informed of the true facts."

Despite these criticisms, however, there is nothing to suggest that the PT expected the return of a Labour Government after the war, let alone the massive electoral defeat that occurred. Members of the Progress Trust assumed that the country would hardly turn against Churchill in his hour of victory. The PT concluded a month before polling day that:

> … following on the General Election the work of the Trust will increase rather than diminish. The new House of Commons will contain many whose experience in regard to National affairs will be extremely limited and much educational work will, therefore, require to be undertaken. The members of the [PT] Council look forward to the period lying immediately ahead as being very critical and one which will call, more than ever, for a really well-informed House of Commons. (Council minutes, 7th June 1945)

3

1945–1951:

They're the Masters Now

"The general sense of the meeting was that it could not definitely oppose the principle of nationalisation as being entirely detrimental to the public interest as to do so would be to fall into the Socialist error of theorising."
(8th January 1946)

Shortly after VE day (8th May 1945), the Progress Trust was irritated by "the deference being paid to high-ranking German Officers and the indignation which was being aroused". But the indignation would soon be directed against them. The PT lost almost half its members in the massive defeat suffered by the Conservatives in the General Election of 1945.

It was an election which many in the PT regarded as unnecessary, undesirable, and even unpatriotic. A main task of the PT's Research Department in advance of, and during, the election had been to summarise in digestible form relevant press comment. Sometimes these summaries included letters from the public, such as one from a gentleman named Mr Levy who lived in Herne Bay and who wrote to *The Sunday Times* on 10th June 1945:

Would Mr Bevin and his Socialist colleagues in the Cabinet explain to a mystified public how they can compel people to stay in their posts until the end of the Japanese War (and still less direct them to work as they think fit through the Labour Exchanges) when they themselves have thrown up their posts at the end of the European War after being requested by Mr Churchill to carry on to the end of the Japanese War in the interests of the country. Are they the privileged class?*

The author of this letter would have assumed, along with everyone else, that a quick victory over Japan was impossible. On the contrary, the Japanese war was expected to continue for years, and would almost certainly have done so were it not for the dropping of two atomic bombs. Nevertheless, the Labour Party insisted upon a General Election. The wartime coalition Government ended on 23rd May 1945; Parliament was dissolved on 15th June; the election was held on 5th July; but the results were not counted until 25th and 26th July when the country was still at war with Japan.

Between the break-up of the coalition and the results of the General Election, the so-called caretaker Conservative Government was in office, with Churchill hoping it would survive intact. This Government included a few members of the PT, which led to their resignations from the Trust, as dictated by the rules, although they continued to receive PT material on the same basis as Council members. The best known of these new Ministers today is Lord Dunglass, Neville Chamberlain's former PPS, who was appointed Parliamentary Under-Secretary for Foreign Affairs, and would many years later become Prime Minister as Sir Alec Douglas-Home. Other PT members of the 'caretaker' Government appointed on 29th May 1945 were:

---

* This letter is printed in a series of daily notes published by the PT in the days leading up to the 1945 Election Campaign under the heading *News & Views*.

Commander T. D. Galbraith, Parliamentary Under-Secretary for Scotland

Mr R. E. Manningham-Buller, Parliamentary Secretary to the Ministry of Works

Mr R. Donald Scott, Parliamentary Secretary to the Ministry of Agriculture and Fisheries

Mr G. Spencer Summers, Parliamentary Secretary, Department of Overseas Trade (appointed 23.3.45)

Captain W. P. Sydney, Parliamentary Secretary to the Ministry of Pensions

Mr Henry Willink, Minister of Health (appointed 11.11.43)

At its final meeting before the dissolution, the PT's Political Committee resolved to meet again at 6pm on Tuesday 31st July "followed by a dinner at the Dorchester Hotel" at which they hoped to celebrate a Conservative victory. It was a forlorn hope. Amongst the PT members who had lost their seats were members of the caretaker Government – Lord Dunglass, Spencer Summers, and Donald Scott were all defeated. Captain Sydney had succeeded to the title of Baron de L'Isle and Dudley on the death of his father, and therefore didn't contest the election. Henry Willink managed to retain his seat – but only by 607 votes, and he left Parliament a few years later.

Whether or not the intended dinner at the Dorchester took place, the minutes of the Political Committee record that on 1st August "it was unanimously decided that the Progress Trust should continue." The PT members who took that decision were:

Sir Alexander Erskine-Hill, in the Chair
Hon. Lionel Berry

Captain E. C. Cobb
Lord de L'Isle and Dudley
Comdr. T. D. Galbraith
Wing Comdr. Sir Archibald James
Major Guy Lloyd
Mr R. E. Manningham-Buller
Colonel Harold Mitchell
Major J. G. Morrison
Sir Joseph Nall
Major B. Neven-Spence
Mr K. W. M. Pickthorn
Comdr. Sir Archibald Southby
Mr H. G. Strauss
Major H. G. Studholme
Mr Spencer Summers
Sir Douglas Thomson

This meeting also allowed defeated members of the Political Committee who intended to continue their political careers and stand again for Parliament to "remain members of the Committee with exactly the same rights as members who are in Parliament"; and also, as a modification of the rules, that ex-members who became Ministers shortly before the dissolution in the caretaker Government "would be re-admitted to full membership".

Adjusting to the loss of office after a long period is always a painful process, especially when unexpected. Some twenty years later the atmosphere at this moment was poetically described by Enoch Powell, who had joined the Conservative Party's Parliamentary Secretariat in March 1946:

The Conservative front bench looked around them and

blinked. It was autumn 1945 and a strange world. For one thing, Mr Speaker was in the wrong place. They were sitting on his left instead of on his right. This wholly unaccustomed position – unknown for fourteen years and only briefly experienced in twenty – made everything seem the wrong way round, not to say upside down. Then, feeling in their pockets, they pulled out a lot of creased White Papers, the White Papers which they had so recently – yet how long ago it seemed! – presented to Parliament: on a national insurance scheme, on a national health service, on land values and planning: there was even a faintly Keynesian one on full employment. They stuffed them back again, and wondered what to do.*

The reference to "creased White Papers" is poignant. Powell chose to highlight the fact that many of the new Labour Government's policies had been shaped by Conservative as well as Labour Ministers belonging to the wartime coalition Government. As late as 1964, Powell still believed this largely accounted for the failure of post-war Conservative Governments to make a clean break from the socialist, interventionist policies which prevailed so long.

It certainly complicated the task of Opposition. In the aftermath of the election, the Conservative Party in depleted numbers was obliged to react to a mass of legislation introduced by the confident new Labour Government for which Conservatives bore a measure of past responsibility. This led

---

* This series of three articles for *The Times* was written under the pseudonym '*A Conservative*'. The true authorship of Enoch Powell was kept secret for many years, although he was often suspected of having written this widely commented-upon critique. The articles appeared on three consecutive days 1st – 3rd April 1964 under the general heading "A Party In Search Of A Pattern".

to the PT's Business Committee instructing Fells on 22nd August 1945:

[a] to continue with the work he has on hand and when completed to send copies to all Conservative Members of Parliament;
[b] to attend all meetings of the Political Committee unless specifically asked not to; and
[c] to submit his weekly report to the Director [i.e. Captain E. C. Cobb] prior to the Business Committee meetings.

The Trust also decided to "aim to provide lectures of an educational nature at schools, colleges, etc. and to have articles written for the Press", and on 4th October "that they needed to recruit six to ten new members at the earliest possible date but not before there had been a full opportunity to judge form nor without the approval of the Political Committee". Already the Political Committee, which every PT Member of Parliament was entitled to attend, was beginning to supersede the Council and Business Committee, at least in terms of political strategy.

The debate on the King's Speech took place between 16th and 21st August. Sir Alan Herbert had tabled an amendment to the Speech which PT members were inclined to support, but which was not called. Sir Alan, however, was able to state other objections beforehand. In opposing a sittings motion moved by Herbert Morrison, Sir Alan complained of the precedence to be afforded to Government business throughout the new session and the implications this had for the rights of backbench members, especially in respect of time allocated to private Bills. Sir Alan exclaimed that, should the Government's wishes be implemented, "I might just as well be a member of the German Reichstag or a stuffed exhibit in the Natural History Museum."[*] This was interesting language to deploy so soon after a war against fascism – it suggests Churchill wasn't alone in believing that a socialist Government "would have to fall back on some form of Gestapo". And today when Parliamentary procedures are often dismissed as obsolete, it is salutary to be reminded of Sir Alan's defence of the privileges of Parliament. Throughout its existence, the PT was always alive to the importance of Parliamentary 'time' as a 'weapon' and as a method of holding the executive to account. One of its future members, Sir Marcus Kimball,[†] was an expert in Parliamentary procedure and his warnings in the 1990s – which I heard personally – against the timetabling of Bills and preventing 'filibusters' have been vindicated.

In 1945, the PT's main task was to scrutinise the Labour Government's first legislative acts, including the proposed repeal of the Trade Disputes Act, the nationalisation of the Bank of England, and legislation connected with Housing. Internationally, the situations in Palestine, Egypt and the Middle East were the priorities. But because Parliament departed for the summer recess almost immediately after the King's Speech, it was not until 4th October that the PT's Political Committee reassembled "to hold a Conference to discuss the long-term policy of the Committee".

From having been the dominant Party in British politics

---

[*] Hansard, 16th August 1945 c. 133.

[†] Sir Marcus Kimball (1928–2014), later Lord Kimball of Easton, was the Member of Parliament for Gainsborough from 1956–1983. He was a farmer and active member and champion of Lloyd's. He was easily classified as a 'knight of the shires,' with views to match. But he was a skilled Parliamentarian.

since 1922, the Conservatives had now lost all prospect of power for the foreseeable future. This gave rise to another anxiety – that the election of a socialist Government with a vast majority would prove to be the precursor of something even worse. This fear was behind the PT's frequent references to the Communist threat during the 1945–50 Parliament. For example:

25.2.47: Mr Horner, Secretary of the National Union of Mineworkers, "has also shown his hand as a syndicalist as well as Communist by admitting that his various proposals will 'inconvenience other sections of the nation and close certain unessential industries…' It is being said that the miners' leaders are determined that this country shall never have adequate stocks of coal again."

1.4.47: PT members agreed with the sentiment behind three Parliamentary questions tabled by Sir Waldron Smithers MP (Orpington), but which had been ruled out of order, implying that the loyalty given by Communists to Russia should exclude them from Government employment. Attention had also been drawn to the 'Treasonable Activities of Communists' as a consequence of the announcement of the results of an MI5 probe among scientific civil servants.

21.10.47: Continuing concern over the influence of Russian Communism in Britain, especially "the infiltration of teachers as personified by The National Association of Labour Teachers. Should there be a Conservative Teachers' Association?"

7.4.48: Need for a debate on "the Communist purge, when it should be stressed that people were to be moved from one department where loyalty was very important to a department where loyalty was less important".

5.5.48: Concern over the "Communist Manifesto series of

broadcasts on the BBC Overseas Service."

21.7.48: Alarm at the Communist Party of GB's call "for the liberation of Africa from Economic Exploitation". The last issue of TRIBUNE has an attack on Unilever and the United Africa Company. Could we not be a help to these two concerns?"*

The PT was not alone in fearing a Communist takeover; Conservative Central Office was similarly fearful. In February 1948, an attempt was made by the General Director of Conservative Central Office (Mr S. H. Pierssene) and Galbraith to co-operate together on a Committee "which the National Union has set up to enquire into Communist and Fascist Activities" and which was to be chaired by Mr H. G. Strauss MP, who was also a member of the PT.† Strauss had suggested that Fells should act as Secretary to the Committee (which he was keen to do), and agreement was given to this proposal until it was noticed that "in the terms of our Trust Deed we might be acting *ultra vires* in giving the services of one of our employees to an outside body." Galbraith felt that the Trust's legal advice was too cautious and could be ignored, but eventually he gave way while allowing Fells to

---

* The Chairman of the United Africa Company was Viscount Trenchard, known as "the Father of the Royal Air Force" and held in deepest respect by both Churchill and the Conservative Party. It was natural, therefore, for the PT to ask whether they could not "be a help to these two concerns?"

† Henry George Strauss was the Conservative MP for Norwich 1935–1945, re-entering Parliament in 1946 for the Combined English Universities and then for Norwich South 1950–55. He resigned from Churchill's Government over the Yalta Agreement, but served under Churchill again between 1951–55 when he was raised to the peerage as Lord Conesford.

assist Central Office's work unofficially as part of his work for the Trust.

Looking back, this is easily dismissed as a 'reds-under-the-bed' scare. At the time, however, it was an anxiety shared by many Conservatives, and especially by those who remained uncomfortable that the defeat of Hitler had been secured through an alliance with a creed they deplored. They could not forget also that there were figures on 'the left' whose commitment to the war had, at best, been lukewarm until Hitler attacked Russia. Now, they feared that the wartime alliance with Russia permitted certain newly elected Labour MPs to disguise their primary allegiance to the Communist Party. On 18th November 1947, the PT considered a paper on Labour's foreign policy which argued that the Foreign Secretary, Ernest Bevin, was circumscribed between three strands of thought within his own Party. There were those who gave Bevin "the same general support which he has received from the Conservative Party"; there were others "who strongly oppose Mr Bevin whenever his policy clashes with that of the Soviet Union"; but

> The third group takes a middle position. Men like Mr Crossman and Mr Christopher Shawcross believe that British policy should seek the closest possible union with the Socialist states of Western Europe and so create a third world power, equal in strength to capitalist America and Communist Russia and free from the evils which they profess to see in both.

The search for some sort of 'union' with Europe, on the assumption that "Western Europe is predominantly Socialist and will remain so," is interesting in light of what we know now. While it was an assumption which the PT rejected, it strengthened its suspicion that a significant section of the Parliamentary Labour Party's loyalty was to a Russian-style Communism. At this same meeting, the PT asked "would it be reasonable to consider the assumption that Sir Stafford Cripps will be Prime Minister by the spring, but only for a short time, as he will succeed in splitting the Labour Party wide open?" Today, one might almost substitute the name Corbyn for Cripps to ask a similar question.

The PT's other priority was to play a part in the Conservative Party's reappraisal of policy following the election defeat. From its formation, and until the creation of the Conservative Party's Parliamentary Secretariat (later to merge with the Research Department) in 1946, the PT's research resources exceeded anything that Churchill permitted the Conservative Party to deploy during the war. Even when the Conservative Party's research capacity was restored, the PT was still able to pay Fells around £1,300 per annum (equivalent to some £50,000 per annum today), and his assistant a salary of £500 per annum. The Trust also now employed the former MP Captain E. C. Cobb* as Director "in general charge of the Trust's work" now that he was "freed from his Parliamentary duties".

By the end of the war, apart from Fells, the PT employed eight people including an accountant, librarian, and an additional research assistant as well as secretaries. This amounted to a salary bill of around £40 per week (equivalent to some £1,600 today). In addition to salaries and wages, regular expenses included the purchase of books for the PT's

---

* Captain Edward Charles Cobb was a soldier and politician, who was the Member of Parliament for Preston in the House of Commons between 1936–1945. He contested unsuccessfully Eton and Slough in both 1945 and 1950.

library; office equipment extending from filing cabinets to "the purchase of a new vacuum cleaner"; and miscellaneous requirements such as the need for an atlas since "we have wanted an atlas from time to time and have been unable to get a good one during the war period." The PT also incurred expense in taking its messages to an external audience. In February 1946, for example, the PT agreed to "finance a trial course or lecture by the Abbey School in London or in one of the Constituencies" as an indication of its wish to look beyond Parliament.

The volume of work undertaken by PT staff was formidable. At each monthly meeting of the Business Committee, Fells would list the Research Notes which had been circulated over the past four weeks. These invariably numbered between five and fifteen, covering current legislation to broader policy areas such as Industrial Relations and the efficiency of British industry; or more obscure international issues such as the Montreux Convention.* An element of this research work involved suggesting policy initiatives or a line to take in debate. Mostly, however, it was a compendium of already published press and external comment which relieved Trust MPs from the need to scrutinise the newspapers themselves, while providing them with an array of helpful statistics for debates.

Such material deserved a wider circulation. In July 1946, the PT decided to launch a news service with the intention of increasing the reach and influence of its Research Department. A report to the PT Council stated:

---

* The Montreux Convention Regarding the Regime of the Straits became relevant to one of the crises associated with the Cold War and the Truman doctrine of containment.

For some time it has been considered that the large amount of factual material collected by the Research Department should receive a much wider circulation than it has hitherto been getting. But up till now it has not been possible to obtain the services of a suitable person to edit the material in a form suitable for wider consumption. The Trust has now secured the services of Mr Colm Brogan, the author of two well-known books – *Who Are The People?* and *The Democrat At The Supper Table* – and look forward with confidence to this development of the Trust's Work. (Report to the PT Council, 24th July 1946)

Brogan's remit was not only to produce a newsletter but to "do journalistic work and write a series of books". Two of these – *Patriots? My Foot!* (a satirical attack on Michael Foot) and a pamphlet *Socialism Conquers Labour* – were described in October 1949 as "selling very well". But what became known as the *Political Digest* was the PT's most important regular publication, and the first printed edition was distributed in January 1947. Within six months, the *Political Digest* (of Parliamentary debates and questions, new Bills, forthcoming legislation, etc.) was issued monthly, providing "factual information for distribution among industrial workers and Political associations. Its present circulation is limited to 2,500 copies per month." It had certain guiding principles which sometimes it was tempted to ignore:

that it should give factual information rather than political comment;

but that those 'facts' chosen should be supportive of the Conservative case; and

that it should not repeat what was easily available in the Press.

The first *Political Digest* included in the PT files covered six areas under the overall heading of 'EVENTS' and included Foreign Policy; Public Opinion; Collective Responsibility; Conscription; the King's Speech; and Railways. It was governed mostly by the Parliamentary agenda, and one constant theme was "the large dissident minority" within the Parliamentary Labour Party, and disagreements which were evident even between Ministers and their Parliamentary Private Secretaries (of which five instances were quoted).

The *Political Digest* was the most important example of the PT reaching out to a political readership beyond Parliament, including Conservative Central Office itself, the new Conservative Secretariat, the Conservative Political Centre and its bookshop. But there were others. For example, the PT turned its attention to Conservative Workmen's Clubs, observing:

> … It has sometimes been pointed out that one of the reasons why the Labour Party can get at the working man is that it is so often in the position to be able to give him advice and information on his problems and on his rights, either through the Party officials or through trade union officials, who often are one and the same. Would it be considered worth exploring whether the Conservative Party could not do something of the same kind through these clubs?

How the PT gained the necessary funds to carry out these activities was seldom reported in the minutes, and was left to the Chairman of the Council to manage. A charge was made for some PT products. In December 1945, for example, it was decided that Research Department material could be distributed to non-Trust MPs and adopted candidates "for a subscription of 10/6 for six months and £1.1.0 for a year to cover the cost of paper and postage". Notably, it was stipulated that "the material should not have the name of the Trust printed on it but a separate slip with the name and address to be enclosed."

This, however, was merely to help defray expenses. More generally, the salaries and office costs of the PT required a regular and reliable source of income. In those days, little regard was paid to demands for 'transparency' or disclosure. Attempts had been made unsuccessfully for the PT to be treated as a charity for the purposes of income tax (April 1946), but these were not pursued in light of a negative response from the Inland Revenue and private legal advice. Thus, the PT's Chairman and Council were constantly seeking out new individual donors and "further possible channels" for finance. The names of individual donors were seldom noted in the minutes, or divulged to members. If support was given by an organisation, there was less secrecy. Aims of Industry, for example, became an important source of finance, although in the early years (prior to 1946) "it was not desired that the Progress Trust should be known to be taking any particular interest in the organisation." Subscriptions were also forthcoming from the British Industrialists and the Home Counties Industrialists. On the other hand, both ICI (through Sir Wallace Akers) and the Imperial Tobacco Company (through Sir Robert Sinclair) failed to respond to PT overtures for financial support.

In all these areas, the Business Committee was answerable to the Council, which in turn acted in compliance with the Trust Deed for which the Trustees were responsible and which exercised control over the Trust Fund. The Trustees now included the Duke of Devonshire and Lt. General Sir

Charles Lloyd. Meetings held between the Trust and Council took place at regular intervals, and the Trustees were charged with ensuring that adequate funds were held in reserve to cover future contingencies, especially relating to the Trust's principal asset, the property in Great College Street.

Trust MPs as a whole, however, were not expected to concern themselves with raising money. Their aim was to promote, in the words of Major Guy Lloyd[*] in a speech in Manchester on 27th July 1946, "a unified policy for an anti-socialist front". He argued this meant "To conserve the Constitution which has made Britain great, powerful, respected, and prosperous"; and also "To ensure that there shall be equality of opportunity for the talented boys and girls in the community, but that those specially gifted or specially industrious shall not be handicapped by any false notions of such 'equality'."

Nothing could be achieved, however, until the country's economic weakness was addressed. In this regard, the PT had sympathy with the assessment given in the *Review of World Affairs,* published in May 1947:

Certainly Britain's economic difficulties could hardly be greater. At present she is not able to produce enough goods to sell abroad to supply the foreign currency she needs for the purchase of the basic means of life, because she has not the coal to keep the factories going. But presently even though she has the coal her production costs will be so high that people abroad will not be able to afford to buy British goods – unless, of course, the British worker wakes up and really works ... The Leftists are seeing more and more clearly that there is no half

---

[*] Major Sir Guy Lloyd (1890–1987) was on the first PT Council formed in 1943. He was the Member of Parliament for East Renfrewshire from 1940–1959.

way house; it is either a question of totalitarian Communism with a world government, or a reversion to private enterprise and the profound influence of Americanism. It boils down to a struggle between Russianism and Americanism.

Fells preferred to concentrate his labours in the economic sphere. He sought wider readership for a note he had written on Keynes and suggested sending it to City Editors "because you may feel that this is a piece of work which might definitely mark the Trust as interested in exposing the current cant of the day in relation to monetary matters" (22nd October 1946). He also wished to target certain members of the Conservative Party when it came to Keynesian 'fallacies' such as "Mr Thorneycroft, who might profit from it" and "Mr Harold Macmillan, who also accepts the Keynesian theories" (note from Fells to Business Committee, 26.11.46).

The constant problem for the Conservative Opposition, however, was how to reconcile its support for social reform with economic policies which were easily branded by its opponents as *laissez-faire*. Under constant attack for their record in the inter-war years, Conservatives were divided over how far to press opposition to the Government's programme. This is apparent from a discussion of the PT Political Committee at the beginning of 1946 on the subject of nationalisation:

> Although no member was able to accept any form of Nationalisation so far put forward, the general sense of the meeting was that it could not definitely oppose the principle as being entirely detrimental to the public interest as to do so would be to fall into the Socialist error of theorising. Accordingly every proposal for Nationalisation should be considered on its merits and from the point of view of its effect on

the freedom of the individual, efficiency, and national defence.

The following views were expressed:

(a) All the present schemes for Nationalisation should be opposed to the utmost…
(b) Our opposition should not be to Nationalisation in general but against the Nationalisation of particular industries and on the particular Bill.
(c) Nationalisation of a single industry is very different from Nationalisation advocated as a means of carrying through a complete plan of State Socialism.
(d) While we favour free enterprise we should be prepared, as practical men, to examine any scheme on its merits.
(e) Industries in danger of Nationalisation cannot expect their battles to be fought adequately in Parliament unless they co-operate in providing the fullest information and themselves put forward proposals for remedying existing defects, or giving proof that defects do not exist and that progress is continuous. (8th January 1946)

The summary of this meeting may have been accurate, but it was not welcome. At the following meeting of the Political Committee on 23rd January 1946, while there was no challenge "as to the accuracy of the record nor that opinions recorded had been stated at some time during the course of the meeting" it was nevertheless felt "that the minute did not give a true picture since it appears to indicate a half-hearted opposition to Nationalisation which is contrary to the general feeling". Like the entire Conservative Party, the PT was scared of being branded obstructive to the Socialist programme, even though it agreed that it could not be afforded. In a wide-ranging speech in Manchester, Churchill had stated, on receiving the freedom of the city (5th December 1947), that Government expenditure "should be reduced by £500 million." The PT's response was to ask for "guidance on what public expenditure could be reduced immediately on a change of government". However, there was no enthusiasm for pressing the point. In framing the PT's response to the Labour Government's last Budget of this Parliament, and in deciding what amendments to press on the 1949 Finance Bill,

> Opinion was divided as to the benefit to be derived –
> (a) by supporting amendments for a reduction in taxation, i.e. income tax, surtax, etc. or
> (b) a general statement that under Socialism and a Welfare State expenditure on the present level was necessary and must be accepted.
> It was agreed that both points of view should be stated in the proper quarter.
> On consideration of the purchase tax there was again a divergence of opinion, some favouring an overall reduction say of 10 per cent and others the removal of the tax from a specified range of goods and commodities. There was further agreement that in one form or another protests should be made about the continuance of this tax. It was unanimously agreed that there should be the strongest protest in regard to the death duties proposals in the Bill.

Maybe it was prevarication of this type which had led Jack Wilkes, the Parliamentary Commentator of *The Tribune*, to complain two years earlier in February 1947:

The most serious Parliamentary problem which the Government faces is the ineptitude of the Opposition. Here is the Government in a jam on coal. Mistakes have been made. Confidence has been shaken. Yet the Government in the House gets clean away with it. Its spokesmen, day after day, massacre the spokesmen who are pushed in their direction by the Opposition. With that happening day after day, the Government may easily become complacent and fail to hear the voices that are beginning to raise themselves outside. In the interests of this Government and in the interests of the well-being of the nation it is essential that the job of Opposition, left vacant these eighteen months, should now be taken over by the Government backbenches.

In other words, the PT's timidity was merely a symptom of a more serious malaise within the Conservative Party for which some blamed Churchill personally. The PT and Churchill were not close, at least in a corporate sense. He was invited to dine on four occasions between 1945 and his retirement as Leader of the Conservative Party – in 1948 he was given "a number of dates from which to choose" – but they never resulted in a meeting.* However, Churchill did attend a PT dinner following his return from Cairo. No date is mentioned, but Strathclyde remembered the occasion in his letter dated 17th February 1980 to Sir Paul Bryan quoted earlier:

W.S.C. came to dinner – there were 12 perhaps 16 of the PT

---

* The occasions were 22.5.46, 5.11.47, 15.12.48, 22.3.50 and finally on 4.5.55 when Churchill regretted his inability to attend a dinner with the PT Political Committee "as he was not now making engagements of this nature".

present. W.S.C. arrived in a bad humour, sat through dinner and never spoke. Suddenly when the Brandy appeared he said "You will see these two will fight." Naturally we all stopped talking. After a pause; "I won't tell you their names, you have never heard of them" – then another pause – "Yes I will, then you will know whether or not I am right. One is called 'Montgomery', the other 'Alexander'."

Whether this was during or after the war is unclear, but it must have been early enough for the comment to be of interest, irrespective of the ironic tease that "you have never heard of them."

Apart from Churchill, other leading Conservatives dined regularly with the PT, providing a confidential and informal opportunity to express views to the leadership. Rab Butler, for example, was a regular guest of the PT from its formation to his retirement from Parliament in 1966. But he was never a soul-mate, and – as will be seen – the PT's attitude towards him was on at least one occasion injurious.

By November 1946, PT dinners took place regularly at their premises at 16 Great College Street:

Gunters ['society caterers'] stated that they would probably employ three waiters. Would 10/- each be considered a suitable tip? I would suggest Mr Fells' room as the room to be used for hats and coats. Sherry to be served in the reception room. May I suggest to the Perrotts that their son should help by opening the front door, showing guests to Mr Fells' room and then to the reception room. If so, and they agree, he could be given 5/-. He could be used to help in other ways, too. (Note from Mrs Ballard to the Chairman)

Conservative leaders sought out by the PT as dinner guests during this period also included Anthony Eden, Harold Macmillan, Brendan Bracken and Lord Salisbury.

Despite the hesitations of Opposition, discontent with the conduct of the Labour Government grew in intensity in the years leading up to 1950 and there was mounting distrust of the prevailing socialist consensus. As early as November 1946, Fells suggested that the PT should approach Kemsley Newspapers (which included *The Sunday Times*, *The Daily Sketch* and *The Sunday Graphic* amongst its titles) to consider "promoting an exhibition of Government forms, for which a large building would be necessary ... There would also need to be sections showing all the forms necessary for the building of a house, the establishment of a new business, importing any commodity, etc. One or two people to whom I have talked about this idea think that it would be one of the most damaging things that could be done to affect the Government."

There were three other policy areas where the PT accused the Conservative leadership of timidity and where Butler was already in their sights:

Trade Unionism – "Is the Party's conception yet clear, and is the conception that a man need not be a trade unionist if he does not want to be one?" (29.10.46)

Education – "It seems certainly the case, both in this matter [raising the school leaving age, which Butler supported] and in others, that the Party is not gaining an inch of ground in relation to the present situation. There is obviously a very widespread feeling that this immediate raising of the school age in current conditions is a major lunacy..." (25.2.47)

Industrial Policy – "A document embodying the industrial policy of the Party, said to have been prepared largely under the direction of Mr Butler is to be published shortly. Ought not Members at the 1922 Committee meeting be told something of the main points before this is put out to the country as a *fait accompli*? It might be considered particularly desirable to enquire to what degree the emphasis is put on planning in general and in detail and to enquire whether the document is sufficiently Conservative." (25.3.47)

This document on industrial policy was entitled 'The Industrial Charter' and seriously divided Conservative opinion. The PT shared the depth of press criticism which its publication aroused. Anthony Howard, in his biography of Butler,* believed this document represented probably "the most memorable concession a free enterprise Party ever made to the spirit of Keynesian economics". If so, it was a concession 'too far' for many Conservatives. *The Daily Express* said "This is simply another version of the old planned economy of the Socialists … It is bitterly disappointing that the Tory Charter, infected by Socialist ideas, should think in terms of State interference and State 'guidance'." *Crossbencher* in *The Sunday Express* asked "Can the Tories hope to recover power on a diet of Socialism and water…?" Such criticisms encouraged a response from Harold Macmillan a few months later who, speaking at Westminster on Saturday 14th June 1947, said that among the critics (of the Charter) were Sir Herbert Williams[†] and Sir Waldron Smithers[‡] and that "with them are

---

* *RAB: The Life of R. A. Butler* by Anthony Howard, Jonathan Cape, 1987.

† Sir Herbert Williams had been Conservative MP for Croydon South until his defeat in 1945, but was returned to Parliament for the new Croydon East seat in 1951 which he represented until his death in 1954. He was a staunch opponent of the Beveridge Report.

‡ Sir Waldron Smithers was a Conservative MP from 1924 until his death

associated other gentlemen for whom time does not merely stand still, but, if anything, runs backwards." Were the "other gentlemen" he had in mind members of the PT?

If so, he would have been unfair. Both Sir Herbert and Sir Waldron occupied, in today's parlance, the 'far right' of politics, and yet they were *not* members of the PT. Also, the position adopted by Sir Herbert Williams on Beveridge was in stark contrast to that of his fellow Croydon MP Henry Willink who, as already mentioned, was both a champion for social reform and a former member of the PT.

Nevertheless, the PT had reservations over the Industrial Charter, as it did over a related statement on equal pay issued by the Conservative Central Office at the same time. The Business Committee considered whether this merited "an inquiry into who is ordering the statements of policy … and whether it is wise to argue, on the one hand, that the Industrial Charter is not yet official Party Policy, but at the same time to use a statement in the Charter as justification for issuing an official pronouncement about equal pay."*

Amidst growing unease over the Opposition's performance, the PT persisted in operating behind the scenes. Its main method of doing so was to achieve strong PT representation upon Conservative Party Committees, where places were keenly contested in Party elections. PT members were

---

in 1954, described by John Boyd-Carpenter MP as "an extreme Tory out of a vanished age".

* This statement proclaimed "we wish to see every step taken in industry to bring about one rate for the job, provided that the services rendered and the results achieved by men and women are the same. Apart from the justice upon which this is founded it will help to make industry more attractive to women and add new members to our industrial forces at a time when they are urgently needed."

expected to support a PT 'slate' of candidates. Sometimes they failed to oblige, and there was one particular incident involving John Boyd-Carpenter* that sheds light on the process involved. In a letter to Galbraith dated 21st November 1946, Boyd-Carpenter complained that:

> ... in view of all the kindness I have had from you, it wouldn't be frank or honest if I failed to tell you that I do feel rather sore over the whole business of the Labour Committee election.
>
> You will remember that I did not care to be put forward for the Vice-Chairmanship of the Labour Committee. But when it was suggested at our special meeting last week, I was very pleased because (1) I am very keen on the subject and (2) I don't think that so far that Committee has pulled its weight. For these reasons had I not known that I was being put forward as PT candidate for the vice-chairmanship, I would have tried to arrange to be nominated for Secretary.
>
> You will also remember that at the meeting in question I refused the suggestion of being run for the Electricity Committee because my interest lay with Labour.
>
> I only mention above facts to put in perspective my feelings as to what happened.
>
> I have no doubt that it would have been more prudent to have attended the meeting of the Labour Committee, although I think you yourself accept the validity of the reason for my absence. Incidentally, I can't understand how a Committee which is concerned with Labour could have met at that particular time! But if for that, or any other reason, I had been

---

* John Boyd-Carpenter, later Lord Boyd-Carpenter (1909–1998) was the Member of Parliament for Kingston-upon-Thames 1945–1972. He occupied a number of senior jobs in Government including at the Treasury and as Minister of Pensions and National Insurance.

defeated for the job by anyone outside the PT, so far from having any grievance I should have thought that I owed an apology for having been so bad a candidate, and having "let the side down".

But I did, and do, feel that where we had a meeting and selected our candidates, good or bad, in advance, it is a moral obligation on us all to support these candidates when it comes to the vote. And it is surely all the more the case that we should not allow ourselves to be nominated against the selected candidate. I don't see how we can work together with confidence in each other or with effect on any other basis.

I have had a word with Christopher Hollis, and I am sure that as far as he was concerned there was some misunderstanding despite the circulation of our list of candidates. But I don't feel that the matter should or can be left there.

Sorry to inflict this on you. But as you will have gathered, I do feel strongly on the matter, and, more important than personal feelings, I think it does go the root of our successful working as a team. And that is vital.

This letter goes further than the personal slight of which Boyd-Carpenter complained. It is also a reminder of how, by this time, the PT aimed to work "as a team". Boyd-Carpenter's complaint was taken seriously, and the Political Committee laid down the law a few weeks later:

The Chairman drew attention to the failure which had occurred in securing the nomination of members for positions on important Committees … it was agreed that members must on all occasions support decisions of this nature taken by the Committee and that to avoid any dubiety in the future one member would be entrusted with the duty of making any particular nomination. (27ᵗʰ November 1946)

During this period, the PT grew uneasy over its strict adherence to the provisions of its governing Trust. For example Mr G. I. Woodham-Smith, the Trust's solicitor, once raised the possibility of "getting a contribution out of certain Liberal Trust Funds" but hesitated because "apparently one has to be very careful not to suggest one is asking for support for a Conservative programme." To this, Galbraith replied,

> I do hope that you will pursue your enquiries in regard to the Trust Funds you mentioned to me. You can say that we are a non-party organisation and that the Liberals are represented on the Council by Lord Teviot, while Colonel The Hon. Arthur Murray is one of our Trustees. The other two Trustees were of course non-party, but unfortunately one of them, Lord Tyrrell, has just died. (27ᵗʰ March 1947)

But by 1947, the PT's main objective was to advance the Conservative interest, and it was impossible to claim that it was "a non-party organisation". As with today's think-tanks, Galbraith reflected the tension between the Trust's educational and political objectives, and specifically the PT's avowed purpose of increasing Parliament's knowledge of industry. Constant attempts were indeed made to extend the PT's reach outside Parliament and politics. On 30ᵗʰ July, 1947, for example, the Business Committee met to consider "means of increasing the effectiveness of the Trust's work":

> After discussion it was decided that the Chairman and Mr Pickthorn should ask Colonel Birch if he would undertake the work of organising an extension of the Trust's contacts

and its network of information and particularly to explore the possibility of obtaining the co-operation of the Commodity Exchanges, Lloyds, the Baltic Exchange, the private banks, etc.

On 4th February 1948 a formal Agreement was concluded with Aims of Industry, which was the culmination of discussions over an extended period and which provided regular financial support in the future. One of the objectives of Aims of Industry was to preach the benefits of free enterprise to 'the millions', which is further evidence of how this agreement might have stretched the Trust's deeds beyond their limit. The terms of the Agreement were set out in a letter of 6th February 1948:

1. The Progress Trust will, subject to its own discretion, act as a channel for stimulating parliamentary interest in industrial matters.
2. The Progress Trust will keep Aims of Industry informed of the impact of projected legislation upon industry.
3. Aims of Industry will put at the disposal of the Progress Trust its machinery for obtaining information from its contacts in Industry on any matter of service to the Progress Trust.
4. The facilities of the two Organisations in the matter of Research to be mutually available.

This was consistent with many of the policies pursued by PT members during the remainder of the 1945–50 Parliament. Here are some concerns and opinions expressed by PT MPs which indicate the direction in which many of them were now travelling:

Viscount Hinchingbrooke, who had joined the PT in 1947,

stated in the Budget debate of 1948 that "I regard inflation as a worse danger than the temporary putting off of increased educational and Social Service expenditure." As a result, the PT was keen for him to expand upon this in an article for the popular press.

PT conveyed agreement with a speech by David Eccles (5th March 1948) in which he said: "Inflation had not been caused by the increases in wages, profits and dividends which had frightened the Prime Minister and the Chancellor into their new policy. These unhealthy increases were the consequence of creating too much money, and the responsibility was the Government's." The PT asked in hope whether this could be taken "as official policy".[*]

PT members were concerned over the remarks of Butler in September 1948 that "Rather than re-open the question of ownership of nationalised industries we envisage more elasticity, a decentralisation of management and a simplification in operation."

PT shared widespread scepticism over 'Savings Weeks' launched by The National Savings Movement, which was expressed by one of its regional Chairmen, Mr Carson, in these words: "If you have saved Government stock for six years, believing it safe, the Government is going to take it from you in the form of a capital levy. But if you spend your money on racehorses and loose living, you can get away scot free. It is useless to say that if you save up to a certain amount you are a patriot but that if you save over that amount you are a parasite. I have opened my last savings week. In future they can get a Socialist MP to do the job." (April 1948)

---

* David Eccles regarded himself as a potential Chancellor of the Exchequer, and had hoped to succeed Selwyn-Lloyd following the 'Night of the Long Knives'. See p. 110.

Another indication of PT priorities was their support for a lengthy letter from Lord Elton on industrial co-ownership and profit sharing, published in *The Times* on 30th March 1949. Lord Elton was a cross-bencher opposed to socialism, and was concerned that "what has ensured the present hold of Socialism on the electorate is not nationalization but the apparent establishment of the welfare State – that is to say, the redistribution of the national wealth, at second hand, so to speak, by means of the social services." Elton argued that the choice facing Conservatives was either "the whole hearted conversion to the ideal of the welfare State" – which, to some extent, was the line advocated by the Tory Reform Committee – or "a revolution which would assign a greater direct share of wealth, and responsibility, to the rank and file of industry." Arguably, it was not until Margaret Thatcher that this course was followed. But certainly, Lord Elton's concern that the Conservative Party stood merely for a "milder and reluctant form of Socialism" was shared by many PT members.

There were also serious reservations over Labour's foreign policy. In November 1948, Kenneth Pickthorn suggested to the PT Research Department that it should try, as a matter of urgency, to tie together

all the administrative failures in the conduct of our external affairs in which he included as examples: "Neglect of sailors murdered by the Albanians; our continuing to export rubber from Singapore; continuing commercial negotiations with the Russians; our making trade agreements with Hungary & Poland; the line that has been taken about the German generals; the trial of Mr Sylvester and others in Palestine; the contrast between Britain & the USA's official attitude to commercial men. PT members had also expressed great scepticism over the Defence White paper's assumption of the same year that there would be no war for ten years. This was judged to be "a very unsound basis on which to calculate our defences".

However, despite widely held dissatisfaction with the Opposition's Parliamentary performance, the Conservative Party was by the time of the General Election on 23rd February 1950 again in contention. The PT, through its work on Committees and its publications, had played a part in the great renewal of policy launched by Butler and others, and had done its best to provide opposition to the Government. One study by Sue Onslow goes so far as to claim "By the late 1940s many MPs had come to regard the PT, even more than the 1922 Committee, as the backbone of the Tory Party."[*]

Perhaps; but the extent to which the Conservative Party opposed socialism, or accepted the post-war settlement, had not been resolved. Neither was the PT always sure how far to press its opposition to socialism, as a trifling yet concise minute of the Political Committee dated 23rd November 1949 reveals:

> Members felt that if plans for the Festival of Britain were carried forward they could not oppose plans for the building of a 'Fun Fair'.

---

[*] Sue Onslow: *Backbench Debate Within the Conservative Party 1948–1957*, published 1997. Sue Onslow is the daughter of Cranley Onslow MP who was Chairman of the 1922 Committee 1984–1992.

4

1951–1964: "THIRTEEN WASTED YEARS"?

"Why not start a State Lottery which certainly cannot be any less moral than Football pools?"
(The PT, November, 1952)

"To be quite frank, your party's record in the past three years has been deplorable ... The handling of African independence has been disastrous ... The immigration Act does not go far enough. I am one of the greatest opponents of the colour bar, but we can't let all these people in until our own people are properly housed ... we are all heartily sick of Mr Marples [Minister of Transport]."
(A letter from a constituent to his Member of Parliament Sir Spencer Summers, November 1962)

The political fortunes of the Conservative Party were improving in the lead-up to the 1950 election, but this was of no advantage to the PT. While the Conservatives were on the threshold of thirteen uninterrupted years in office, the PT was living beyond its means. At the beginning of 1949, "subscriptions" were reported to have only "just covered expenditure". Economies were necessary.

Accordingly, the PT Council decided on 26th January 1949 that their premises at 16 Great College Street "should be sold and accommodation found elsewhere". This led to a meeting between the Trustees and the Council on 2nd March 1949 at which the following were present including three of the Trust's most active MPs:

Major Guy Lloyd, DSO, MP (in the chair since Commander Galbraith was ill)
TRUSTEES
His Grace The Duke of Devonshire, KG, MBE, TD
Lt. Gen. Sir Charles Lloyd, KCB, DSO, MC
Lt. Col. The Hon. Arthur Murray, CMG, DSO (who resigned at this meeting)
Lord Teviot, DSO, MC (who was the replacement of Colonel Murray as a Trustee)
COUNCIL/BUSINESS COMMITTEE MEMBERS
Major E. A. H. Legge-Bourke, MP
Major J. G. Morrison, TD, MP
Mr G. I. Woodham-Smith

The disappointment of having to sell the property was softened by the realisation that its fabric was in a sorry state and would have been too expensive to repair. The conclusion of the meeting was that the Trustees should "retain the sum of £10,000 held by them in security" (equivalent to over £300,000 today); that "the premises should be sold as soon as possible for the highest possible sum"; and "that enquiries for alternative accommodation should be pursued as soon as possible after the sale of No. 16 Great College Street".

The sale was completed by November 1949 to a firm of solicitors at a price of £3,200 (equivalent to over £100,000 in today's money). By 1st March 1950 alternative premises had been found in Buckingham Gate, fairly close to Westminster. These were described by Bridget Lakin – who joined the Trust shortly after the move from Great College Street – as two service flats and "a bit depressing". Nevertheless, they remained the Trust's offices until 1960 when it moved to a flat in Ebury Street which had been offered by the Grosvenor Estates* at a rental of £625 p.a. plus an estimated £50 p.a. for rates (total annual cost equivalent to some £14,000 today). Neither premises was ever held in such affection as Great College Street. In a letter of thanks for a retirement gift (23rd March 1950), Margaret Ballard said she would keep it "in remembrance of the days passed in the little panelled room at 16 Great College Street with its view over the Abbey Gardens – days of war and of peace and of many political happenings".

Reductions in staff and output accompanied the move. Long before the elections of 1950 and 1951, the Conservative Research Department had regained its pre-eminent position, including, as it did, some of the brightest young brains of the Conservative Party. It was inevitable, therefore, that the PT's research role diminished in importance. Even so, a decision in March 1950 to discontinue the *Political Digest* was significant. The Labour Government was still in office but with a much reduced majority. Its fragility reduced its capacity to legislate, which in turn provided the PT with an excuse to cut back its coverage of Parliament. This also suited Fells because, as he explained to the Chairman, it would allow him to concentrate upon fewer policy areas in greater detail:

The role which the Political Committee will take for itself and the instructions which will be given about research raises the issue of the future of the Digest. Occasional highly specialised memoranda would not provide suitable raw material for the Digest though they might for occasional printed publications.

---

* Grosvenor Group Holdings Limited was another source of finance for the PT in its later years.

In the light of the King's Speech and the possibility of long recesses it also seems probable that there will not be enough material of adequate importance and interest to fill the Digest even on its present lines which also means the continuance of research on its present lines.

In these circumstances the question arises whether the Digest should cease. It could die a natural death now with the calling of a new Parliament; if it is continued tentatively it would have to do so maybe for at least a year until another Election and another Parliament offered a natural excuse for its disappearance.

The Digest was originally started to attract financial support. Occasional published specialised memoranda particularly on financial and economic subjects may not be any less attractive. (6th March 1950)

This advice was taken. The Business Committee decided two days later "to cease publication of the *Digest* from this issue; to be resumed if and when it is considered worthwhile". Colm Brogan and three other employees ceased working for the PT as a result, although the parting was amicable. Brogan wrote to Galbraith on 12th July 1950:

I feel that I cannot see the end of my connection with the Progress Trust without saying how deeply I appreciate the invariable sympathy and generosity with which I was treated. My four years with the Trust were not only happy in themselves, but I believe they will prove to be enormously useful in the future.

Galbraith said in reply the following day:

We are indeed glad that during the period of our association your name became so well known to the public in England that you were enabled to make contacts in the journalistic and publishing worlds which … will be of the greatest value both to you personally and to the political philosophy to which you adhere.*

By the end of 1951, a cheque for £16/5s was enough to cover the weekly salaries bill (equivalent today to nearly £6,000 p.a.), representing, in today's money, a reduction of some £300 p.a. over the start of the year. A total establishment of nine at its peak had been reduced to four, and Fells was now free to delve more deeply into a range of economic and industrial subjects of particular interest to the Trust.

Sources of finance
The PT continued to receive regular funds from industry. Two of its main donors were the United Industrialists Association (UIA) and the British Industrialist Association (BIA). In 1962, these merged into one body called the British United Industrialists (BUI) and the BUI continued its support of the PT throughout its existence. At times, this organisation was perceived by its detractors as part of a secret mechanism to channel money discreetly into the Conservative Party and other like-minded bodies such as Aims of Industry (which also, as already noted, had links with the PT). It represented a formidable array of businessmen, as evidenced by those

---

* It is pleasant to know that Colm Brogan was, at this time, a constituent of Winston Churchill (he lived in Woodford Green E18). The PT recommended his services to Conservative Central Office in March 1963 "as he is a satirist and we live in the age of satire". As well as being a journalist on *The Herald*, he wrote a number of pamphlets and books. He died in 1977.

attending a PT Council dinner on 10th November 1953 at the House of Lords. On the guest list were:

Sir Charles Colston, CBE, MC, D.C.M., Chairman of U.I.A. & of Hoover Ltd

Sir Frederick Handley Page, Kt., CBE. Director U.I.A. and B.I.A. and Chairman of Handley Page Ltd

Sir Charles Percy Lister KC, Chairman of R. A. Lister & Blackstone & Co. Ltd

Sir Richard Powell, Bt., MC General Manager of U.I.A. and B.I.A.

Mr Halford W. L. Reddish, F.C.A., Director of B.I.A. and Chairman of Portland Cement

Sir Robert Renwick, Bt. KBE, Director of U.I.A. & B.I.A., and of W. Greenwell & Co.

Sir Henry J. Ross, Director of U.I.A. and of Distillers Co. Ltd

The Hon. Randal H. V. Smith, Director of U.I.A. & B.I.A., and of Morgan Grenfell

Major Gen. Sir Edward (Louis) Spears K.B.E., MC, Chairman Institute of Directors

Those MPs representing the PT (as its senior members) were:

Mr Assheton
Lord Bennett
Commander Galbraith
Colonel Gomme-Duncan
Lord Hawke
Lord Hinchingbrooke
Major E. A. H. Legge-Bourke
Major Sir Guy Lloyd
Major Morrison

Brigadier Rayner
Lord Teynham
Lord Teviot

The industrialists' presence at this dinner confirmed their readiness to develop closer links between Parliament and industry. In the following year (July 1954), the UIA and BIA together donated a further £5,000 to the PT. At another dinner held on 16th February 1955, Colonel Hobbs – who had recently commenced working for the BUI – was introduced to the PT. He became one of the Trust's most important supporters and often came to its rescue when funds were urgently required. Life for the PT became harder after his retirement in 1977.

Another group of PT financial supporters, especially towards the final years of its life, was the Estates Business Group (previously the Landowners' Group), which occupied an office in Portman House. Their support encouraged the Trust to keep up with agricultural and land heritage developments. However, the PT needed little encouragement to do so as some were either landowners themselves, or represented constituencies where agricultural issues were important.

To what extent PT donors expected something for their money was never stated explicitly. Occasionally, the PT would give political advice on a particular piece of legislation and, if appropriate, the matter would be taken up with the relevant Minister. More generally, however, industrial supporters of the PT were content merely to be kept informed of Parliamentary proceedings, and to receive the PT's publications and research output. The PT provided its donors with political insight and intelligence, but little else. As a lobbyist on any specific industrial issue, the PT's instinct was to steer clear. Also, once a Conservative Government was returned to office, the PT's enthusiasm for the political game tended to be a distraction from its mission to bring industry and Parliament closer together – especially when a crisis had the capacity to shape politics for decades.

The Suez Crisis

One such crisis was President Nasser's nationalisation of the Suez Canal in 1956. Up to then, Middle East affairs had been intermittently on the PT's agenda. The political minutes of 5th February 1947, for example, record Major Legge-Bourke* as mentioning the "possibility that there would be an announcement of the Government's policy for Palestine shortly which might be partition in favour of the Jews". The minutes continued "This was not felt to be the solution of the problem." In March 1949, following the occupation by British troops of Aqaba, the PT noted Dr Weizmann's warnings that the Egyptians could close Suez to Jewish shipping and that at some stage a new canal might have to be cut between Tel Aviv and Aqaba. It was argued that threats to the Suez Canal made it essential for Aqaba to be placed in Jewish hands.

But the PT's first acknowledgement of a potential crisis was on 28th October 1953 when the Political Committee held "a general discussion on Foreign Affairs, with special emphasis on the Suez Canal". This discussion took place in advance of a foreign affairs debate in the House of Commons which prevented the Foreign Secretary, Anthony Eden, from dining with the PT that evening as planned. Since this debate was

---

* Sir Harry Legge-Bourke (1914–1973) was the Member of Parliament for Isle of Ely from 1945 until his death in 1973. He was another member of the PT who was also Chairman of the 1922 Committee (1970–1972).

upon 'European Affairs and Trieste', Eden had no reason to make any reference to Suez. But PT members must have had fresh in their minds Churchill's Parliamentary speech a few months earlier during Eden's enforced absence through illness:

> Naturally, we do not wish to keep indefinitely 80,000 men at a cost of, it might be, over £50 million a year discharging the duty which has largely fallen upon us, and us alone, of safeguarding the interests of the free nations in the Middle East, and also of preserving the international waterway of the Suez Canal ... Of course, if the boastful and threatening speeches of which there has been a spate in the last few months, and, in some instances, even in the last few hours, were to be translated into action and our troops in the Canal Zone were to be the object of renewed attacks by saboteurs or even by the Egyptian Army, which is being aided and trained by Nazi instructors and staff officers in unusual numbers, and our soldiers were being killed, we should have no choice – I am sorry to say this to the House, but we must face facts – but to defend ourselves. I am advised that we are entirely capable of doing this without requiring any physical assistance from the United States or anyone else. (Hansard, 11th May 1953 c. 853–892)

In this speech, it was Churchill who held out the prospect of a war over the Suez Canal which ultimately led to Eden's downfall, and which, with its ramifications, divided the country for generations to come. But for the PT, the crisis developed slowly. The issue was only discussed twice in 1954. After the meeting on 19th May when Major Mott-Radclyffe* gave "the Committee the benefit of his views, following his

---

* Sir Charles Mott-Radclyffe (1911–1992) was the Member of Parliament for Windsor between 1942 and 1970.

recent visit to Egypt and the Suez Canal zone", it was not discussed again until the crisis broke in 1956, despite the strong views held by some of its members. No doubt one explanation for this apparent lack of interest was that nine members of the PT were also active members of the Suez Group which, prior to the crisis, existed to oppose what it suspected was Government weakness in its negotiations with the Egyptians.* One of these, Major Legge-Bourke, actually resigned the Tory Whip in July 1954, and became an independent Conservative MP, because of his opposition to the Government's resumption of Anglo-Egyptian negotiations. The Whip was restored to him in October. Since Suez was such a divisive issue, and a Suez Group already existed, it made sense for the PT to steer clear of the issue, and leave it to others to pursue.

However, this changed on 10th September, when members of the PT received the following telegram:

PLEASE ATTEND SPECIAL MEETING 78 BUCKINGHAM GATE 12 NOON WEDNESDAY SEPTEMBER 12 TO DISCUSS SUEZ — GUY LLOYD

Fourteen members of the PT attended this meeting, but no record of the discussion was taken.† The situation was

---

* PT members of the Suez Group included Ralph Assheton, Captain Duncan, Christopher Holland-Martin, Lord Hinchingbrooke, Harry Legge-Bourke, Guy Lloyd, Angus Maude, Charles Waterhouse and Paul Williams.

† Those attending, with their titles, were: Major Sir Guy Lloyd, Major John G. Morrison, Major Sir William Anstruther-Gray, Bt., Captain J. A. L. Duncan, Colonel Sir Alan Gomme-Duncan, Mr Alan Green, Viscount Hinchingbrooke, Major E. A. H. Legge-Bourke, The Rt. Hon. J. S. Maclay, Lt. Commander S. L. C. Maydon, Major C. E. Mott-Radclyffe, Sir Spencer

discussed throughout the crisis on seven future occasions, however, including:

> 24th October 1956, "when Lord Hinchingbrooke undertook to pursue certain suggestions in the appropriate quarter";
> 31st October 1956, the day of a debate on Suez in the House of Commons in which PT members Hinchingbrooke and Legge-Bourke spoke in support of the Government;
> 7th November 1956, when exception was taken to an article on Suez which had appeared in *The Guardian* of 1st November;*
> 5th December 1956, with special reference to the Foreign Secretary's announcement in the House two days earlier which, in effect, acknowledged the failure of the Government's policy;
> 12th December 1956, which considered "the political situation" following the two-day debate on the Suez Crisis on 5th & 6th December 1956.

During the December debate, some Conservative MPs who had been most supportive of the Government's original decision to take military action now became the fiercest critics of its retreat. On 6th December, 327 Conservative MPs opposed the Labour Opposition's motion on Suez; but when it came to supporting the Government's own motion, this number dropped to 312. Two PT members spoke in the debate – Captain Charles Waterhouse† and Angus

---

Summers, Captain the Rt. Hon. Charles Waterhouse and Mr Paul Williams.

* A number of critical articles appeared in *The Guardian* of 1st November, but this probably refers to a piece by Max Freedman describing intense anger in the United States over Suez: "Veteran reporters cannot remember ever seeing American opinion ... so incensed and so critical of British policy."

† Charles Waterhouse (1893–1975) was the Member of Parliament for Leicester South between 1924 and 1945 and Leicester South East between

Maude[*] – and both withheld their support in the division. Legge-Bourke wasn't called by the Speaker, but did his best to speak through interventions. Eden's resignation as Prime Minister followed shortly in the New Year (9th January).

Some thought Butler should be Eden's successor, but Macmillan gained the prize. How this came about is controversial, with the PT implicated in Butler's failure to succeed. During the Suez crisis Major John Morrison[†], the Vice Chairman of the PT's Political Committee, was also Chairman of the 1922 Committee (he was elected to this post on 3rd November 1955). He therefore carried great influence within the Parliamentary Party at this crucial moment. A former High Sheriff of Wiltshire, he was once described as "the cartoonist's dream of what every Chairman of the 1922 Committee should look like."[‡] Lord Lambton provided a further description:

> ... he is no way representative of the new Conservatism – his main recreations are those of a nineteenth-century sporting patrician with the hounds, his shooting records and his country tastes ... he is completely disconnected with ambition, but that in everything practical he does he excels.

One of Morrison's practical tasks was to contain the Suez

1950 and 1957.

[*] Angus Maude (1912–1993) was the Member of Parliament for Ealing South between 1950 and 1958 and then Stratford-on-Avon between 1963–1983.

[†] Major John Morrison, later Lord Margadale (1906–1996), was the Member of Parliament for Salisbury from 1942–1965. He was Chairman of the 1922 Committee between 1955 and 1964.

[‡] Philip Goodhart, *The Story of the 1922 Committee*, published 1973.

rebellion within the Conservative Party. He had been a former member of the Suez Group himself, but resigned before it began to make life difficult for the Government. Morrison's dual role partly explains why, when on both occasions Butler was in contention for the leadership (i.e. 1956 and 1963), the PT was suspected by Butler's friends of undermining his chances of becoming Prime Minister. A direct reference to the first of these occasions was in an article by the left-wing journalist Hugh Massingham for *The Sunday Telegraph* written some ten years later on 28th August 1966:

> Because of his ambivalent attitude Rab had few friends at the end of the crisis. Those on the Left of the party felt that he had deserted them and those on the Right had become his implacable enemies. In Eden's last fading days he probably had very little influence, but the Right was united, important and resolute. They were not very numerous, but about a dozen of them belonged to a curious club that was comically called the Progress Trust. The name is typical of the double talk of our declining nation. Even the right wing of the Tory Party feel compelled to use words that give a wholly misleading idea of their real thoughts and philosophy.
>
> The members of this small group canvassed. They worked. Like Eden, they did not care very much who was the next Prime Minister, but they were determined that it should not be Rab. In every struggle for the Tory leadership what matters is not so much who is for you as who is against you, and the Right made so much noise, Rab's friends were so dispirited and out of favour, that the honest, bewildered member naturally came to the conclusion that Macmillan was the only man who could unite the party.

Massingham was not a friendly witness – his natural home was *The Observer* rather than *The Sunday Telegraph*. Butler's lacklustre performance in front of the 1922 Committee on 22nd November 1956 was much more fatal to his chances of becoming Prime Minister than anything the PT could have said against him.

Nor is it certain that the PT as a whole was 'anti' Butler. True, there were members of the PT who, long before Suez, had accurately remembered Butler as a supporter of Neville Chamberlain and, less fairly, a detached member of Churchill's wartime Government. Butler had even been suspected of favouring negotiations with Germany to bring the war to an early conclusion, an accusation which carried weight for those already ill-disposed towards him. Also, there were some in the PT who still held against him his 'modernising' approach in Opposition between 1945 and 1950.

On the other hand, Butler was one of the PT's most regular dinner guests. Perhaps it was because he knew the PT so well that at a dinner during the Suez crisis, on 14th November 1956, he opened up in a way which, according to his biographer Anthony Howard, he came to regret:

> Whatever credit he (Butler) might have attracted as a result of his bewildering, belated defence of the Government's Suez policy in the Commons on 13th November 1956 had been dissipated the very next night when, in the supposed privacy of a Commons dining-room, he had rashly blurted out all that had gone on (not leaving out the threat to sterling) to some twenty right-wing MPs who were members of the so-called Progress Trust.*

---

* *RAB: The Life of R. A. Butler* by Anthony Howard, Jonathan Cape, 1987.

Ian Gilmour in *The Oxford Dictionary of National Biography* also described Butler's behaviour on this occasion as "being almost suicidally imprudent at a dinner of right-wing MPs", using again 'right-wing' in a pejorative sense.

It is odd, however, that Butler should have spoken so frankly to a supposedly hostile audience. If Gilmour was correct about the PT's sympathies, why did Butler take such a risk? Moreover, the frequency of past contacts between the PT and Butler – not just as a dinner guest, but also as one always ready to receive PT deputations – suggests that relations between him and the Trust were cordial. Butler's own account of this particular 'Suez' dinner captures perhaps more accurately both the PT's character and occasion:

> It was my misfortune and perhaps my miscalculation that at precisely this moment in time, when we were making up our minds to withdraw, I dined with twenty influential Conservative members of the Progress Trust, and was very open with them in speaking privately of some of the realities of the situation, particularly in relation to sterling, which no one had hitherto had done. The small private room became like a hornets' nest. They all hurried off to the Carlton Club to prepare representations to the government. Whenever I moved in the weeks that followed, I felt the party knives sticking into my innocent back. (*The Art Of The Possible, The Memoirs of Lord Butler*, Hamish Hamilton, 1971)

Butler's complaint, if it be a complaint, was that "they all hurried off … to prepare representations to the government" – but not, let it be noted, to the press. Most members of the PT were opposed to bowing to American pressure and regretted the Government's change of policy. But their opposition was not necessarily directed at Butler personally; and, along with many others, they failed to notice at the time that if anyone was guilty of changing his mind, it was Macmillan who subsequently earned the epithet with regard to Suez 'First-in, First-out'.

Eight Conservative MPs opposed to military action over Suez had abstained from supporting the Government in the House of Commons on 8th November 1956 – none of these was a member of the PT. However, in May of the following year a further eight MPs who had supported Eden originally but opposed the subsequent 'climb-down', resigned the Conservative Whip in protest at the Government's abandonment of its boycott of the Canal.* Three of these rebels were members of the PT – Viscount Hinchingbrooke, Angus Maude and Paul Williams[†] – and this led to their suspension from the PT. Their departure was handled by Sir Guy Lloyd who informed the PT "that he had personally spoken to the Members concerned … as requested, and it was now mutually understood that their Membership of the PT was regarded as being in suspense until such time as they again accepted the Party Whip" (Business minutes, 29th May 1957).

Foreign Policy

The Suez crisis may have been the most dramatic example of Britain's changed place in the world, but it was Dean Acheson, the former US Secretary of State under President

---

* Other Tory MPs who resigned the Whip in May 1957 were John Biggs-Davison, Anthony Fell, Hon. Patrick Maitland, Sir Victor Raikes and Lawrence Turner.

† Paul Williams (1922–2008) was the Member of Parliament for Sunderland South from 1953 until his defeat in the election of October 1964 when he subsequently became Chairman of the Monday Club.

Truman, who six years later struck the rawest of nerves with his celebrated remark that "Britain has lost an Empire and has not yet found a role" (5th December 1962).

Conservatives had been sensitive to such sentiments ever since 1945 when their reluctant acquiescence in the loss of Empire was skilfully portrayed by the Labour Party as an eagerness to wage war in compensation. At the Durham Miners Gala of 21st July 1951, for example, Herbert Morrison proclaimed:

> If you had seen the semi-hysteria of backbench Tory MPs in the last fortnight, if you have read the more excitable of the Conservative newspapers, you will find it difficult not to conclude that if they had had their way, we should have been involved in two wars in the last ten days or so.[*]

Since those with direct experience of fighting a war are normally the least enthusiastic over waging a new one, it was unjust to charge Conservative MPs of that generation of 'war-mongering'. But it played to popular sentiment that Conservatives had a sentimental regard for a declining Empire and were prepared to protect their interests overseas more actively – and, if necessary, by military intervention – than Labour's more pacifist stance.

The PT believed that the primary objective of Britain's defence and foreign policy should be to protect her security at home and her commercial interests abroad. How best this was done was not always obvious. The 1948 Conservative Party Conference in Llandudno, for example, was accused by various commentators of "re-dreaming an old dream of

---

[*] This was presumably in reference to the Abadan crisis and the nationalisation of the Iranian oilfields.

Imperial Preference" and Churchill himself of proclaiming simultaneously the benefits of both Imperial Preference and "the new hope of Western Union". The PT noticed "that among economists and financial journalists there is a feeling that the Conference got itself hopelessly tied up about the sanctity of Imperial Preference".

Russia was a separate issue. There were those in the PT who during the war, and in anticipation of the Cold War, had always suspected Eden of showing too much leniency towards the Russians – and not just Eden. The Political Committee discussed on 20th November 1945 a report that "Mr R. A. Butler, speaking at Wimbledon on Tuesday, is reported as calling for less suspicion of Russia." The PT asked "whether this is Conservative Policy?"*

Underlying the PT's mistrust of Russia was a fear of the spread of Communism; and this fear determined, in turn, whom the PT counted amongst Britain's true friends and allies. One minor incident serves as a reminder of how sensitive this question was to become. In the early months of 1952, following his illness, King George VI was due to go to South Africa as a guest of D. F. Malan, the Prime Minister of South Africa, to convalesce by the coast.† Six Labour MPs objected to this and proposed that an address be presented to the King praying that he will take into consideration "the distress caused to many of his subjects" by his decision to stay in Dr Malan's official residence. Six Conservative MPs reacted by tabling an amendment "rejoicing at the continued

---

* This is the first of many references to R. A. Butler in the minutes of the Progress Trust.

† The term 'apartheid' had been introduced in 1948 as part of Dr Malan's election campaign, although racial segregation had been in force for many decades before.

improvement in his health and praying that His Majesty will disregard mischievous attempts to embroil the Crown in controversy following His Majesty's gracious acceptance of the Hospitality offered by his Prime Minister in the Union of South Africa". Three of these MPs (John Vaughan-Morgan,[*] Angus Maude, and Sir Edward Boyle[†]) were future members of the PT, although Sir Edward had little in common with either of the others. He was associated with the 'left' of the Conservative Party, would resign from the Government over Suez and quarrelled with Angus Maude much later over education policy. On the other hand, his gentle, civilised approach to politics was very much to the PT's taste.

The PT's defence of the King's visit to South Africa was as much constitutional as political:

> The King of England is constitutionally quite separately the King of South Africa and separately the King of each Dominion. How can his dealings with each Dominion be properly brought within the purview of the House of Commons? Ought not the propriety of the Speaker allowing such tablings be considered by the highest legal authorities? (Business minutes, 6th February 1952)

In defending the constitutional rights of the King, the PT also demonstrated its habitual reluctance to delve into the internal affairs of a 'friendly' country. Nowhere was this reluctance more evident than in Africa and, especially, Rhodesia, where hostility to majority rule was the cause of deep divisions

---

* Sir John Vaughan-Morgan (1905–1995) was the Member of Parliament for Reigate between 1950 and 1970.

† Sir Edward Boyle (1923–1981) was the Member of Parliament for Birmingham Handsworth between 1950 and 1970.

within the Conservative Party throughout this period.

As far back as 1948, the PT had taken notice of the Communist Party's call for the liberation of Africa from 'economic exploitation' and by the early 1960s Africa was a regular topic of discussion by the PT's Political and Business Committees. Iain Macleod had been appointed Secretary of State for the Colonies in October 1959, in which capacity Lord Salisbury had famously described him in the House of Lords as "too clever by half" (7th March 1961), a sentiment shared by many in the Trust. A few days earlier on 22nd February 1961, the PT discussed Rhodesia almost for the first time,* and concluded "that Mr Macleod has lost a lot of confidence here and in Africa" although it was also agreed "that he should not resign at the moment, and that we must back the plan".†

This was only a temporary respite. On 15th March 1961, the PT felt the Government had become "too stubborn" towards Rhodesia, was adhering to the White Paper too strictly, and that "the Chairman, if he had the opportunity, should give this view to Mr Butler, and if not speak to the Chief Whip." As well as being Home Secretary, Butler was at this moment Chairman of the Conservative Party and Leader of the House of Commons. A week later, amidst fears that South Africa might leave the Commonwealth, the Trust believed "that as

---

* The PT had prepared a Research Note on the Federation of Rhodesia and Nyasaland in anticipation of a meeting with Sir Archibald James on 21st November 1956 "on the subject of the Federation of Rhodesia and its problems." At the time, *The Economist* stated "The real issue is to make partnership more of a reality to the African population, and out of African co-operation and contentment to recreate the sense of European security."

† This plan was Iain Macleod's proposal for a new constitution to govern the Central African Foundation.

many links as possible should be kept with South Africa".

On 10th May, the PT brought their concerns to Macleod personally in a PT deputation comprising Morrison, Legge-Bourke, Commander Maydon,* John Peyton† and Stephen Hastings.‡ The delegation was instructed to raise the position of Jomo Kenyatta and to suggest to Macleod that "he should have better relations with the white settlers in Africa." Macleod was replaced as Colonial Secretary by Reginald Maudling in October 1961, who was soon described by Macmillan as being even more enthusiastic than Macleod to pursue a new Northern Rhodesia constitution. Rhodesia was the subject of a further PT meeting with Butler on 4th April 1962 which was thought to have gone "quite satisfactorily and it was agreed that it would be a good thing to maintain contact with Mr Butler on this subject". Butler had just been appointed head of the newly created Central African Department, while remaining as Home Secretary.

Macleod, however, was the architect of the policy and the conflicting emotions surrounding it were symptomatic of Conservative divisions, which became more acute as the 1960s progressed. They encouraged, for example, the creation of the Monday Club in January 1961.§ The break-up

---

* Lieutenant Commander Lynch Maydon (1913–1971) was the Member of Parliament for Wells between 1951 and 1970.

† John Peyton (1919–2006), later Lord Peyton of Yeovil, was the Member of Parliament for Yeovil between 1951 and 1983. He was Minister of Transport from 1970–1974 but an opponent of Edward Heath.

‡ Sir Stephen Hastings (1921–2005) was the Member of Parliament for Mid-Bedfordshire between 1960 and 1983.

§ The Monday Club was an active 'right-wing' pressure group within the Conservative Party whose influence was at its strongest throughout the 1960s and 1970s.

of the Central African Federation was the Monday Club's chosen topic for its first public meeting in September 1961, and opposition to majority rule in South Africa and Rhodesia was one of its principal purposes. The PT made no comment on the Monday Club's existence until February 1962 when it thought it would be useful to meet its representatives and "help to steer them along sensible lines". But the PT's mind quickly changed. On 7th March 1962, Fells was asked to "draft a letter for next week arranging a meeting between Mr Bristol and Mr Fells, but it was agreed that the meeting should not take place on the PT premises, and that the PT should not be mentioned." A week later "It was agreed that Mr Fells should not proceed with the idea to meet Mr Bristol of the Monday Club." So the meeting never took place; and in the event only a few MPs associated with the PT were active members of the Monday Club.*

Nevertheless, the PT was sympathetic to some of its beliefs. Broadly, the PT was aligned with anyone who shared a dislike of interference in the internal affairs of friendly African countries, even discussing in February 1962 "how speedily independence should be given to the Rhodesias". For most PT members, Africa was not an issue upon which to rebel or 'go public'. One exception, however, was Sir Harry Legge-Bourke. By 1962, he was totally out of sympathy with the Party's leadership, and when he criticised Macmillan personally and in public, stating it was time the Prime Minister stood down, he decided he should resign from the Chairmanship of the Conservative Party's Defence Committee. At the same time, he also resigned from the PT:

---

* The most prominent of these were Victor Goodhew, Stephen Hastings, Lord Hinchingbrooke, John Peyton and Paul Williams (a future Monday Club Chairman).

The Political Committee agreed to accept with deep regret the resignation of Sir Harry Legge-Bourke. It was also agreed that in due course should it be mutually agreed his name could be reconsidered for membership. (PT Committee minutes, 14th February 1962)

On 28th February 1962, Reginald Maudling spoke in the House of Commons following the recent violence and disorder in Northern Rhodesia, when he expressed the "earnest hope of Her Majesty's Government that all parties in Northern Rhodesia will now co-operate in the new Constitution and fight the election, when it comes, on this basis". The final reference to Rhodesia in the PT's minutes during this period was on 3rd April 1963 when "it was agreed that Southern Rhodesia should be given the right of independence now ... and that the Chairman, Sir Charles Mott-Radclyffe and Sir Tufton Beamish* should have a word with the Chief Whip on these subjects today."

Iain Macleod's approach to Africa distanced him from the PT. Hitherto, they had enjoyed cordial relations. Indeed, when Macleod was first elected to the House of Commons, he was short-listed as a potential PT member although for some reason this was never pursued (15th November 1950). His rapid promotion to Minister of Health in May 1952 was welcomed by Conservatives, and led to his receiving a PT delegation only a few months later.

But by the time Macleod became Chancellor of the Duchy of Lancaster, Leader of the House of Commons and

---

* Sir Tufton Beamish (1917–1989), later Lord Chelwood, was the Member of Parliament for Lewes between 1945 and 1974. He always remained on the backbenches and was Chairman of the PT between 1970 and 1973.

Conservative Party Chairman – he was appointed to all three roles on 9th October 1961 – he habitually attracted criticism from those who believed "the winds of change" in Africa were raging too severely. On 18th April 1962, the PT decided "that there should be a formal Progress Trust approach over the point that the same man (i.e. Macleod) should not hold the two posts of Leader of the House and Chairman of the Party, and that an individual approach should be made as well." Two months later (25th July 1962), the PT described a letter by Macleod to Conservative Constituency Chairmen as "tactless and unnecessary".

By November, the PT had softened its criticism of Macleod as Party Chairman and felt "he was doing a good job" (28th November 1962). But his conduct following Macmillan's resignation quickly dispelled this impression. The PT deplored Macleod's famous article in *The Spectator* attacking the process through which Sir Alec Douglas-Home had 'emerged' as Prime Minister, declaring "the less said about Mr Macleod's article in *The Spectator* the better."* Macmillan's resignation, and the appointment of Douglas-Home, was the second occasion when the PT's influence was suspected of damaging Butler's chances of becoming Prime Minister, although here again it was probably the personal intervention of John Morrison that was more significant. This was the famous occasion when Morrison is reported to have said to Butler that "the chaps won't have you." Macleod and Powell disagreed – they wanted Butler and thought that, if only he had displayed the necessary ruthlessness, he could have become Prime Minister. Whether or not they were right,

---

* This lengthy article appeared in *The Spectator* on 17th January 1964; it was when Macleod referred to "the tightness of the magic circle" in choosing Macmillan's successor.

there is no doubt that both Macleod's and Powell's refusal to serve under Douglas-Home was a loss to the Conservative Government.

Domestic Policy

In his *Spectator* article, one of Macleod's main contentions was that "the Tory party for the first time since Bonar Law is now being led from the Right of the centre." In foreign policy terms, the meaning of 'right of centre' was clear. It described anyone unhappy with the speedy dissolution of Empire, with defence cuts, and with the withdrawal from 'East of Suez'. But Macleod was speaking also of domestic politics, where the terms 'right' or 'left' are harder to define.

From the moment the Conservatives were returned to office in 1951, there were members of the PT who voiced disappointment with its performance. Captain Waterhouse, for example, "expressed alarm at the tendency of certain Ministers to reject any proposals which did not meet with the approval of the trade unions", a view "supported" by the rest of the Committee declaring "the matter should be very carefully watched." At the same meeting (28th November 1951), Brigadier Rayner* "thought it was deplorable that under the new Government, small enterprises were being forced to cut down or close down because of lack of raw materials". For such disappointments to be voiced so early on in a new Government's life was unusual, and was indicative of the suspicion that Churchill's Cabinet was 'not being Conservative enough'.

Sections of the press felt the same. Although the PT had little formal contact with the media, a joint luncheon took

---

* Brigadier Sir Ralph Rayner (1896–1977) was the Member of Parliament for Totnes between 1935 and 1955.

place on 22nd May 1952 with five journalists who included Hugh McMichael, the editor of *The Scotsman*. Most of the journalists' comments related to 'spin' and their own personal convenience:

> contacts with Ministers and even MPs were "nothing like so good as it used to be";
>
> the 'timing' of various popular or unpopular announcements might be greatly improved if only the Government would seek the 'lobby's' advice;
>
> there was no opportunity for press and MPs to mingle given "the disparity in refreshments" and the "lack of a bar to be used by lobby and Press Gallery". The refusal to allow the press to use the Terrace was objectionable and "Annie's Bar was greatly missed – there should be some bar where members of the government, private members and members of the lobby and Press Gallery can stand each other a drink."

Their most surprising comment, however, was that most of the press was "behind the Government" but, because of bad liaison, Ministers were not "reaping the full advantage of their support". The PT was also worried at this time by the negative press comment concerning Churchill himself "ranging from *The Economist* to *The Sunday Pictorial. The Evening Standard* complains that there is no retort to these criticisms from backbench members of the Party and that this silence if it continues will greatly damage the Party."

A general sense that Churchill's Government was not acting with sufficient energy to reverse the socialist direction of policy was felt most directly in the economic sphere, but it pervaded many other domestic topics in which the PT took an interest – in particular the Health Service, and agriculture.

On health issues, the work undertaken by Fells led to the already-mentioned deputation to see Macleod on 11ᵗʰ November 1952. Principally, this was to discuss a PT survey on the general state of the Health Service which had been sent personally to Macleod "explaining the motives for having had it prepared". At the meeting, which lasted over an hour, the PT's focus was to stress the need for a proper accounting and costing system within the Health Service. Most of the questions raised were therefore of a technical nature. Nevertheless, Conservative fears that under Bevan the National Health Service had taken the wrong path were never far from the surface. So at this meeting, Macleod was asked whether he was considering charging "for X-ray and for food provided in hospitals?" He replied that he was opposed to charges for X-ray treatment, "believing that the saving would be comparatively trivial"; and on charging for meals, the PT was reminded "it would, undoubtedly, be unpopular: it would require a means test and, for various reasons, he considered that the actual saving would not amount to more than five or six million pounds." Macleod was also asked whether hospitals should receive block financial allocations over a number of years: Macleod agreed it was desirable, but doubted whether "Parliament would approve block grants involving many millions of pounds."*

Somewhat inconsistently, the PT also argued at this meeting against private patients having to pay the full charge for their medicines, even though any change here would have cost the Health Service a considerable sum. Many Conservatives believed that Bevan, for political reasons, had

---

* The Minister of Health was not, at this time, a member of the Cabinet: this remained the case until Enoch Powell, as Minister of Health, was promoted to the Cabinet in 1962.

created an unnecessarily large division between the private and public sectors. One way of bridging this division was to allow private patients to obtain their prescriptions on the same terms as those under the Health Service, especially as this had once been Conservative Party policy. Macleod needed no reminding of the political dangers of this advice, but was in agreement that there should be greater awareness that "the cost of the Health Service comes principally from taxation" and he too was concerned over "the unfortunate relationship which has developed within the Health Service between General Practitioners and Consultants". He also agreed that there was potential for greater use of voluntary help within the NHS.

Following the meeting with Macleod, the PT's interest in the NHS remained primarily financial. In June 1958, the PT hoped "that the Select Committee on Estimates would look further into the cost of the Health Services". In November 1959, the PT returned to the inability of private patients "to obtain free drugs under the Health Act" emphasising again this was in breach "of a party promise made ten years ago". The issue was raised again in November 1963 although, by then, "it was not the time to press it." During Enoch Powell's tenure as Health Minister (1960–63), the only aspect of health policy which the PT discussed was nurses' pay, where "the inequality of the differential seems to be the main trouble."

As already suggested, the PT's involvement in agriculture derived partly, but not entirely, from the interests of its donors. At the beginning of 1953, the PT formed an Agricultural Controls Sub-Committee, which on 28th April visited the Minister of Agriculture, Sir Thomas Dugdale.* The delegation

---

* The PT was represented by Major Sir Guy Lloyd, Major Morrison, Mr

informed the Minister that the PT was broadly supportive of the Government's agricultural policy. They accepted the need for regular price reviews in the short term, but were "anxious to wind up the Ministry of Food as soon as possible to restore trading in food to private enterprise". For the longer term, they conceded "that some form of support prices for farm produce may be necessary but we hope that it will be possible to get away from annual price reviews with all the unpleasant negotiations associated with them". In particular, they opposed any Government interference "to check a rise in prices above the level brought about by consumer demand".

But their principal concern involved the rights and duties of landowners. The PT argued that the protection of these rights was key to increasing the productivity of land. Amongst a long list of recommendations, the PT advocated:

- the restoration of the landowner's right to give notice to quit;
- greater use of the leasehold system thus providing greater security of tenure;
- the need for a very substantial increase in rents, otherwise no resources for land improvements would be available;
- no aggregation of land with other assets for death duty purposes, and "only a nominal rate of duty should be paid unless and until the land is sold."
- modification of the ultimate sanction of dispossession.

Today, this list is easily branded as selfish. At the time, however, it was seeking to do no more than restore a balance distorted by the war. The Minister was sympathetic, but timid in light of the political and practical constraints in turning

---

Assheton, Lord Cranborne, Captain Duncan, Major Legge-Bourke, Mr Mott-Radclyffe and Brigadier Rayner.

back the clock. One of his objections to the raising of rents was that it would provide the landowner with little benefit until taxation had been reduced, even though "in principle it would help production." The Minister also favoured regulatory as opposed to legislative remedies "owing to the [Parliamentary] opposition otherwise involved." On dispossession, the Minister saw no alternative but to maintain the ultimate sanction "although he did not like it, at any rate in the meantime".

Another deputation to the Ministry took place on 16th March 1955, concentrating upon "the alleged powers of the Milk Marketing Board"; but by the 1960s, agricultural issues were dominated by the implications of entry into the Common Market. Until then, the PT and Government were aligned in believing that agriculture should participate in a general move towards greater economic freedom. But hints of self-interest were never far away. In February 1954, for example, John Morrison had voiced concern that, under the Housing Repair and Rents Bill, the new principle involved "the landlord being responsible for interior decoration and repair".

Resale Price Maintenance

How the PT justified its support for farmers and land-owners was also mirrored in its opposition to Resale Price Maintenance – an issue long forgotten, but at the time divisive and dangerous for the Conservative Party.*

Those in the Conservative Party who, in 1964, opposed

---

* Resale (or Retail) Price Maintenance was a system whereby manufacturers and distributors essentially collaborated to prevent prices from falling below an agreed level in order to maintain the viability of small traders and shopkeepers.

the abolition of Resale Price Maintenance (RPM) were sometimes branded as 'right-wing' because of their innate conservatism and their wish to protect the interests of the small shopkeeper. But if it is 'right-wing' to be laissez-faire and economically liberal, as the term is understood today, the description fits more accurately those opposed to the practice of fixing prices at a minimum level. At least, the PT acknowledged the issue's complexity and its political sensitivity. As early as 16th June 1950 (although RPM had been on and off the agenda since 1920), PT members were encouraged to attend a Private Members' Debate on RPM in the House of Commons. The subject was selected by a Labour MP (W. T. Williams), and the debate developed into something of a fiasco when the motion he proposed attacking RPM turned out to be inconsistent with his speech which, in many respects, supported it. One leading member of the PT – Spencer Summers* – responded:

> The thing which is important … is that this is not a simple matter; that any attempt to do away with such abuses as may exist are quite capable, unless treated with discrimination, of doing more harm than the good they seek to do. I therefore hope that in dealing with this matter the complexity and variety of its nature will be recognised, and that it will be dealt with on a realistic ad-hoc basis, doing away with such abuses as can be proved to exist, where they exist, without at the same time, by the crudeness of the methods intended to do away with these abuses, doing more damage to the public in other directions. (Hansard, 16th June 1950 c. 771)

---

* Sir Spencer Summers (1902–1976) was the Member of Parliament for Northampton between 1940 and 1945 and then Aylesbury between 1950 and 1970. He was Chairman of the PT from 1965–1970.

The curious aspect of this debate was that Conservative MPs who were supportive of RPM found themselves defending practices which Labour MPs argued were uncompetitive and led to higher prices. On 9th May 1951, the Political Committee decided they should attempt to reach unanimity on the question, and by February 1955 the PT was sufficiently of one mind to approach the President of the Board of Trade (Peter Thorneycroft) to urge caution.

With the intervention of both a General Election and the Suez crisis, RPM disappeared from view, but resurfaced early in 1962 when once again the PT approached the President of The Board of Trade, who was now Frederick Erroll and a former member of the PT. By then, not a single member of the PT's Political Committee was in favour of the abolition of RPM, and "it was agreed that the Chairman should try and have a word about it with Mr Erroll and that Mr Kimball should speak to Sir Keith Joseph, Minister of State for Trade" (2nd May 1962). This was followed up a fortnight later by a letter to Erroll "urging that this was not a good time politically to abolish the system of Resale Price Maintenance, owing to the resentment it would cause amongst small traders". The PT received from Erroll "a rather non-committal answer" (30th May 1962).*

After Macmillan's dramatic reconstruction of his Government (13th July 1962):

The Chairman [Major John Morrison] said that he had spoken to the President of the Board of Trade [Erroll had survived the re-shuffle] and that it looked as though the Government were

---

* At about the same time (11th July 1962) nine members of the PT declared themselves against local commercial radio, amounting to another illiberal and 'left-wing' stance.

still going to go ahead and alter the present system. It was agreed that the Chairman should write to Mr Alan Green [the new Minister of State] and give the views of the PT that it was suicidal folly politically to alter the status quo at the moment. (Political Committee, 18th July 1962)

Morrison was correct in his assumption that the Government was still going ahead. By January 1964, following the abolition of the office of President of the Board of Trade, Edward Heath was appointed the first Secretary of State for Industry, Trade and Regional Development – and he too was determined to end RPM:

There was a full discussion on Resale Price Maintenance. It was agreed that shop hours should be prolonged but not to touch Sunday opening at the present time ... that those trades who had been through the Monopolies Commission should not have to go through the mill again ... that the timing of the abolition had been bad and that there would be no time for reaction before the Election. It was agreed that the subject should be discussed next week after Mr Heath had been to the 1922. (Political Committee, 22nd January 1964)

By then, the PT had been forced to abandon its principled objection to discontinuing RPM, and concentrated instead upon mitigating the consequences of doing so, through amendments to the Bill. Never wishing to be in open rebellion:

The Chairman [Morrison] referred to a suggestion from Mr Goodhart* that a Committee should be convened including

---

* Philip Goodhart, who was not a member of the PT, was the

some of the rebels to discuss the RPM Bill at the same time as it is being discussed on the floor of the House. It was agreed that this would be useful providing that HMG is willing to give way a bit and that the rebels would be prepared to make it a workable Act and co-operate. (Political Committee, 4th March 1964)

But a week later, when RPM was again discussed, "it was agreed that Mr Heath must be more accommodating to the reasonable amendments otherwise the Government may find themselves beaten on one or two amendments." On the 15th April:

RPM and Clause 5 amendment 59 was discussed fully, it was agreed that this was not a "wrecking" amendment and should be allowed to go through otherwise there would be another row. It was agreed that the Chairman should report the views of the Committee to the PM, and that Sir Charles Mott-Radclyffe, Sir Tufton Beamish, and Sir Richard Glyn should speak to the Chief Whip (William Whitelaw). Mr Kimball and Mr James would speak to their area Whip. It was further agreed that the Bill should not be lost but go through as quickly as possible and that unless Mr Heath was more flexible on this amendment it was thought he ought to lose his job.

The suggestion that Edward Heath "ought to lose his job" was, for the PT, unusually censorious and confirmed how

___

Conservative MP for Beckenham. He is most well-known for his championing of holding local referendums to ascertain the electorate's views on joining the Common Market, and he wrote a respected account of the 1975 Referendum itself. He also wrote a history of the 1922 Committee, besides holding junior ministerial posts under Margaret Thatcher.

contentious the whole issue had become. The PT was uncompromising in its representations mainly because the measure was deeply unpopular with Conservative voters; indeed, there were Conservative MPs who later argued that the abolition of RPM was a significant cause of the Conservative Party's election defeat of October 1964. Whether the measure itself was, or was not, consistent with Tory economic philosophy was of little importance to the PT, although perhaps it should have been. This, after all, was the moment when Enoch Powell from the backbenches began his advocacy of a very different economic policy from all that had gone before. It was ironic that, on this issue, Heath and Powell were united.

Good relations with Heath were soon restored. He first dined with the PT on 20th November 1963, and the evening was described as "a great success". He was a regular guest in the future, and always regarded the PT as a body worthy of his attention. He was also on friendly terms with John Morrison and his family. But there was no PT enthusiasm for his determination to abolish fixed pricing.

The Objectives of Economic and Fiscal Policy

So often in its life, the PT's resolve to fight socialism had been plagued by uncertainty over how best to do it. The arguments advanced in its early years still have a resonance today. No wonder that, in June 1952, Fells drew the PT's attention to an article in *The Tablet*:

Douglas Jerrold[*] writes that constitutional reform is impera-

---

[*] Douglas Jerrold (1893–1964) was a journalist of 'the right' who was suspected of fascist sympathies before the war, and a former editor of *The English Review*. A fairer description was that he was a Tory out of sympathy with the direction of the Conservative Party. It is of interest that Fells

tive in the light of the nearly equal division of the electorate. Without such reform there can be no confidence, no long term planning by private enterprise, no thrift and no 'free' currency. We run the risk of everything being turned upside down every five years and this must produce economic ruin. He says the Conservative Party runs the risk of never again holding office if it does not get cracking in fortifying a free enterprise economy and asserts that in its present comatose condition and indifference to principles it deserves what is coming to it.

This criticism was reflective of Jerrold's pessimism, but one which many shared. One Tory pamphleteer a year earlier had noted that out of seven million new voters since 1931, "the Socialists took 6,500,000 and the Tories 500,000."* Amongst the reasons he gave, joyfully reported by Cross Bencher in *The Daily Express* on 25th June 1951, were:

1) The Tory Central Office is too autocratic; its constitution out of date.
2) Local associations are snob-ridden.
3) The Party's choice of unsuitable candidates – suspected of Fascist, anti-Semitic or anti-trade union attitudes.
4) The attitude to state controls. There is no firm lead on nationalisation, some of which may be necessary and some not.
5) Tories opposition to 'contracting out' of the political levy instead of demanding that every man should be able to earmark his contribution for the party he favours.
6) Tories are not active enough in looking after the poorer

considered his article worthy of circulation.

* 'Britain's Future, Tories' Future?' by William Martin, 1951.

wage earners. "Why are they not foremost in condemning any firm that achieves an increase in profits, but fails to make any increase in wages?"

7) Tories should win over the Liberals, even at the price of some form of proportional representation.

Fells suggested that this attack was motivated by Cross Bencher's dislike of "Old Etonians of the Conservative Party" – and perhaps of the PT, since there were plenty of them there also. However, in singling out the Government's accommodating attitude to state controls and its failure to provide a lead on nationalisation, this criticism struck home.

There was some comfort for the Government, however, in the Labour Party's own problems. In a by-election in Wycombe on 4th November 1952, the Conservative candidate (John Hall) was returned with an increased majority. Fells had spent time in the constituency during the campaign and explained the result:

A notable feature at the meeting addressed by Mr Attlee at Wycombe was the paucity of younger people in the audience of about 1500. A journalist told me he had made a tour of the Wycombe shops and was surprised at the extent to which the young shop assistants – particularly the young women – favoured the Conservative candidate.

More and more Labour Party speakers are dubbing anyone earning £20 a week as "rich". The candidate, at the Attlee meeting, asked his audience to compare their lot with that of those getting £1000 a year and this was much to the liking of the audience which responded heartily to all appeals to envy, hatred and greed but got rather bored with the last portion of Mr Attlee's speech when he described in quiet ecstasy and a super dose of his usual smugness his vision of the Socialist world when the good inherent in man would have full play. He said his Socialist colleagues on the Continent, whom he had recently been meeting, were broken-hearted over the interruption to Labour's plans for building a new Jerusalem in England's green and pleasant fields. Nothing that Mr Attlee said indicates that he is less of a Socialist than Mr Bevan.

When Butler, as Chancellor of the Exchequer, dined with the PT on 16th July 1952, the PT raised the following as economic priorities and concerns:

1) G.A.T.T.
2) Is rest of sterling area pulling its weight in restoring strength to sterling particularly India and Pakistan?
3) Is he worried about leakages through the Exchange Control?
4) Is there no way of providing loans for local authorities except through a national budget surplus?
5) Can the possibility of including taxation rates in a cost of living index be examined?
6) Can a calculation be made of the percentage addition to costs of exports due to social insurance and other welfare payments? It is often stated that social insurance payments in France add 25 per cent of costs of production so presumably such calculations are possible.

However worthy this list, it steered clear of challenging the Government's overall economic direction. In November 1952, the PT noted that Mr Butler, in his search for economies and new revenue sources, had said on several occasions that "he is willing to look at any proposition however unorthodox or novel." The best which the PT came up with was to suggest a State Lottery "which certainly cannot be any less moral than Football pools?" This was prescient, but gave no guidance on where significant savings might be made. The following year, the PT was more precise over what it wanted from the Budget. It opposed any increase in taxation, and argued that if any tax relief were possible, "three quarters should go towards a reduction in the standard rate of income tax" and "the remaining quarter should go towards such a reduction in purchase tax as would give the maximum benefit to the ordinary family budget."

The PT never had any inhibition in arguing for lower taxes, but only on a few occasions did it offer concrete suggestions as to how these might be financed. The PT was, for example, an early enthusiast for selling council houses to tenants, and recommended this in a letter to Butler on 3rd December 1959. His less-than-encouraging reply led the PT to write to him again on 17th February 1960 "suggesting that the Local Government Circular should be distributed by Central Office to Conservative agents and … that Local Councillors should encourage the sale of council houses to tenants".

This forerunner of Thatcherism, however, was an isolated example and the PT failed a significant test in its reaction – or, more accurately, its lack of reaction – to the Treasury upheaval of 1958. The resignation of Peter Thorneycroft, Chancellor of the Exchequer, and his entire Treasury Team on 6th January passed without any comment from the PT, even though the issue in contention – the level of public spending – was crucial to the whole conduct of economic policy. From July 1957, inflation had been regularly discussed by the Political Committee but, along with the rest of the Conservative Party, there was little agreement on its causes.* The Conservative Party could not decide whether inflation was more a monetary phenomenon, caused by an expansionist monetary policy, or was due to excessive wage settlements which caused prices to rise. Most in the PT favoured this latter explanation, which might explain why no PT support was forthcoming when Thorneycroft, Enoch Powell and Nigel Birch all resigned together believing the opposite.†

It doesn't excuse, however, the PT's lack of interest in the resignation. Derick Heathcoat-Amory, Thorneycroft's successor, filled his place at dinner only a month later when the PT's priority was:

> ... to consider at this meeting ways and means of reducing the burden of certain Social Services on the Exchequer, basing a proportion of the costs of the Services on contributions, or higher charges, subject to a means test, without depreciating the value of the Services and amenities provided (5th February 1958)

In March, the PT submitted a "confidential memorandum" to the new Chancellor on the subject of a reformed profits tax.‡ Two years later, the PT's attention shifted again, this time towards death duties.

When Selwyn-Lloyd§ became Chancellor on 27th July

---

* The PT actually sent a letter to the Prime Minister expressing concerns over inflation around 24th July 1957, but no copy is retained in the PT files.

† Along with Powell, Nigel Birch had been a member of the PT before joining the Government.

‡ A flat rate Profits Tax of 10 per cent was introduced in 1958, replacing a Differential Profits Tax introduced by Hugh Dalton in 1947.

§ John Selwyn-Lloyd (1904–1978) was the Member of Parliament for the

1960, his appointment was unexpected – it had been widely assumed that Sir David Eccles would be given the job. Some journalists suspected the 1922 Committee of blocking Sir David's appointment, and on 13th July 1960 Morrison felt it necessary to inform the PT of his assurance to Sir David "that the reports that had appeared in the *Daily Sketch* and the *Daily Herald* that the 1922 Committee had written a letter saying that he was unsuitable for the office of Chancellor, were untrue."* Whether or not there was strength in the rumours, a former member of the PT was now Chancellor of the Exchequer, and in this capacity he dined with the Trust on 7th December 1960. Here, the "scope for general economy"; the need for "streamlining of the Social Services"; and the "abuses of National Assistance" were all raised. But while spiralling costs of the 'welfare state' were always natural targets for the PT, too often they provided an excuse to leave unchallenged the functions of Government overall. In particular, the PT still failed to engage on the causes of inflation, and the interminable debate between cost/push and demand/pull pressures which eventually led the Conservative Government towards the fateful step of adopting a prices and incomes policy.

In the meantime, however, a political scare emerged which proved to be well founded. On 1st November 1961 members of the Political Committee "wondered what the Chancellor

---

Wirral between from 1945 to 1976 when he was elevated to the House of Lords. He was a member of the PT twice: during the 1945–51 period until his first ministerial post in the Foreign Office. And then again briefly from 1966 before his election as Speaker in 1971. Few members of the PT served for so long at the highest levels of Government.

* Sir David Eccles was then Minister of Education, but the Chancellorship was the job to which he aspired and felt qualified to fulfil.

is going to do about a short term Capital Gains Tax" and raised the subject with him at a dinner on December 5th. On 27th February 1962 the Chancellor made an Economic Statement to the House which was in itself unusual given its proximity to the Budget. Selwyn-Lloyd informed the House of a failure to contain public expenditure within agreed limits – the Government's target had been exceeded by some £111 million. Bringing this fact to Parliament's attention by way of a statement in advance of the Budget, but with no policy proposals to deal with it, was widely criticised. It also raised expectations of a new tax. The PT tried to be helpful, concluding the day after that the Chancellor "was working on the right lines and should be encouraged rather than attacked" although it was worried that the country was being told "one thing one moment and something else the next".

The PT was less amenable when it transpired that the rumoured Capital Gains Tax was not only likely but might be retrospective. As the Political Committee pointed out on 7th March 1962, "there would probably be a row over this and the Chairman [John Morrison] agreed to convey the Committee's feelings to the Chief Whip." A week later:

> The Chairman read a letter from the Chancellor saying that he had noted the views on making a tax on short term gains retrospective, and that although, of course, he could not disclose Budget secrets rumours were not always accurate.

In the event, Selwyn-Lloyd's Budget of 9th April proposed a "speculative gains tax", in the hope that, by giving it a different name, it wouldn't attract as much opposition as a tax on "capital gains". Since this new tax was to be levied on the gain in price of shares sold within six months of acquisition – or of land sold within three months – this was a forlorn hope. As expected, the measure was very unpopular with Conservative supporters while doing very little to satisfy Labour – a combination experienced many times before and since. In the Budget debate, a former member of the PT voiced angrily the concerns that many Conservative MPs felt privately. Viscount Hinchingbrooke asserted that this tax was a sop to 'left-wing' opinion following the disastrous by-election defeat at Orpington on 15th March 1962; that it would raise no revenue in the current financial year; and that it was a hostage to fortune which the Socialists would take up and develop.*

An existing member of the PT – Edward du Cann† – voiced more diplomatically these same concerns. He praised the Chancellor and the Government for the "fact that the standard of life in this country is very high", felt the increased threshold for death duties was welcome albeit still too high, but concluded:

> I am a strong supporter of this Budget. I believe that it has many good features. But it has one thoroughly bad feature – the capital gains tax. It is ... as Lord Hinchingbrooke said in his excellent speech, the thin edge of the wedge ... If ever we have a Labour Government or a Lib–Lab coalition it is true that they would grind the knife in a little deeper. (Hansard, 12th April 1962 c. 1603)

The unpopularity of this Budget encouraged Macmillan's

---

* As indeed happened. The Labour Government introduced a Capital Gains Tax in 1965.

† Edward du Cann (1924–2017) was the Member of Parliament for Taunton between 1956 and 1987. He was another member of the PT who became Chairman of the 1922 Committee (1972–1984).

dramatic reconstruction of his Government on 13th July 1962 – the 'Night of the Long Knives' – which resulted in Selwyn-Lloyd losing his job. Both this new tax, and the row over RPM which was to follow, suggested that the Conservatives were out of touch with their supporters – something which always alarmed members of the PT. But they were less sure of what would be popular. Despite the intellectual influence of Enoch Powell and Keith Joseph, the PT was slow in the 1960s to identify and debate new options to make Conservative Party policy more distinctive.

The Verdict Upon Thirteen Years in Government

During the 1964 election, Labour's main accusation against the Tories was that they had presided over "thirteen wasted years". While few Conservatives went that far, there were some who felt that the Conservative Government had run out of steam and had lost the opportunity to pull back the ratchet of socialism. Protecting free enterprise was a duty imposed on the PT by the terms of its Trust Deed, but it did not extend to providing a doctrinal definition. No wonder, therefore, that the PT felt that the three 'anonymous' articles in *The Times* published in early 1964, and quoted earlier,* "should be played down as much as possible" (8th April 1964). However, these articles by Enoch Powell became the political creed of those Conservatives who felt the Government, in its pursuit of 'Butskellism', embraced too readily the need for state planning and Government intervention in the economy.

Associated with this approach was the Government's attempt to control prices and incomes, which inevitably had implications for relations with the trade unions. In the early years, the PT's fear was that the Government would

---

* See pp. 38–9.

do anything to buy-off the prospect of a strike. But while the PT wished on occasions for a more robust stance, it showed no enthusiasm at this stage for any move to curtail the trade unions' legal privileges. In February 1964, the Political Committee discussed whether a Royal Commission "to look at the trade unions" should be established. Opinion was divided on this suggestion, because there was still a sense that the issue of trade union power was beyond the reach of a Conservative Government to address.

Although, on 6th March 1963, the PT believed that William Deedes* "was doing a very good job in getting Ministers' speeches well publicised", there was a pervading sense of unease in the Parliamentary Party. One manifestation of this unease was discontent with the Speaker, Sir Harry Hylton-Foster, whose impartiality was called into question for giving too much time to the Labour Opposition – despite being a former Conservative. He became involved in an acrimonious correspondence with Lord Hailsham, which the PT thought should be published until they remembered that "as we cannot afford any more trouble at the moment, the Whips should try and deal with it as quietly as possible" (23rd June 1963). A few weeks later, John Morrison told the PT in confidence "that he had had a word with the Speaker on giving too much time recently to the Socialists, and that the Speaker took the point but was unrepentant" (11th July 1963).

This was a symptom of a deeper fear that the Conservative Party had lost both the initiative and its confidence. On 27th March 1963, the Political Committee held a discussion "on Members signing anti-Government motions so near the Election". A few months later, the atmosphere had

---

* William Deedes (1913–2007) was the Member of Parliament for Ashford between 1950 and 1974, before returning to journalism.

deteriorated still further so that John Morrison informed the Political Committee "that the Chairman of the [PT] Council – Lord Strathclyde – had reminded him that the Progress Trust was formed to preserve Conservative principles and that we might all remember that" (24th July 1963). But what were these principles? And what did they have to say about growing concerns within the country over other issues such as immigration and the Common Market?

Ever since the Orpington by-election on 14th March 1962, in which the Government lost a safe Conservative seat to the Liberals, Conservative MPs were aware of growing public hostility towards themselves. Fells gave the PT his assessment of the Orpington campaign which sounds, in some respects, uncannily familiar:

There is one grievance or grave annoyance which has been overlooked in Press Comment and which in fact may have been as important as any. These people were put to the gravest inconvenience by the period of working to rule adopted without union sanction by the electric train drivers on Southern Region some weeks back and over a spell of very bad weather … Not even a loud word of sympathy for their plight came from Government quarters … one asks whether there is not something radically wrong with the committee member-ship of many of our Constituency Associations in the light of developing social trends. The Orpington Association seems to have been out of touch with the make-up of the Orpington electorate otherwise it is difficult to account for their choice of candidate (chosen it is said from ninety applicants) … Is there any Conservative Member of Parliament who can say that the official line of the Party on all matters has been so in tune since 1959 with what the hard core of supporters believe that they can be relied upon to spread the gospel with all sincerity and enthusiasm ... Why did the women of Orpington make this mass protest against the Government?

The PT believed the country's dissatisfaction rested "with the Government's lack of decision over practically every problem, and dissatisfaction over the continual economic crises". PT members shared with each other the feedback they were receiving from their constituents. One such letter is preserved in the PT files, written by a member of the public in November 1962 to his constituency MP, Sir Spencer Summers. Nothing could describe better the level of dissatisfaction that overwhelmed Conservative MPs at this time. The young man described himself as a 27-year-old bank clerk, newly married to a school teacher aged twenty-four, and whose salary was just under £1,000 p.a.:

The only reason we are living here [in Chesham] is because we could not find a reasonable house for under £3,500 nearer London. By reasonable, I mean a 3 bedroomed semi-detached house with garage or space, nothing less ... The [commuting] journey takes over an hour despite the recent £10 million modernisation scheme, and it is a very cold depressing affair ... [inflation] has added £26-10 to my essential household bills in a year ... I have had one increase in salary in these years [one and a quarter years] – £30 – which after tax leaves £21 ... the worst chancellor [i.e. Selwyn-Lloyd], apart from Dalton, we have ever had ... The only luxuries we enjoy are television which costs 9/-d a week in rent and I smoke cigarettes – approximately 12/6d a week ... We possess a refrigerator but no washing machine, spin drier or car ... Out of my monthly income I have £8 left ... This, Sir, is not a hard luck story!

We are very happy and content, but this is so typical of many people today ... and this is the main reason why the so-called 'white collar' worker is protesting in by-elections ... When the pay pause was in operation it was the chap who threatened strike action who got the money ... To be quite frank, your party's record in the past three years has been deplorable ... The handling of African independence has been disastrous ... The Immigration Act does not go far enough. I am one of the greatest opponents of the colour bar, but we can't let all these people in until our own people are properly housed ... we are all heartily sick of Mr Marples...

It was hoped that Harold Macmillan's resignation in 1963 might arrest this decline, and to some extent the Government regained a sense of direction and energy after his departure. But however well disposed personally the PT was to Sir Alec Douglas-Home – he was, after all, the first former member of the Progress Trust to have become Prime Minister – members soon expressed doubts as to whether he was the right man to resist Harold Wilson. Even the PT was doubtful over his image "and the fact that the photographers concentrate on taking photographs of him shooting". On 5th February 1964, the Political Committee thought "it would be a great mistake for the PM to have any duels on TV with Mr Wilson" and John Morrison was "asked to convey this informally to the Chief Whip". Another reason for wishing to minimise appearances on television was because otherwise "it would make it much more difficult to avoid debating with the Opposition in constituencies."

The Tories did better than many expected in the General Election, held on 15th October 1964. But there was little cause for comfort in their modest defeat when faced with the analysis which Sir Charles Mott-Radclyffe shared with his fellow PT members:

> Over past years, the Government have spent too much time knocking their own supporters without telling them why they thought this was necessary ... large numbers of ex-service pensioners voted Liberal as a gesture of disgust at the niggardly way in which they had been treated over their pensions ... [Re. Common Market] it is a mistake to suppose that the British electorate are not still very insular ... Once the veto was exercised, MPs then had the unenviable task of explaining to their constituents, without much help from Ministers, that the country was not going to be bankrupt by staying out ... [Re. Immigration] the fact remains that the people in Slough, not to mention other areas, don't like living in the same street with a lot of West Indians and Pakistanis, and if they have an opportunity of moving elsewhere, then they do so very quickly. Very grave social problems have been created in Slough by coloured immigrants and as a Party we really must face these facts...

As a former member of the Government, Enoch Powell was coming to the same conclusion. Even so, in troubled times members of the PT could always be trusted to maintain a sense of proportion. Here are a few examples of the distractions that exercised the minds of certain PT members during "thirteen wasted years" of Government:

7th May 1952: Major Morrison discussed the question of a closed season for red deer;

5th June 1957: Press comment on the removal of the British Flag from B.E.A. was discussed;

29th October 1958: Concern was felt about the handling of hecklers at the Conservative Party Conference;

4th February 1959: Alarm was expressed that there should be any thought of televising proceedings in the House of Commons;

8th April 1959: Major Morrison reported that MPs are encouraged to appear on Television by Central Office, but not at election time;

27th January 1960: There was a discussion on birching;

2nd March 1960: It was agreed that although it would be a good idea [for MPs] to have better facilities for writing letters, etc., that too many private rooms for Members of Parliament would remove the essence of Parliament;

30th March 1960: There was a discussion on the Channel Tunnel;

29th March 1961: It was agreed that the Breathalyser test was a bad idea, and that it would be extremely difficult to implement owing to different people's reactions to alcohol;

18th April 1962: Major Morrison said he would speak to the Chief Whip on the matter of the length of the Minister's speech on potatoes last night;*

8th April 1964: Mr Kimball said that there were suggested plans to alter the dates of the State School holidays *and this would affect public school holidays* [author's italics]. It was agreed that a letter should be written to Sir Edward Boyle asking him to clarify the position, and that Major Morrison should have a word with the Chief Whip on the subject.

The PT would have had an answer to those who considered

---

* The Minister of Agriculture, Fisheries and Food had begun speaking on the Potato Marketing Scheme (Amendments) at 10.31pm on 17th April 1962 and concluded just under an hour later at 11.29pm.

this list an irrelevance. It is better that politicians know their limitations, and "do not itch to interfere with matters which they do not understand" (*Iolanthe,* W. S. Gilbert).

5

1964–1979:
The Natural Party of Government? From Heath to Thatcher

"... There is such an enormous amount of legislation pouring out at the moment that it is physically impossible to digest it all; the troubles of the PT are the troubles of the whole Party..." (Sir John Eden, 2ⁿᵈ February 1966)

"Mrs Thatcher will not be accepted by the constituencies, and Mr Heath is gathering support outside Parliament ... The Conservative Party should not have to tear itself apart when the present Government is doing so badly." (19ᵗʰ December 1974)

Between 15ᵗʰ October 1964 and 10ᵗʰ October 1974 there were five General Elections. Labour won four of them: the other led to an embarrassingly brief, albeit significant, period of Conservative rule (June 1970 – February 1974). Thus, Harold Wilson succeeded in undermining the Conservative claim to be the "natural party of government". Edward Heath stretched Conservative loyalties to breaking-point by abandoning any attempt to champion free enterprise, and by his determination to join the Common Market. And three issues which remain potent today – immigration, the EU and the state's role in the economy – came to dominate British politics. With hindsight one can therefore see how, during the 1960s and 1970s, the seeds of Thatcherism were sown.

Throughout this period the PT maintained an anxious interest in all these policy areas, normally united and occasionally exercising influence upon the Party's leadership. However, the changing nature of the House of Commons brought its own complications, especially as the general conduct of politics had become less susceptible to the PT's gentlemanly approach. Members found it "increasingly hard to attend the [PT's] Political Committee" because of the growing volume of Parliamentary and constituency business (12th July 1976), and they attracted a smaller audience from within the Conservative Party. At a PT Council Meeting in February 1966, most of the discussion centred upon the role and purpose of the PT in Opposition:

> Although it was agreed that the role is a difficult one when out of power it was nevertheless felt that the PT had lost influence in the Party committees and that they were not in touch with what was going on in the various policy committees. It was agreed that the Party was divided on most issues and that the Trust must try and present a united front and support Conservative principles and that when choosing new members they should pick men of like mind … It was noted that the PT still had very good relations with the Chief Whip [William Whitelaw], and that any strong views of the PT would always be sure of a sympathetic hearing.

Changes in the PT's leadership followed the Conservative election defeat of 1964. While Lord Strathclyde remained Chairman of the Council, John Morrison – who became Lord Margadale on 1st January 1965 – was succeeded as

Chairman of the Political Committee by Spencer Summers. Strathclyde reminded the Council on 11th November 1964 (the first meeting after the election):

> ... the Council was entirely responsible for the running of the Trust. The Council, however, had handed over responsibility during the past few years for the actions of the Political Committee to the Chairman of the Political Committee ... the Council had always left the choice of new members to the Political Committee and it was agreed that this practice should continue.

This is a reminder that MPs were *invited* to join the PT – they did not apply – and that while a spread of opinion was tolerated, most held similar views on the important topics of the day.

Sir Tufton Beamish's new appointment as Vice Chairman of the Political Committee was also significant as this had a bearing upon the PT's attitudes towards Europe. Sir Tufton was often, and unfairly, categorised as a traditional 'right-winger'; but while his views on Africa and Defence may have supported this description, on other issues – and especially given his undiluted enthusiasm for Britain's membership of the Common Market – the classification was inaccurate. At the same time, there were various additions to the Political Committee during this period which introduced a younger and more 'Heathite' element to the PT – such members included Charles Morrison[*] (the second and much more left-wing son of Lord Margadale, whose wife was a

---

[*] Charles Morrison (1932–2005) was the Member of Parliament for Devizes between 1964 and 1992.

notable supporter of Edward Heath); Paul Channon;[*] and David Lane[†] (who, along with the former PT member Sir Edward Boyle, was a prominent member of the left-wing group PEST).[‡] None of these new members, however, was chosen to undermine the PT's core character which, as again reiterated on 4th May 1966, was "unanimity of opinion on important issues, and of keeping consistently in mind the guiding principles of the Conservative Party; together with the Trust's traditional support of individual freedom and free enterprise".

There was also a pressing need for funds. By the time the Conservatives were returned to office in 1970, the PT's annual expenditure was some £4,000 p.a. (equivalent to over £60,000 today). This was less than in the 1960s but still more than could be afforded. The Trust's cash balance on 8th November 1967 stood at around £14,000, soon to be reduced to £7,000 following an ex gratia payment to Fells on his retirement. As a consequence, the Council decided that it could not afford to purchase the lease of the PT's premises in Ebury Street which had been its home since 1960 (and

---

[*] Paul Channon (1935–2007) was the Member of Parliament for Southend West, the seat which his late father, Chips Channon, had represented, between 1959 and 1997. He held senior ministerial office, but was perhaps never as famous as his father, whose diaries provide a fascinating political perspective of the years 1934 until his death in 1958, which caused the by-election at which his son entered Parliament as the youngest MP.

[†] David Lane (1922–1998) was the Member of Parliament for Cambridge between 1967 and 1976. He was the first director of the Commission for Racial Equality.

[‡] PEST (Pressure for Economic & Social Toryism) was a pressure group on the 'left' of the Conservative Party, formed in the 1960s largely to counter the influence of the Monday Club.

which still had twelve years to run). Bridget Lakin solved the accommodation problem by providing an office and dining room in her mother's house in Eaton Terrace for a rental of £300 per year. She also reduced her hours to three mornings per week. Donations from the Brewers became more spasmodic during this period and eventually were discontinued. But Colonel Hobbs continued to facilitate donations from the industrialists. Between November 1966 and May 1979, Hobbs produced over £17,000 in total as and when required.

Given that Bridget Lakin was now working fewer hours at much cheaper premises, with Fells soon to be replaced by a part-time research officer, expenditure was considerably reduced. The only other item of regular expenditure was a small payment to a journalist to provide the Political Committee with 'lobby notes' (which, mainly, reported lobby gossip concerning the Labour Party). These had been provided since late 1964 by the lobby correspondent James Margarch, who in 1976 was replaced by Keith Renshaw and whose remuneration, by 1979, was some £450 p.a. By the time the Conservatives returned to office in 1979, the PT's salary bill amounted to around £4,000 per year – in other words, the same as in 1970 but in reality, because of inflation, much less. It was now equivalent to over £20,000 p.a. in today's money, as opposed to £60,000 ten years earlier.

The last task of Harry Fells before his retirement was to conduct an Inquiry into 'taxation and disincentive' which involved contact with a wide range of industrial concerns and professions. On the PT's behalf, Fells was commissioned to seek evidence on "the effect of Income Tax and Surtax on personal effort and promotion of both salary and wage earners". The intention was to compile a confidential report for "the exclusive benefit" of those who provided evidence. In the event, the memorandum seeking their support concentrated more upon the issue of industrial relations:

> A small number of Conservative Members of Parliament, who from time to time have collaborated together, have become increasingly concerned at certain features of the industrial situation, to which frequent reference is made in the Press. They have in mind such matters as the widespread belief that in most factories and offices surplus labour is employed, which could advantageously be redeployed, but this is not done because management fears the consequences of trying to do so; that management does not pay enough attention to labour relations and particularly to the art of communication; that the chief obstacle to the removal of restrictive practices is unreasonable resistance from the trade unions; that the virtual absence of discipline gravely prejudices efficiency and that unofficial strikes are far too common.
>
> Attempts may be made through legislation to try and improve matters – e.g. by compulsory strike ballots, early warning system, enforcement of contracts, etc. They are anxious to be in a position to judge the likely effect of any such proposals, and their reception in industry, but in so much as Members of Parliament just have not the time to discuss such matters on the spot with those directly concerned, this is not easily accomplished. No publicity will be sought, or permitted, in connection with the assignment, and in no circumstances will the origin of any information given to Mr Fells be disclosed.
>
> It is hoped that his visits, made possible through personal introductions, will induce frank comment and so enable opinions to be formed and advice to be tendered, based on

sound foundations and a common sense Conservative point of view.

For a number of years, this group of Members have been assisted by the research and in other ways by Mr H. J. Fells of 58 Ebury Street, S.W.1. Arrangements have now been made whereby Mr Fells has accepted the assignment of studying these matters on behalf of the group, with a view to compiling a confidential report for their exclusive benefit.

Companies which co-operated included Shell, United Biscuits, Schroders, GKN, Scottish and Newcastle Breweries, Lithgow, Sedgwick Colline and many other smaller concerns. No copy of the final report exists in the files, although they contain a few summaries of individual meetings which demonstrate little industrial support at the time for radical reform. The report was discussed by the Political Committee on 29th November 1967, and a copy of the memorandum was sent to the Shadow Chancellor, Iain Macleod. It was the last occasion when the PT independently compiled external data from business and industry with a view to influencing policy. The PT had always shown an interest in labour relations, but this initiative was an acknowledgement of how far the issue of strikes and trade union power was now worrying Conservative voters. The PT disliked 'buying-off' strikes in the early years of Churchill's Government; they disliked even more the strikes which resulted in resisting trade union demands in the 1960s. It would take some time, however, before the link between militancy and attempts to control inflation via an incomes policy was accepted.

The departure of Fells resulted in less statistical compilation from outside sources, and a greater concentration upon political comment. On 19th March 1971, the first of the Ebury Research Notes was produced and circulated to PT members – the chosen subject was 'The growth of the civil service'. From that moment, it was the task of the PT's Research Officer to produce a Research Note for the weekly meeting of the Political Committee. Usually, the subject was at his discretion, and was drafted more to invite discussion than to present dry facts. The notes did not represent the policy of the PT, but their production each week guided topics for discussion which sometimes led to action. The part-time Research Officers were:

R. M. (Jim) Stuttard: 1971–75
Brendon Sewill: 1975–82
Richard Ritchie: 1982–2005

Virtually all PT notes survive, and are listed in Appendix II.* Leaving aside the value (or not) of their content, they provide a useful chronological list of when political issues first surfaced in the PT's consciousness, and for how long they remained topical. Some subjects are returned to frequently; others are quickly forgotten. Sometimes the notes display prescience; but on other occasions, they lack all the benefits of hindsight. At least, however, they encapsulate many of the debates which preoccupied the Conservative Party as a whole at moments of significance or crisis.

Although the PT had reduced its expenditure and activity, it still wished to exercise undiminished influence. But this was a tall order. On 2nd February 1966, Sir Spencer informed the Political Committee "that he was worried about the PT and that it had not the grip that it once had". Sir John Eden,†

---

* They are kept in the Conservative Party Archive at the Bodleian Library.

† Sir John Eden Bt., later Lord Eden of Winton (b. 1925) was the

a nephew of Anthony Eden and an important PT member of this period, responded by reminding the PT "that there was such an enormous amount of legislation pouring out at the moment that it was physically impossible to digest it all and that the troubles of the PT were the troubles of the whole Party."

Another concern in 1966 "was that little was known about what was going on in the various Party Policy Committees, and what was Party policy on the main subjects". But this should not have been a surprise. 1966 was the first time for sixteen years that the country was governed by a Labour Government with a commanding majority; and therefore, in what was expected to be a long period of Opposition, the Conservative Party could be excused for reconsidering afresh its fundamental beliefs. It is often claimed that the Conservative Party's only interest is in winning elections and retaining office, and there were some in the PT who gave this impression. But there were others who, while just as anxious for power, felt that a lukewarm Conservative Party, uncertain of what it stood for, had no chance of regaining office or making a difference if it did.

When the dire economic situation encouraged the press to speculate on the possibility of a National Government, Lord Strathclyde informed the Council that "should this occur the Progress Trust would be very necessary to see that Conservative principles were maintained and not allowed to be forgotten either by the Party or by such a Government." (13th July 1966). There was little unanimity within the Conservative Party, however, on what these principles any longer were – and Enoch Powell for one was determined that the issue could no longer be fudged. Ever since his refusal in

---

Member of Parliament for Bournemouth West between 1954 and 1983.

1963 to serve in the Government of Sir Alec Douglas-Home, Powell had, in a series of speeches, revisited the whole notion of what 'Conservatism' was about. Even after the Conservative defeat of 1964, when he rejoined the Conservative front bench, Powell persisted in speaking regularly and forcefully on all aspects of Conservative policy and principle. Like him or loathe him, it was impossible for anyone in politics to ignore his speeches during this period. How Conservative politicians reacted to his analysis was a useful pointer to their place in the political spectrum.

For a very short period, Powell had been a member of the Progress Trust. He was invited to join in July 1955 (at the same time as Angus Maude), but waited until 26th October to attend his first Political Committee meeting. The following month he became a Vice Chairman of the 1922 Committee. But only a few weeks later, Anthony Eden appointed him as Parliamentary Secretary at the Ministry of Housing under Duncan Sandys. This meant that Powell had to resign from both Committees. He had attended just five meetings of the PT, and had little contact with it thereafter. Powell belatedly accepted an invitation to dine on 13th July 1966 when it was agreed "to ask him to develop his philosophy on Defence and Economic Affairs with particular reference to the relationship between Industry and Government".

As Shadow Secretary of State for Defence, Powell's views on the nuclear deterrent and Britain's role 'East of Suez' were at variance with many members of the PT. As Sir Tufton Beamish pointed out on 19th October 1966, following the Conservative Conference,

It was noticeable that when Mr Enoch Powell spoke on Defence after Sir Alec (the reverse order to last year) he revealed a marked difference in emphasis and priority to that of Sir Alec whose speech was the only one during the Conference which offered forward policy in precise terms.

Defence, however, was not the issue which divorced Powell from the leadership and eventually ended his membership of the Conservative Party. His views on economic policy, immigration and the Common Market were the causes of his exile. Immigration and Europe are the subjects of the next two chapters. But it was the economy, and in particular the re-imposition of an Incomes Policy, which led to the early collapse of the Conservative Government, the departure of Enoch Powell from the Conservative Party, and the replacement of Mr Heath by Mrs Thatcher.

Ironically, Powell's views on economic policy were, in the eyes of most PT members, his least contentious. But Powell and the PT were never natural bed-fellows. The previous chapter noted the PT's surprising lack of concern over the en-bloc resignation from the Treasury in 1958. By the late 1960s, however, the disputed causes of inflation were central to the entire political debate, and it was impossible for the PT to be neutral over whether or not there should be a 'Prices and Incomes Policy'. This was the issue which Powell chose as one of his chief criticisms of the prevailing economic consensus. In doing so, he was loyal to the principles behind his resignation from the Treasury, since these lay at the heart of the disagreement over the causes of inflation.

The PT's first specific reference to the issue was made on 18th January 1967:

The Party's policy on Prices and Incomes was discussed and it was agreed that this should be discussed at the dinner with the Chief Whip. Sir Spencer Summers felt that the country wanted to know what the Party's policy is on a number of subjects on which differing views had been expressed and it was agreed that some steps must be taken in this direction.

More significantly, three weeks later:

> There was a discussion on the continuance of the wage freeze and it was agreed that the Chairman should tell the Chief Whip that the Committee were in agreement that the Party should oppose any Government legislation which introduced the element of compulsion on a permanent basis. (8th February 1967)

Usually, the PT's minutes do not record how a Chief Whip responded to such representations, but on this occasion William Whitelaw replied with a pertinent remark which summed up the pusillanimous attitude of industry leaders (including, naturally, the CBI) at the time:

> The Chief Whip said that the trouble is that management do not mind [an incomes policy] as many welcome the chance to pass their responsibility [for wage settlements] to the Government for saying 'No'. (15th February 1967)

The PT, however, was still reluctant to take sides in the debate. A recent speech by Edward Heath on economic policy, for example, merely caused the PT to comment, on 19th July 1967, "that the speech was far too long". If pressed, the PT was sceptical of any attempt by the state to control by law wages and prices. When, for example, Sir Spencer Summers stated, on 24th January 1968, "that the Achilles heel of the Party seems to be how to keep wages from rising", other members of the PT retorted "there was far less infla- tion under the 'free for all system' and that the wage freeze had produced more inflation." A month later, and true to form, the CBI issued a statement in February 1968 urging the Labour Government to seek new reserve powers on prices and incomes: the PT's response a few days later (6th March 1968) was again to rule out "a Compulsory Prices and Incomes Policy in Opposition" but hinted that "a voluntary system" might be more acceptable even though it would be hard to gain Conservative acceptance.

The issue was soon to become less academic from a Tory per- spective. The Conservative Party was unexpectedly returned to office in June 1970 on a manifesto which "utterly rejected the philosophy of compulsory wage control", a fact recalled by the PT on 11th November 1970 in the light of the 'Dirty Jobs' strike when it repeated "the Party is pledged not to introduce a Statutory Wage Freeze." This remained the PT's view in April 1971, despite signs even then that the resolve of Heath's Government was faltering. Jim Stuttard, who had recently taken over from Fells as the PT's Research Officer, brought to the PT's attention an article in *The Economist* (24th April), which advanced the case for an emergency incomes policy. While the PT agreed "that it was worrying that the Government has not yet got a grip on inflation", neverthe- less "it could not go along with the ideas pressed for" by the paper and article.

However, this is what eventually happened. The PT had approved of Tony Barber's first Budget, but when the PT took a delegation to see the Chancellor in June 1971 on double surtax, the Government's enthusiasm for reducing taxes had disappeared – Barber told them "he had helped the high tax payer all he could for the moment."* By 1972, the Government's economic policy was unravelling. On 1st March, the PT expressed alarm "over the decision to prop up the Upper Clyde Shipbuilders and what it would lead to with regard to other requests". Marcus Kimball, who seldom expressed strong views on economic policy, "said he would like to raise the subject of 'lame ducks' with the PM at their forthcoming dinner on Wednesday 22nd March". Sir John Eden emphasised at a dinner on 26th April 1972 "how unhappy he had been about the huge size of the DTI, and the power of the civil servants in the Department". On 21st June, "it was agreed that there were now 'no more tricks' to be tried to stop inflation except as Mr William Benyon† suggested by the control of imports." Fears over strikes and growing industrial unrest sapped the PT's morale, as it did the Government's. The circulation of free market articles by commentators such as Sam Brittan were not enough to maintain the PT's resolve against compulsory wage and price controls. On 2nd August 1972, "it was agreed that Conservative philosophy on the nationalised Industries and the private sector must be re-thought." On 6th November, the Government imposed a ninety-day standstill on pay, prices, rents and dividends.

It is difficult to resist the impression that fears over trade union militancy blinded the PT, and most in the Conservative Party, to the fundamental flaws in the Government's

---

* Anthony Barber (1920–2005) was the Member of Parliament for Doncaster between 1951 and 1964, and then Altringham and Sale from 1965–1974. Before a long period in Government, he was a loyal member of the Progress Trust, and always available to meet his former fellow members.

† William (Bill) Benyon (1930–2014) was the Member of Parliament for Buckingham, later Milton Keynes, between 1970 and 1992.

economic policy and resulted in a general disinclination to defend capitalism. A statutory prices and incomes policy was a gift to those in the trade union movement who wanted to bring down a Conservative Government. But this was never fully appreciated. Instead, during the economic debate at the Conservative Party Conference of 1973, the significance of the Government's Prices and Incomes Policy was glossed over – at least in view of the relevant Ebury Note (No. 76), which quoted with approval a former PT member, Angus Maude:

> His few crisp phrases rallied the centre, dealt blows against purist critics to left and right, pin-pointed a few areas for cleaning up capitalism whilst further encouraging enterprise and, finally, ended as he started with an infectious confidence that we could win an election even on the present polls.

This summed up the prevailing view of the PT. But by November, when industrial opposition to wage controls was mounting and the miners' overtime ban had started to bite, the PT's only response was to discuss the case for a possible state of emergency. On 12th December the PT's suggested remedy was "that the Prime Minister should speak to the country at the first opportunity", and that this message should be passed to Whitelaw. More insidiously, the PT wanted it hinted to "the strikers" that it was in their interest to "accept the offers made to them under phase III as there was bound to be a phase IV which would be far stricter". Moreover, "it was agreed that doing something about property speculators would be a sop to the strikers."

On 19th December, in reply to an overture from the Chief Whip, the PT advised against an emergency election but added "most people present were in favour of an early Spring

Election as long as there has been some settlement with the miners, etc." On 6th February 1974, however – and ravaged by the experience of the 'three-day week' – "everyone agreed that it was now necessary to have an election, and that the issues were clearer than three weeks ago."

Once the election had taken place and Heath's Government was defeated, with Enoch Powell no longer a member of the Conservative Party, Conservative MPs faced the challenge of whether or not to break from their 'Heathite' past. In respect of economic policy, this meant tackling the issue of a prices and incomes policy specifically, and the need for Government intervention in the economy generally. But the PT still showed no inclination to address either. An Ebury Research Note (No. 123) raised the issue of a wealth tax – in the false expectation of its introduction by the Labour Government – and suggested that it might have appeal to Conservative thinking if it led to a "lower rate of income tax on high earned incomes". The Political Committee somewhat reluctantly "agreed that a wealth tax could be acceptable on the German pattern but only if Income Tax does not go above 53 per cent". One member – Stephen Hastings – objected more strongly, and argued the Conservative Party should be "stiffer against the egalitarian propaganda being put forward".

Jim Stuttard also encouraged, via a series of Research Notes (Nos. 132 & 134–37), the Political Committee to discuss Incomes Policy, but they did so with little enthusiasm, merely stating on 19th February 1975, that "despite continued Government denials, a return to some form of statutory control was inevitable." The PT at this time was more interested in the prospect of a National Government. Only a few months earlier, they had judged the economic situation "so serious that [the Party's] leadership may not be an issue next year as there may be a coalition by that time" (27th November 1974). Whether or not this prediction was born of wishful thinking, it demonstrates how mistaken even front-row spectators of the political game can be: there was no National Government, and on 4th February 1975 Edward Heath was challenged successfully by Margaret Thatcher and forced to resign the Party's leadership.

Most in the PT had been against a leadership challenge and thought it unlikely that Heath would be deposed:

> Mr Charles Morrison explained the rules just out for electing the leader of the Party. The present situation was discussed, and it was thought that Mrs Thatcher would not be accepted by the constituencies, and that Mr Heath was gathering support outside Parliament. It was regretted that the Conservative Party should have to tear itself apart when the present Government is doing so badly. (19th December 1974)[*]

On 15th January 1975 it was again agreed "that the Constituencies were fed up with the continued pre-occupation with the leadership". But once Mrs Thatcher won through, Michael Hamilton[†] – who had become the PT's new Chairman in 1974 – stated on 12th February,

> … that he would be writing to the new Leader to invite her to

---

[*] Those attending this meeting were Sir Paul Bryan, David Crouch, Rear Admiral Morgan Giles, Marcus Kimball, Charles Morrison, Jim Spicer, John Osborn, Peter Rees and Jasper More.

[†] Michael Hamilton (1918–2000) was the Member of Parliament for Wellingborough between 1959 and 1964, and subsequently Salisbury between 1965 and 1983.

dine on 12th March* … that the experiences of the last week had been damaging to the Party and that there should now be total support for the new leader. It was agreed too that the rules for election of the leader must be looked at again.

The PT had never shown any enthusiasm for confronting the prevailing economic orthodoxy in the way Mrs Thatcher intended, although some PT members, notably Peter Hordern, were intellectually sympathetic to the economic direction which eventually she followed. While there was always support for lower taxation, the PT gave no credence to reductions on the scale of Enoch Powell's 'Morecambe' Budget of 1968 when he advocated, to general derision, income tax at "4/3 in the £" (ironically, still a little higher than the current standard rate). Nor was the PT in the vanguard for calls to 'denationalise' the state industries. At its first dinner with Margaret Thatcher on 24th March 1976, the three suggested topics for discussion were the Party in Opposition; détente with the trade unions ("we hope that Mr Prior will say no more on this subject"); and Rhodesia. If, at this time, the PT had an overriding economic concern, it was more to do with the threat posed by the trade unions, than with any theoretical objection to an incomes policy. By and large, however, the central assumption behind economic policy, namely that neither political Party had much scope to behave differently in respect of inflation, went unchallenged. The PT accepted Mrs Thatcher as Leader, but gave her little encouragement for a radical change of direction. For a long period following the Conservative defeat of 1974 the PT

---

* Unsurprisingly, Mrs Thatcher was unable to accept this invitation. Her first dinner with the PT as Leader was scheduled to take place on 12th November 1975, but this had to be postponed until 24th March 1976.

was uncertain as to whether it was policy or leadership failures which were responsible for the Party's plight. Labour's
return to office so soon after their defeat in 1970 suggested
that the Conservative Party's claim to be 'the natural party of
government' was no longer credible. The PT had little hope
at this early stage that Mrs Thatcher was capable of coming
to the rescue.

6

IMMIGRATION

"The main object of the new Immigration Act [1972] ... was to control immigration; to control coloured immigration – let that be quite clear. It was not said so in print because we are sensitive about these things."
(Sir Paul Bryan, future Chairman of the PT, 22nd November 1972)

"It was agreed that there should be no step down the Enoch road of repatriation." (27th June 1984)

"We have been good at absorbing migrants in the past, but the present trouble is that Muslims do not want to integrate, and we must avoid having 'bloc ethnic' voting as in the States." (21st July 1989)

On 6th July 1948 the PT suggested, to some forty constituency agents, six motions which their Conservative Associations might consider tabling for debate at the forthcoming Conservative Party Conference. One of these related indirectly to immigration, and is the PT's first recorded reference to the subject:

That this Conference recommends that population settlement within the British Commonwealth and Empire should be reviewed and co-ordinated in the light of Imperial, economic and strategic needs.

A few months later on 13th November, at a by-election in Edmonton, the Labour majority over the Conservative candidate was slashed from 19,069 (in 1945) to 3,327. On being informed of the result, Churchill said "it is another El Alamein."* But the local Labour Party complained of an "insidious irresponsible doorstep anti-Labour campaign of denigration and defamation" and, in particular, "We are happy to say that we overcame race-prejudice, spite and the more usual exploitation of the nation's post-war difficulties." The PT noted that the Edmonton Conservative Association "emphatically denied that the Tories introduced race prejudice and spite into their campaign" adding "it was the followers of the Socialist cause who first brought up the matter."

Ten years later, on 12th November 1958, the PT's Business minutes made their first mention of "coloured people", although the Political Committee had raised the immigration issue a few times previously, notably on 12th and 26th May 1954:

> The question of free entry into this country of penniless West Indians, and others, without jobs, thus becoming a burden on the state, was referred to. Mr Spencer Summers intimated that he hoped to have some information available on this matter in the near future... (12th May 1954)
>
> It was agreed to postpone discussion of the question of entry into this country of penniless West Indians and others until a later date when Mr Summers' report would be available. Mr Erroll indicated that he was exploring certain channels in connection with this matter. Meantime, Mr Fells was asked to watch the position... (26th May 1954)

---

* *The Times*, 15th November 1948.

Immigration, therefore, was now under PT scrutiny. Frederick Erroll* raised the matter most often during this early period. On 16th June 1954 he "outlined the action which he had taken in connection with the entry into this country of penniless West Indians and others, as well as being in correspondence with Sir Hugh Lucas-Tooth" who was Parliamentary Under-Secretary of State at the Home Office. A few weeks later, on 7th July 1954, the Political Committee referred to "the entry into this country of persons whose sole purpose is to attempt to get free medical and surgical treatment".

As soon as the Political Committee met after the summer recess, the issue was again discussed. Another member of the PT, Malcolm McCorquodale,† agreed to "watch the position" while Sir Guy Lloyd as the PT's Chairman raised the issue within Government. On 3rd November, he "reported on the results of his enquiries concerning Coloured Immigrants ... and undertook to arrange a deputation to see Mr Lennox-Boyd." As ever, the discretion of the PT's secretary of this period led to sparse minutes, but it is clear that it was immigration from Jamaica which caused the PT most concern. Alan Lennox-Boyd was Secretary of State for the Colonies, and a month later Sir Guy was able to report that he had agreed to receive a deputation on 9th December, which would consist

---

* Frederick Erroll (1914–2000), later Lord Erroll of Hale, was the Member of Parliament for Altrincham and Sale between 1945 and 1964. His most senior jobs in Government were President of the Board of Trade (see page 98) and Minister of Power.

† Malcolm McCorquodale (1901–1971), later Lord McCorquodale of Luton, was the Member of Parliament for Sowerby between 1931 and 1945 (despite fighting in the RAF). He was the Member of Parliament for Epsom between 1947 and 1955.

of Sir Guy himself together with "Captain Duncan,* Colonel Gomme-Duncan,[†] Mr F. J. Erroll, Lord Hinchingbrooke, Mr Ramsden[‡] and Captain Waterhouse" (military titles were still meticulously recorded during this period even though the war had ended almost ten years previously).

No details are given of this meeting, but it is likely that Lennox-Boyd expressed himself relatively powerless in the matter as on 2nd February 1955 Sir Guy informed the Political Committee that arrangements had now been made for the same deputation to discuss "the problem of Jamaican immigration" and "the possible consequences" with the Home Secretary (Hon. Gwilym Lloyd-George) on the following day. Once again, no record exists in the PT files of what was said, although Fells was asked in March to prepare a paper. A General Election intervened on 26th May 1955, but it was agreed by the Political Committee on 20th April "to pursue the points raised concerning the immigration of coloured people into the United Kingdom after the General Election".

Familiar and widespread Conservative concerns over immigration were expressed as early as 1954, and the issue kept resurfacing. Although it has been suggested that Churchill personally was more concerned than many in his Government to limit 'coloured' immigration, lack of action began to attract criticism during his post-war administration.

---

* Captain Sir James Duncan (1899–1974) was the Member of Parliament for Kensington North (as a Conservative) between 1931 and 1945 and South Angus (as a National Liberal) between 1950 and 1964.

† Colonel Sir Alan Gomme-Duncan (1893–1963) was the Member of Parliament for Perth between 1945 and 1959.

‡ James Ramsden (b. 1923) was the Member of Parliament for Harrogate between 1954 and 1974. He was the last person to hold the office of Secretary of State for War.

After the election of 1955, the issue went quiet within the PT until, on Sir Guy's initiative, the Political Committee was invited on 12th November 1958 "to give their views on the problem of coloured people in this country" and Fells was again asked for a paper. As before, it was decided that this was an issue which the Chairman "should pursue in the appropriate quarter" although on this occasion the issue was now referred to as "Colonial immigration" (19th November 1958).

The PT's renewed interest may have been sparked by the Conservative Party Conference a few weeks earlier. Butler as Home Secretary came under pressure at this event when the rank and file demanded that the Government should revise the country's immigration laws. But it took until June 1961 when, in the words of Anthony Howard, Butler gave his "reluctant acquiescence to the need to bring in immigration legislation". In May 1961, there had been correspondence between the new Chairman of the PT (John Morrison) and Butler on "coloured immigration with regard to the housing programme". But in essence, the PT was now pushing at an open door, which explains why the PT left the subject alone once Butler had introduced new legislation. There were moments when the Immigration Bill ran into stormy waters in Committee, and on 6th December 1961 the PT wondered "how big the rebellion on the Immigration Bill would be. It was thought that it would not be more than about twenty, so it was agreed that no action should be taken." It is not clear what specifically this 'rebellion' was about, but it probably concerned the ability of citizens from the 'Old' Commonwealth (i.e. mostly 'white' citizens) to enter the country under the proposed new legislation. There was no significant Conservative resistance to the Bill on the grounds it did not go far enough; but the Labour Party opposed the need for immigration control on principle, with Hugh Gaitskell describing it as "cruel and brutal anti-colour legislation".* The Act received Royal Assent on 18th April 1962.

In common with most of the Conservative Party (including Enoch Powell), the PT's assumption following the new legislation's enactment was that immigration would now be subject to effective control, and public anxiety on the subject would therefore diminish. The PT did not consider the subject again until January 1964, but this was only as part of a general review of Labour Party policy in an election year. As Fells reminded the Committee, the Labour Party still opposed the 1962 Act and was committed to new legislation which, while acknowledging the need for a measure of control over the number of Commonwealth immigrants entering the country, would allow for no discrimination on grounds of either race or colour. Their proposed legislation promised to contain what would now be understood as a large 'race-relations element', with the emphasis on 'integration'.

The Labour Party was as good as its word at least in this latter respect. Following its victory in the October 1964 General Election in which immigration had been a controversial topic (not least the campaign in Smethwick which led Harold Wilson as Prime Minister to brand the newly elected Tory MP Peter Griffiths as a "parliamentary leper"), the new Government moved quickly to introduce a new Race Relations Bill which the PT was in no doubt "the Opposition must vote against" (14th April). Thirteen PT members of various strands of opinion attended this meeting.†

---

* It is of interest that in the Act's long title, reference is made only to "*temporary* provision for controlling the immigration into the United Kingdom of Commonwealth citizens".

† Those attending were: Sir Spencer Summers, Sir Tufton Beamish,

New promised legislation to control immigration, however, was not forthcoming from the Labour Government – it was not introduced until 1968 – and in 1965 the PT was keen that "attention be drawn to the fact that the Government had completely somersaulted over the immigration issue". That was as far as it went. There is no evidence of any PT discussion of immigration between 1964–68, despite its growing potency. It remained largely an unspoken topic, except when, on 3rd May 1967, the PT realised that Labour's Race Relations Bill "would prove a dilemma for the Conservative Party as to what view to take" and again on 29th November 1967 when "it was agreed that the more the Government try to legislate against racial discrimination, more trouble and difficulties would arise which will be very difficult to deal with."

The expulsion of Kenyan Asians from Kenya in 1968 marked the next stage in the UK's immigration debate. In order to prevent their unrestricted right to settle in the UK, following persecution in their own country, the Labour Government was forced reluctantly and speedily to amend the 1962 Immigration Act. This new Bill went through Parliament in just three days, and received Royal Assent on 1st March 1968. It received all-party support, although there was backbench opposition from within the Labour Party as well as from a few Conservative opponents of the measure (including Iain Macleod and Michael Heseltine). The PT discussed the measure twice (on 28th February and 6th March), when it was felt that "the Opposition had lost an opportunity of nearly defeating the Government." But had this opportunity been taken, it would have been an opportunist tactic to embarrass

---

Humphrey Atkins, Paul Channon, Sir John Eden, Charles Morrison, Lord Margadale, Sir Charles Mott-Radclyffe, John Temple, William Roots, George Younger, John Osborn and David Webster.

the Labour Government rather than a principled belief that Kenyan Asians should be permitted unrestricted access to Britain. Many felt genuinely torn at the time between a conviction that immigration must be controlled, and a duty to honour this country's obligations.

During this period, Enoch Powell was a member of the Shadow Cabinet. But he held an old-fashioned view as to what constituted collective responsibility within Opposition, as opposed to Government. As Shadow Secretary of State for Defence, he felt free to speak on a wide range of matters outside his brief so long as he was in compliance with Conservative Party policy. These matters were normally in the economic and constitutional sphere, concentrating on the very nature and purpose of Government. But he now regarded immigration as a far more urgent issue than before, mainly because the 1962 Act had clearly not secured its purpose of controlling immigration amidst rising public discontent prompted by the Kenyan Asian crisis.

His first significant and public intervention in the immigration debate was on 21st May 1965 in Wolverhampton when he spoke at a Conservative Women's Coffee Morning. He made three other immigration speeches after that (prior to the famous speech at Birmingham on 20th April 1968), the most important being in Walsall on 9th February 1968. None of these caught the attention of either the PT or of the press.

All this was to change after Powell's Birmingham ('Rivers of Blood') speech, which shook the political establishment to its foundations and transformed the way immigration has been debated ever since – although it is worth recalling that Powell argued at the time that his speech was in support of the Conservative Party's official position to oppose Labour's

Race Relations Bill on Second Reading and in defence of its official policy at the time to encourage 're-emigration'. Four days later, the PT discussed the speech:

> It was agreed that the inflammatory tone was deplorable but that there was tremendous support for the sentiments expressed in the country and that this must be faced. It was also felt that the speech had possibly been a bid for the leadership. It was agreed that Mr Hogg's speech in the debate [i.e. in the House of Commons] had saved the day and that the 'woolly' wording of the reasoned amendment had upset people.* It was felt that Mr Powell having got more response than he expected would now lie low for a little while. (24th April 1968)

This was a forlorn hope. The public's reaction to the speech was overwhelmingly in Powell's support, and unprecedented in its extent. The PT considered Powell's speech had been, in part, "a bid for the leadership". Fair or unfair, there was from this point growing press speculation over the durability of Edward Heath's leadership of the Conservative Party. On 8th May, the PT felt "Mr Heath's speech at the 1922 Committee lunch was sound but a bit long." On 15th May, as there was

---

* This was the debate on Second Reading of the Race Relations Bill on 23rd April 1968. The Conservative Opposition proposed an amendment to the Bill which was rejected by the Labour majority. But the Bill was then given a Second Reading without a division despite the Opposition making it clear that, in its view, the Bill would make the situation "worse". In his speech on Second Reading, Quentin Hogg said of Powell's speech: "If one is going to say, and goodness knows many of us have thought, that the streets of our country might one day run with blood ... then surely one ought to consider whether, in the more immediate future, one's words are more likely to make that happen, or less likely to make that happen."

no sign of the controversy over the speech subsiding, the PT felt that "more information is obviously required about what is meant by dependants and how many are likely to come here during the next few years." The PT agreed "that the immediate family of immigrants should not be refused entry" but that the use of terms such as 'strict control' should not be deployed "without more knowledge of the facts". All this Sir Tufton Beamish, deputising for Sir Spencer Summers, was expected to report to the Chief Whip.

The Race Relations Bill received its Third Reading in the House of Commons a little after 4.30am on 10th July. There followed a few hours later the PT's weekly meeting of the Political Committee which discussed the significant divisions which had been revealed amongst Conservative MPs in this final, ill-tempered debate. This was the famous occasion when Quentin Hogg lost his composure and complained:

> MR. HOGG My Hon. Friends are perfectly at liberty to disagree with me, but I am entitled to express my opinion [i.e. that a vote against Third Reading would be misinterpreted and associated with "ugly manifestations of feeling"]. I have served my Party for 30 years –
> MR. JENNINGS So have we
> MR. HOGG – and I have given up what I believe to be a promising professional career and I have abandoned a great hereditary position. I am not now going to be put down from saying what I believe it is my duty to say by unmannerly people who cannot hear views different from their own in silence. I ask my party to agree with me.

Forty-four Conservative MPs failed to comply with his request, and voted against the Bill's Third Reading. Peter

Hordern, a future Chairman of the PT, was one of them. Sir Spencer Summers who spoke in the debate was very sympathetic to the reasoned amendment tabled by eight members of the 1922 Committee Executive, and refused to support the Bill as a whole. He said: "… those who consider this to be a bad Bill and who intend to vote against it should be acquitted of any suggestion of being racialist by so doing." But once their protest was made, the PT's instinct was, as ever, to be helpful and minimise the damage:

> It was thought important to avoid a row in the 1922 on Thursday and Sir Spencer Summers suggested that Sir Arthur Vere Harvey [Chairman of the 1922 Committee] might say at the main meeting that the Executive had decided beforehand to have a discussion with the Leader on which he would report on the following Thursday, and to affirm to the main Committee the Executive's support for the Leadership. It was agreed that this might take the heat out of the meeting and Sir Spencer said that he would put the idea to Sir Arthur Vere Harvey and the Chief Whip after consultation with Sir Tufton Beamish. (10th July 1968)

A day later, on 11th July, the 'rebellion' was (unusually) discussed by the PT's Council where Sir Spencer reported his anxieties "lest the PT's influence with the Chief Whip might be weakened" as a consequence of two members of the PT signing the original reasoned amendment.

This vote heightened tension within the Conservative Party, emphasising that the consequences of Powell's speech were long-lasting (although Powell himself had remained silent on the topic since April). On 17th July, the PT again discussed Party policy on immigration when it was urged on the Chief Whip to encourage "the Leader now to speak out and say exactly what Tory Policy is on Immigration and define exactly what is meant by 'a dependant' and what is meant by 'strict control'." The Political Committee added that "Mr Heath should speak on these lines at the 1922 meeting on Thursday." A week later, Sir Spencer was asked to speak again to the Chief Whip and emphasise "that there must be a firm party statement made on Immigration before the Party Conference" in which a definition of 'dependant' must be provided.

Enoch Powell spoke briefly and dramatically from the floor at this Blackpool Conference, but his main intervention was on the fringes when he pronounced his 'Morecambe Budget' referred to in the last chapter. Whatever his earlier intentions, Powell now posed a definite challenge to Heath's leadership, despite the PT judging the Blackpool Conference to have been "very successful, and that Mr Heath's speech had been particularly good" (16th October 1968). At least, the PT could not be accused of pandering to Powellite sentiments. As already noted, David Lane became a member of the Political Committee on 27th November. Lane was a standard-bearer of left-leaning Tories.* Whatever the views of individual PT members may have been, the decision to make Lane a member of the Progress Trust suggested little sympathy with Powell or the views he expressed. At this same meeting on 27th November "the activities of the Monday Club" were discussed critically. Although Powell was never a member of the Monday Club, its membership had been boosted by Powell supporters following the Birmingham Speech, and was therefore now regarded with even more

---

* David Lane did not remain a member of the PT for long, because he was appointed Under-Secretary of State for the Home Office in 1972.

hostility by the Conservative leadership.

Any discussion of Conservative immigration policy, therefore, was now bound up with Heath's personal authority. But
when twenty-one members of the PT dined with Heath on
12th March 1969, neither immigration nor the Common
Market were suggested as topics, presumably because they
wished the occasion to be convivial. Instead,

> The main question was how much were the promises already
> made going to cost, and where are the cuts going to be made? It
> was also suggested that they should ask him about the phasing
> out of Capital Gains Tax and that a few warnings should
> be given against too much reform of local government. Mr
> Peyton suggested that tactics in Opposition should be raised
> and the lack of co-ordination between the Shadow Cabinet
> and the various Policy Committees. (12th March 1969)

But ignoring the issue of immigration could not conceal
the support that Powell's views had attracted throughout
the country, including from Conservative Party workers.
On 9th June in Wolverhampton, Powell made his first major
immigration speech since Birmingham. Its emphasis was
on 'repatriation' but it also contained (unlike the previous
speech) an attack on Heath personally, accusing him of "sheer
incomprehension of the very magnitude of the danger". The
Political Committee believed "that his attack on the Leader
was deplorable" but "the Party should not ignore its warnings." Again, the PT concentrated on the need to define
'dependant' but, on repatriation, felt "that the immigrants
would not accept £2,000 to return to their country of origin".

Despite the odium which Powell attracted from the Tory
establishment, the 1970 Conservative Manifesto ('A Better

Tomorrow') promised an immigration policy which was arguably Powellite. It is easily forgotten that the Conservative Party's immigration policy in 1970, as stated in the manifesto, was as follows:

> There will be no further large scale permanent immigration. We will give assistance to Commonwealth immigrants who wish to return to their country of origin, but we will not tolerate any attempt to harass or compel them to go against their will.*

The manifesto commitment to prevent "further large scale permanent immigration" was broken so spectacularly in the years that followed that it marks a significant landmark in the public's disillusionment of politicians. But in the period immediately after the 1970 election there were parallels with the early 1960s – a Government was committed to new legislation which, yet again, was intended to bring under control the number of immigrants entering the country. The question, therefore, was whether this time the legislation would be successful. The PT's view on 3rd March 1971 was "that the Immigration Bill was a good one", although the following week "anxiety was expressed over the Patrial Clause".† Sir Tufton Beamish undertook to raise this aspect with Bill Deedes who was one of the Conservative members

---

* Powell would have argued that he wasn't calling for compulsion or harassment either. But the financial support he proposed to encourage voluntary repatriation was on a totally different scale from that contemplated by Heath's Government.

† The Patrial provisions of the Bill were a complex way of acknowledging the rights of entry of those possessing a family connection with those already settled in the UK. It was the chosen term to define 'dependants' which the PT and others had called for.

on the Standing Committee considering the Bill, along with Powell. Another concern surfaced later over repatriation. On 21st April, the PT agreed "that the Home Secretary should be pressed to get bilateral agreement with countries that admit immigrants with subsidised passages".

Those enthusiastic for further controls on immigration waited to see whether the new Immigration Act would fulfil the promises made in the manifesto. Doubts were raised on 22nd November 1972 when the House of Commons was asked to approve regulations under the new Immigration Act. This was, incidentally, an early moment when it dawned upon MPs that Common Market rules on 'free movement of labour' had implications for immigration policy – although Robert Carr as Home Secretary informed the House that "Judging by experience in the existing six countries of the Community ... the movement of labour into and out of any one country is not likely to be very large and is on the whole showing signs of decline" (Hansard, 22nd November 1972 c. 1360).

Tory MPs, however, were more worried that visitors from the 'old' Commonwealth would suffer restrictions under new rules which they felt should not apply in their case. The PT had decided earlier in the day that, while willing to support the Government, they looked for concessions and an under-taking that talks would be held with the old Commonwealth in order to achieve bilateral agreements. In addition, and perhaps more ominously,

It was agreed that the Government ought to act now in seeing that the country does not get landed with the Kenya Asians as it was felt that the country would not stand for any more. (22nd November 1972)

This was in reference to Idi Amin's decision in August 1972 to expel within ninety days Uganda's Asian minority ('Kenya' Asians was an inaccuracy of the minutes).

One of the four members of the PT present at this meeting was Sir Paul Bryan whose views, as a future Chairman of the PT, were surprisingly direct. He spoke in the House of Commons debate later that day and said that the main object of the new Immigration Act "… was to control immigration; to control coloured immigration – let that be quite clear. It was not said so in print because we are sensitive about these things." He expressed the concerns of many in the PT that new immigration controls intended to limit 'coloured' immigration were going to impose restrictions on movement from Australia, New Zealand and Canada at a time when many expelled Asians from Africa would be allowed to seek asylum in the United Kingdom. On 13th December 1972,

> The Chairman [Sir Tufton Beamish] reported that he had spoken to the Chief Whip about a further influx of Asians. Reciprocity was felt to be the best thing for the future and to avoid patrials. It was agreed that all members should speak to their area whips on their feelings about having any more Asians.

On 1st June 1973, Enoch Powell returned to the subject in a speech in Birmingham, in which he claimed that net immigration from the New Commonwealth had amounted to 87,000 in the two years and a half since the General Election of 1970. So much for "no further large scale permanent immigration". In this speech, however, he shifted his emphasis towards the birth figures of those of 'New Commonwealth origin'. When the Political Committee met for the first time after this speech, on 13th June, "it was agreed that [about Powell] there was not very much that the PT could do." Powell always believed that, without his speeches, Governments would have done even less to control immigration. Others claimed, on the contrary, that Powell's speeches made it impossible for anyone else to argue for stricter controls without incurring the charge of racism. This disagreement is still voiced today.

The PT showed little further interest in immigration until 1976, when Mrs Thatcher herself spoke on the subject. Ebury Note 179 (18th July 1976) suggested that "The Conservative Party needs a new radical, tough, humane immigration policy" and suggested it should comprise "no further immigration – not one single man, woman or child"; and, in addition, proposed "grants of £10,000 for each recent immigrant who wishes to emigrate". It is unclear how many PT members went along with this suggestion but "it was agreed to raise this at the dinner with Lord Thorneycroft on 28th July." A few days earlier, on 30th June, the PT had urged Whitelaw not to "try for a compromise, but to take a consensus of views, and then leave the Leader to make up her own mind as to what the Party line should be". Also, "the Finance racket [i.e. of evasion of immigration controls] ought to be stopped."

Mrs Thatcher was asked about immigration in a television interview in January 1978 when she spoke of people "really rather afraid that this country might be rather swamped by people with a different culture" and there was much speculation at this time that she intended a new and much stricter immigration policy. The PT did not encourage this development. On 1st February 1978, it complained of "the apparent lack of liaison with Mr Whitelaw before making her views known" and on 12th April the PT concluded "that the Party had come out of the immigration argument as well as they could, but it was hoped that they would remain as quiet as possible on the subject in the future". This reaction was prompted more by fears over Mrs Thatcher's tone and temperament than a feeling that immigration was no longer important.

Once Mrs Thatcher became Prime Minister, she moved quickly to introduce revised and stricter immigration controls which some Conservative MPs refused to support. The PT's reaction was to regret their abstentions but "it was at least a good thing as far as the press and public were concerned that the Conservative Party should be seen to have a conscience" (5th December 1979). Admittedly only three members attended this meeting, but this pusillanimous attitude was not untypical of the PT. Ebury Research Notes continued to raise the topic from time to time. Ebury Note 380 (18th June 1984), for example, argued that the issue was still of electoral significance, and that it had adverse implications for attempts to control public expenditure. But the mood of the PT had changed:

> It was agreed that there should be no step down the Enoch road of repatriation. The Sikhs vote Labour but most of the Asians are natural Conservative voters. The second generation of West Indians are as much a problem as their parents. It was thought that there is need for 'positive' discrimination on the American pattern. (27th June 1984)

In November 1987, the new Immigration Bill occasioned a further Ebury Note (No. 488) which was discussed on 18th November (the note had asked whether the practical value of the new legislation "outweighs the grievances it may excite?"):

It was agreed that there must be proper controls to preserve good relations with the ethnic races. People coming into this country for three months and disappearing must be stopped, and the importing of brides from India and Pakistan was regretted ... it is important to create a black middleclass as in America, and that ethnic schools are a mistake as it slows up integration. There was one view expressed by Mrs Virginia Bottomley that a balance in the black–white ratio in schools should be done by social engineering. It was agreed that we must work on good black parents to become school governors.

Two years later, the PT discussed for the first time topics which today would fall into the category of 'multiculturalism' or 'communalism'. On 12th July 1989, on the general subject of ethnic minorities, there were "worries over public order and education ... Teachers are sometimes idle about promoting Christianity and as a result we are losing out. In some areas the nativity play is dropped ... Although the problem only arises in certain parts of the country, some people do feel threatened ... we have been good at absorbing migrants in the past, but the present problem is that Muslims do not want to integrate, and we must avoid having 'bloc ethnic' voting as in the States."

This was the last time that immigration and race relations were discussed formally. On 23rd March 1999, an Ebury Note (No. 802) ventured into the tortuous area of 'institutional racism' following the Stephen Lawrence Inquiry, and the PT's response was "We should take a tougher line on both black and white immigration." On the issue of institutional racism itself, the Committee considered "that the police were incompetent rather than racist" and that "The Labour Party has always exploited race as they were after the black vote, and they exploited the Stephen Lawrence affair."

But by this time, it was much harder to claim that the views expressed at a PT meeting represented the views of the PT as a whole, let alone the Conservative Parliamentary Party. Attendances at these political meetings were too small. By the time immigration again became a major topic in British politics, the PT no longer existed. The immigration debate which had once centred upon the New and Old Commonwealth and the need to control 'numbers' evolved into a debate about 'multiculturalism' and the issue which Robert Carr (and others) had in 1972 dismissed as of marginal importance – namely free movement of labour within the European Union and the failure of the European Union to control its own borders. Immigration and the European Union had become inextricably linked.

7

EUROPE

"It was difficult to persuade Mr Heath, as he is so keen on the Common Market himself, that it is not so popular in the country." (16th March 1970)

"The people are switched off by Europe bashing ... The average person thinks that we must get on with our fellow Europeans." (26th June 1989)

"We always seem to lose the argument in Europe, although we have used both the Thatcher and the Major approach." (1st May 1996)

If immigration led to Enoch Powell's break with the Conservative Party's leadership, Europe led to his exile from the Conservative Party as a whole. In the General Election of February 1974, he refused to stand as an official Conservative candidate in his constituency of Wolverhampton South West, and instead left Parliament urging those for whom the issue of Parliamentary sovereignty was paramount to vote for a Party committed to keeping the European question open – that was the Labour Party. He believed that membership of the European Economic Community (EEC) was so inconsistent with the traditional beliefs and purpose of the Conservative Party that persevering with this policy would result in its destruction.

While the PT was always on guard against anything which threatened the Conservative interest, it did not take this threat seriously at the time. The PT Council simply accepted the advice of Sir Tufton Beamish on 10th November 1971 that "all the members of the Political Committee were pro-Common Market." As already mentioned, Sir Tufton was an enthusiast for membership, so his advice might have contained an element of wishful thinking. But to be fair, there was no need for Sir Tufton to downplay PT criticism of Heath's European policy, because none existed. The PT was part of the Conservative tradition that viewed the Common Market as necessary for trade and as a safeguard against another European war. Only a very few PT members at this time would have been suspected of harbouring secret hesitations.

Much earlier in the PT's history, it was different. There had been misgivings over Churchill's apparent enthusiasm for a 'united' Europe. When it was reported in *The Evening Standard* "that Mr Churchill and his associates are planning to address public meetings up and down the country in support of their [United Europe] Movement", the PT's reaction on 21st November 1947 was to ask whether these meetings were intended "to take precedence over the Party's meetings or will they tend to diminish their number?" Their concern was that Churchill's involvement with the United Europe Movement might become a distraction from the task of preparing for an election. Related anxieties surfaced the following year (14th September 1948) when the PT asked "Is it desirable to examine how far the Party is being pledged to Western Union?" The question was prompted by pressure for a provisional European Assembly, which Churchill was believed to support. A European Parliamentary Congress had also called for the creation of a European Federal Parliament, which met with Conservative opposition.

The first reference in the PT's minutes to the Common

Market itself was on 11th July 1956 when Sir Harry Legge-Bourke, who was deeply opposed to European political federation in the 1950s but whose views on the Common Market were less clear-cut later on, "drew attention to a motion on the Order Paper on the Common Market in Europe". Thereafter, the Common Market was a regular subject of discussion, but it is difficult to judge from the minutes where the PT stood. Mostly, their concerns centred upon the trading implications for countries outside the Common Market and especially for the New and Old Commonwealth; on 26th June 1957, for example, "questions concerning the European Free Trade Area and the Common Market were discussed at some length."

Britain's first application to join the Common Market was widely expected in 1961, although it was not until the end of July that this was confirmed. A few months before – on 3rd May 1961 – the PT had discussed the prospects of Britain applying, when "it was agreed that British Agriculture must have certain safeguards before going into the Common Market." On 10th May, the PT's view was even more sceptical:

It was hoped that there would be no sudden joining of the Common Market … we are pledged to support [agricultural] prices for the life of this Parliament and must not break our word. Some members thought that certain farmers were not unreasonable about the eventual joining of the Common Market but it was agreed that eighteen months were needed for re-thinking.

'Sovereignty' was not mentioned, and there was no repeat of the arguments relating to peace. The PT's interest in Europe had reverted to its traditional areas of comfort – agriculture, international trade, and relations with the Commonwealth. It was from this perspective that the PT wished to consider Britain's application. On 7th June 1961, Morrison undertook to speak to Butler and Martin Redmayne, the Chief Whip, in order to request making "more information available regarding the Government's thoughts on the subject".

The PT also feared that Britain's proposed membership might prove contentious at the forthcoming Party Conference at Brighton in October. For this reason, the intention was for PT members to stay together in the same hotel so that they were on-hand to help draft emergency resolutions "in case the discussion should get out of control at the Conference" and result in "a crisis". In the event, the PT left it too late to book a hotel, but it didn't matter as the Government received endorsement for its application without any difficulty, despite the best efforts of Sir Derek Walker-Smith, the Conservative MP for East Hertfordshire, who led the opposition. It is doubtful, incidentally, whether the PT was equipped to draft any resolution, emergency or otherwise. Before the Conference, on 19th July, John Morrison had asked Fells "to get a copy of the *Daily Herald* pamphlet on how the Common Market works". His request doesn't inspire confidence that the Conservative Party's most senior backbencher knew very much about the subject.

Once the Party Conference had given its approval to the application, and negotiations were underway, the PT was content to let them run their course. These continued until January 1963, and their collapse passed without comment or remorse from the PT's Political Committee. When three years later, in October 1966, Harold Wilson decided to make another attempt, the PT was also relaxed, believing it necessary to "support the Government on this" and sensing that "there were not so many dissenting voices on the Opposition side now" (18th November 1966). Wilson announced to the House of Commons his formal decision to make a fresh application to join the Common Market on 2nd May 1967. Like last time, most Conservative reservations were almost solely related to agriculture and links with the Commonwealth, and the decision to re-apply was warmly welcomed by Edward Heath on behalf of the Opposition. On 27th November 1967, President de Gaulle's veto was again imposed, and again the PT registered no disappointment.

This was the last time that the Conservative Party was broadly united on the subject. Nobody was surprised by Mr Heath's wish to take Great Britain into the Common Market, but two failed applications gave – to those who were never entirely persuaded of the need – an excuse to express doubts over a third attempt. Moreover, Enoch Powell opened a second front in his opposition to Heath by questioning in fundamental terms the whole principle of Britain's membership. Although there were Conservative MPs who had identified the same issues long before him, Powell's opposition to membership was of a different calibre, and would prove to be the greatest threat to Heath in his persuading the Conservative Party of the necessity and desirability of a fresh application.

But Heath's first challenge was to come up with a formula to maintain the Party's unity throughout a General Election, which could not be postponed beyond the spring of 1971. At a dinner with Tony Barber in May 1969, the PT asked "How does the Party put across to the Electorate the price of going into the Common Market?" While the issue was still discussed mostly in terms of agriculture and fishing, the PT now displayed signs of unease that the issue of membership was becoming more controversial. On 19th July 1969:

> The entry of Britain into the Common Market was discussed. It was thought that no move would be made [i.e. by the Labour Government] until after the German Elections, and that if an approach is made we must only make it if it is going to be successful as a third refusal would be disastrous for any Political Party. It was agreed that NAFTA would not come about as the Americans were not keen and it was felt that it was a pity that there was no alternative when bargaining with Europe.

The PT was also conscious of the tactical risks in electoral terms. On 11th February 1970, when few expected the General Election to follow so soon afterwards, the PT considered the likelihood that Harold Wilson might perform an about-turn on Europe, using a recent assessment of joining the Common Market "as a means to justify backing out of our joining" and so put Heath "in a very difficult situation". Clearly, some PT members suspected that Harold Wilson would now oppose membership of the EEC – at least until after a General Election – for opportunist reasons in order to galvanise Conservative opponents of Heath's policy and make it even more electorally divisive for the Conservative Party. For this reason, the PT felt that "if someone, not Mr Heath, warned the country of the possibility of a *volte face* to win the election, it could do no harm." Other extracts from the PT minutes of this period express similar fears. For example:

> The debate on the Common Market White Paper was discussed. It was felt that the Prime Minister was back-tracking.

The Chairman [Sir Tufton Beamish] pointed out that the Treaty of Rome states again the importance of private enterprise and competition, and that Europe does not want Britain whilst she is a Socialist State. (25th February 1970)

The dinner to Mr Heath on March 11th 1970 was discussed and it was agreed ... that it was difficult to persuade Mr Heath, as he is so keen on the Common Market himself, that it is not so popular in the country. (16th March 1970)

The idea of a referendum on the Common Market was discussed. It was agreed that it would be very difficult to compose the questions, and that it was against the Constitution ... the best compromise would be for Members to hold consultations with their constituents and then to have a Free Vote in Parliament. (20th May 1970)

This meeting was the last before the General Election which took place on 18th June 1970 and which led, against the expectations of many, to a new Conservative Government with Edward Heath as Prime Minister. Suddenly, Britain's membership of the Common Market moved from a theoretical possibility to a practical likelihood, even though Enoch Powell believed that the House of Commons would never ultimately give its consent. The wording of the Conservative Manifesto had allowed Powell to reconcile his opposition to the Common Market with standing as an official Conservative candidate. The manifesto had stated that "Our sole commitment is to negotiate; no more no less." Heath himself had also stated in Paris on 5th May that "the full hearted consent of Parliament and peoples" of the new member countries would be necessary if the enlargement of the Community was to be a success. The distinction between 'Parliament' and 'peoples' – and how 'full hearted' consent was to be measured

– lay at the heart of the debate once Heath had secured the 'terms of entry' that satisfied him.

As the negotiations continued, the PT's only comment was that "Mr Rippon was handling the negotiations very well, but that the French were still being very difficult" (10th February 1971). More critically, the PT expected "that getting acceptance in the House might be a very dangerous time for the Tory Party as the Opposition are bound to go against it as their one chance of defeating the Government". In this, the PT interpreted Mr Wilson's instincts correctly, but not those of some in his Party. Along with many others, the PT underestimated the determination of a group of Labour MPs to come to the Government's rescue should it prove necessary. Of one thing the PT was sure: "… there definitely would not be a referendum. All parties were agreed on this" (17th March 1971).

The PT's main concern at this moment was tactical. At a dinner with Mr Whitelaw on 21st July 1971, the PT recommended "the virtues of a free vote". Sir Tufton on this occasion was in a minority, arguing that a free vote would increase the number of Conservative opponents of entry into the EEC (as, by then, the 'Common Market' was known). Sir Tufton was undoubtedly correct, but he failed to allow for a free vote producing the same effect on pro-EEC Labour MPs who wished to support the Government. Once the White Paper entitled 'The United Kingdom and the European Communities' was published in July, the PT's discussion concentrated on "the various ways of putting it across in their constituencies. It was noted that Central Office would be sending out notes on the more complicated issues to help members with questions from the 'Antis'" (7th July 1971). When Parliament returned after the summer recess to enact the actual legislation, the fear again was how Conservative 'antis' would vote given that the Committee stages of the Bill could not be 'sent upstairs' but would have to be debated by all MPs on the floor of the House. Nevertheless, allowing a free vote "had been a good tactical move by the Government" (20th October 1971).

Once the decision of principle was approved by a majority of 112 in the House of Commons on 28th October – 356 MPs supported the Government and 244 voted against – the PT discussed the issue less frequently, despite attempts by its researcher to raise the topic. Following the vote on 28th October 1971, there were nine Ebury Notes on aspects of the EEC leading up to Britain's accession to the Treaty but none was discussed at length. One of these (No. 42, 12th February 1972) even dared to mention the word 'sovereignty', acknowledging the safeguard of "unanimity of voting" but pointing out that Heath did not necessarily see the need for such safeguards, ready as he was "to develop effective institutions" involving an increase of executive power at the centre and the creation of an effective European Parliament.

The Second Reading debate upon the European Communities Bill took place on 17th February 1972 – and was only carried by eight votes. For a moment, it looked as if Powell's prediction that the legislation would not pass might be vindicated. Its passage was now dependent upon the Government's ability to curtail discussion of the Bill by the use of the guillotine i.e. timetabling of the Bill – something to which both Enoch Powell and Michael Foot insisted the House would never consent. But it did; on 2nd May, the House of Commons agreed to limit the time for debate by a majority of eleven, once again with help from members of the Labour Party. This ensured the Bill's enactment and allowed the PT to turn its attention towards the economic and industrial relations problems which were threatening Heath's Government. As the PT remarked on the day after the guillotine vote, "there will be no increase in investment by Europeans in this country until the labour problems are sorted out." So far as most of the Conservative Party was concerned, Britain's membership of the EEC was now settled and at the Blackpool Conference of 1972 the issue provided no drama or excitement. According to an Ebury Note (No. 62):

> What the theme now presented (and the gift was embraced with joy) was the opportunity to be seen as a united Party. Apparent as this was in the debate, the seal was set upon it in the response to the clarion call with which the Prime Minister closed his speech. Rapturously, with generous emotions including hope and gratitude, was he sent away with surely no doubt that, so far as Conference could ensure it, "fair blows the wind for France." (16th October 1972)

Joining the EEC meant that Sir Tufton Beamish could no longer continue as the PT's Chairman. On 1st January 1973 he was appointed as one of the UK's first Members of the European Parliament and while the 'dual-mandate' allowed him to remain a member of the House of Commons (although he stood down at the General Election of February 1974), his attendance was now divided between London, Brussels and Strasbourg. His place as Chairman was taken by John Temple,* but at the meeting of 24th January 1973 Sir Tufton was allowed to continue as a member of the Political

---

* John Temple (1910–1994) was the Member of Parliament for Chester between 1956 and 1974.

Committee. He soon displayed disillusionment with his new role. At a meeting on 13th June 1973, after reporting on the business of the European Parliament, the PT shared his view that "it was sad that so much that is going on there is not reported in this country", and a few months later, on 7th November, there was sympathy with Sir Tufton over the costs he incurred "attending the European Parliament" which "were considered prohibitive enough" to be raised with the Chief Whip.

It never occurred to the PT that Britain's membership of the EEC would soon, by accident, be tested by an early General Election. Not until 30th January 1974, when a General Election caused by the miners' strike was still a matter of speculation (it was not announced until 7th February), did Temple report "that he had spoken with the Chief Whip about the importance of having Europe in the Manifesto". The early election, which took place on 28th February, also brought to an end Temple's brief Chairmanship of the PT as he did not stand for re-election. He was succeeded by Michael Hamilton.

The reasons for Mr Heath's defeat in February 1974 have been widely debated. Whether or not his European policy was a major factor, it is unarguable that one consequence of Labour's victory was to reopen the issue of Britain's EEC membership in a way that could not have happened otherwise. Labour's commitment both to renegotiate the terms of membership, and then to put the result of these negotiations to the British people – by referendum as most people assumed, although Powell argued that it could also be through a further General Election – transformed the outlook. The PT ducked the issue at this stage. On 13th March, at its first meeting following the election, the PT merely put down the "failure of the Election campaign" to the poor selection of candidates and bad timing. "There was also criticism of there being too much of Mr Heath and Mr Wilson on TV." But no mention of Europe.

The period between February and October 1974 was dominated by the prospect of a second General Election – which the PT wished to avoid. There was also speculation on the prospects of forming a National Government, as some doubted whether the Conservatives would be able to govern on their own, even if they recovered a majority. Mr Heath's personal position was discussed by the PT on 12th June 1974 when the Chairman reported that he had received a letter from David James,[*] a rare participant at PT meetings, "suggesting a change of leadership. It was noted that it had been kept out of the press so far." The PT's view as a whole was "that the Party should be firmed up in support of Mr Heath, as this was no time to change the leadership" despite Sir Paul Bryan's earlier view that "as the Party is so divided at the moment, a good look should be taken at what the Party's policies are" (20th March 1974).

The PT did not include 'Europe' as a policy in need of reappraisal. Even after the second election defeat of October 1974, and the replacement of Mr Heath as Leader by Mrs Thatcher, it was agreed on 26th February 1975 "that it was very important, now that the party had improved its standing nationally, that the new Leader and Mr Maudling should be shown to be pro Europe" in the lead-up to the forthcoming referendum campaign. The referendum took place on 5th June 1975, and again it was viewed by the PT from a

---

* David James (1919–1986) was the Member of Parliament for Brighton Kemptown between 1959 and 1964 and subsequently North Dorset between 1970–79.

purely tactical perspective, fearing "it would be very serious if the BBC give equal coverage to the anti-marketeers which appears to be their plan" (9th April 1975).

The referendum over – and Britain's membership of the EEC confirmed – the issue of Europe vanished almost entirely from the PT's gaze until the holding of direct elections to the European Parliament which took place for the first time in 1979, but which had been raised by an Ebury Note in February 1976 (No. 163). When discussed,

> … It was thought that in due course Elections would come at the same time as General Elections here … proportional representation (PR) would be resisted, not because MPs were entirely against PR but because in Europe, in practice, it does not seem to reflect the will of the people … It was thought that the European Parliament would attract a high calibre type of member. (18th February 1976)

Whether direct elections should be based on proportional representation or 'first past the post' was a divisive issue. On 13th December 1977, the Labour Government had recommended to the House the regional list system, but on a free vote this was rejected by 319 votes to 222. A large number of Labour and Conservative MPs conspired together to defeat this proposal, but at least five members of the PT joined Edward Heath and other Conservative MPs in supporting the Labour Government's recommendation. These PT members included William Benyon, Charles Morrison and Robert Rhodes James,* all of whom were active PT members. After

---

* Sir Robert Rhodes James (1933–1999) was the Member of Parliament for Cambridge between 1976 and 1992. He was a distinguished historian and a previous clerk in the House of Commons – and an assiduous attendee

the vote, the PT was of the view "that if the Conservatives want the Bill to go through they will have to vote with the Government on the guillotine" (14th December 1977).

A bigger issue was the European Monetary System (EMS), first raised with the PT on 5th November 1978 (Ebury Note 236). This was when proposals for fixed exchange rates, a European Monetary Fund and a European Currency became concrete. The note suggested six reasons for joining the EMS (including it would "show us to be good Europeans") and five reasons against (including a "common currency can only work if there is a common government to redirect resources to weaker areas"). When the note was discussed, the majority PT view was "to go in at the beginning" despite the problems which might be caused for employment and exports. The PT members who attended this discussion on 15th November 1978 were Michael Hamilton, Peter Blaker,[*] Sir Paul Bryan, Peter Hordern, Jasper More,[†] Charles Morrison and Robert Rhodes James. They were amongst the most active, and representative, of PT members during this period. The EMS was debated in the House on 29th November 1978, when, in anticipation, the PT had regretted "that Sir Geoffrey Howe is sitting on the fence". This did not go unnoticed by the Chancellor of the Exchequer himself, Denis Healey, who began his speech as follows:

---

of PT political meetings.

[*] Sir Peter Blaker (1922–2009) was the Member of Parliament for Blackpool South between 1964 and 1992.

[†] Sir Jasper More (1907–1987) was the Member of Parliament for Ludlow between 1960 and 1979. He was an opponent of membership of the EEC and resigned from Edward Heath's Government for this reason in 1971.

THE CHANCELLOR OF THE EXCHEQUER (MR. DENIS HEALEY): I welcome the opportunity that we have today, in the last few days of negotiations concerning the possible setting up of a European Monetary System, to describe the Government's approach. I also welcome the opportunity to discover the views of the Opposition. I am sure that Sir Geoffrey Howe is looking forward to telling us how he is reconciling the views expressed by Mr Biffen with those of Mr Hurd, and not least those of Mr Nott. (Hansard, 29th November 1978 c. 457)

The EMS was the first of many initiatives by the EEC which forced MPs of all parties to revisit the full implications of the policy which they had supported in 1972. It also provoked divisions within Conservative ranks which would characterise Parliamentary debates ever after. Following the referendum, political attention turned to what was and was not susceptible to UK influence within the EEC as it began its slow but relentless journey towards economic, monetary and political union. This Parliamentary debate on the EMS was, perhaps, the first time when the House of Commons was forced to confront practically, rather than theoretically, the issues which went to the heart of the European 'project'.

It would also prove to be the last time for many years that a Labour Government was obliged to make up its mind on a European question – not to be called on again until Labour's return to office in 1997. In May 1979, the baton passed to Mrs Thatcher whose first confrontation with the European Community involved not the EMS, but the size of Britain's overall net contribution to the EEC budget. She received little encouragement from the PT to press her case. On 19th March 1980, for example, the PT disapproved of her threat "to withhold VAT payments" in order to apply pressure to gain concessions. Otherwise, Britain's place in Europe was hardly discussed by the PT in Mrs Thatcher's first year of office. The subject had again gone quiet, and any interest expressed usually related to the privileges of Conservative Members of the European Parliament whose pay and status within the Palace of Westminster continued to be a source of concern for those on the gravy train. "The cost of European Members" was the only specific European issue raised with the Prime Minister when she dined with the PT on 5th November 1980.

On 1st April 1981, however, the PT discussed an Ebury Note headed 'What's Wrong With Europe' (No. 290). This note referred to "recent polls" showing "the majority of the British people are in favour of Britain leaving the EEC", adding "this may be partly because since we joined in 1973 nothing much has gone right for Britain." This was said at a moment, prior to the Falklands War, when Mrs Thatcher's Government was in serious difficulties and nobody took a second term for granted. Despite the obvious failings of Michael Foot as Opposition Leader, expectations that he would fight an election on the need to recover Parliamentary sovereignty from Brussels posed a threat to a divided Conservative Party. However, the Falklands crisis – which lasted from 2nd April to 14th June 1982 – transformed both Mrs Thatcher's position, and the political agenda which followed.

During the Falklands crisis, the PT's Political Committee met six times. Its first discussion of the crisis on 21st April 1982 was hardly overflowing with confidence and does not read well in retrospect:

> It was agreed that it did not look as though fighting could be avoided, and that all party support would break-up when

the first shot was fired. It was agreed that "British Interests" should be paramount rather than "The Falkland Islanders' wishes should be paramount." There were worries about air cover as the Harrier is no match for the mirage jet. It was also thought that public opinion is fickle over the Falklands and that support could vanish once serious fighting begins, but it was noted that Suez did the Party no harm electorally.

The PT did not have a particularly 'good' war, because not enough of its members had the necessary faith in a clear-cut victory to give Mrs Thatcher their full support. They feared that the risks of fighting the war outweighed the benefits. Thus, when on 12th May the PT detected "a whiff of compromise in the air", it did so without any sense of disapproval. The PT's ambitions went no further than the hope "that the British would at least have a foot on the Islands when the final negotiations take place". Hardly a ringing endorsement, but only two PT members attended this meeting. They were Michael Hamilton (who was about to become Francis Pym's Parliamentary Private Secretary) and William Benyon, who was a Tory of the more patrician tradition. Their misgivings were probably shared by others in the PT who, before hostilities started, were keen to do anything to avoid them.

Of course, these doubts were forgotten once victory was secured. Sir Paul Bryan had become Chairman of the Political Committee on 26th May following Hamilton's resignation, with Peter Hordern and William Benyon becoming Vice Chairmen.* The PT's verdict now was "that

---

* One of their first stipulations was that membership of the PT should be increased and that former Parliamentary Private Secretaries be readmitted. On 21st July 1982, membership of the Political Committee was increased to 25, with the return of all former PPSs i.e. Nicholas Baker, Kenneth Carlisle,

the PM's performance had been amazing, and that there must be a political bonus for the Party" (17th June 1982). Mrs Thatcher's authority had been greatly strengthened, and she was now free to return to her agenda, with much greater hope of securing a second term. The PT likewise lost no time in moving on, while warning that people should not think "we could coast to victory in the Election on the Falklands." They had concerns that the Falklands Inquiry might reveal failures of Government policy which would be to their disadvantage, and hoped that even though the economic trends were encouraging, "we would not have an early election."

The Falklands conflict had diverted attention from a significant development in Europe when, on 18th May, the Council of Agricultural Ministers in effect ignored a British 'veto' and allowed a matter to be settled by majority voting.[*] An Ebury Note (No. 325) drew this to the PT's attention as a further example of the direction in which the EU was travelling while conceding that "at present, it is unlikely that the EEC will play a decisive part in determining the outcome of the next General Election. On the other hand, if the Labour Party wished to play the anti-EEC card, the 'veto' controversy

---

Mark Lennox-Boyd, Richard Luce and Malcolm Thornton as well as John Hannam and Lord James Douglas-Hamilton as new members. Better attendances followed at meetings, especially when meetings were moved to the House of Commons rather than at the home of Bridget Lakin in Eaton Terrace.

[*] This was reported to the House of Commons by the Minister of Agriculture, Peter Walker, who confirmed that what had happened was a breach of the Luxembourg Compromise and was evidence of the Commission's desire for majority voting which HMG opposed. There was widespread opposition expressed in the House of Commons to this development, although not from Roy Jenkins.

would provide it with valuable ammunition."

This was not, however, a fear shared by the five PT MPs who discussed the paper on 23rd June 1982.* The minutes record,

> There was criticism of our attitude to Europe, and although standing up to the Foreigner was popular in the short run it would do the country no good in the long term. Mr Richard Luce was attracted by the suggestion that there should be increased use of majority voting in the Council, but reserving the right of veto for matters considered as being contrary to vital interests of individual states. It was thought that the electorate should be told that a withdrawal from Europe would mean loss of jobs, that there should be a broader attack on tariffs and a stand made against Japan so that we look constructive in Europe.

This extract from the PT minutes is revealing. First, it demonstrates how, seven years after the referendum, the prospect of Britain leaving the European Economic Community was now mentioned as a possibility. Second, the alleged need for Britain to be more "constructive" in order to exercise greater influence within the EEC became a constant theme for those relatively relaxed over the loss of the 'veto' – although it should be noted that hardly anyone was arguing at this time for the right of veto to disappear entirely. Third, as is now known, the increased use of majority voting supported by some in the PT was the path which Mrs Thatcher (perhaps unwittingly) eventually chose in order to gain the advantages

---

* The five MPs were Peter Hordern, Lord Cranborne, Harry Greenway, Peter Viggers and Richard Luce. It is unlikely that Lord Cranborne agreed with the conclusion of the minutes.

of freer trade, paving the way to the Single Market.

The tactical issue of this moment, however, was whether Michael Foot would seek to make Britain's membership of the EEC a major election issue. This was the question raised again by a paper on 14th February 1983 (Ebury Note 341), noting that Foot seemed determined to concentrate more upon the issue of nuclear disarmament than Parliamentary sovereignty; but warning that if the anti-EEC card were to be played effectively, it could be significant. On 23rd February, the PT

> … agreed that it would be quite impossible to leave the EEC as we would immediately get a further 2,000,000 unemployed. It was also agreed that it would be impossible to unscramble the fishing rights. It was thought that the Party should be Euro-realists and fight our corner, and that we are helped by the fact that the Prime Minister is tough with Europe. It was thought that it is not good news that Greece, Spain and Portugal are to join the EEC and that unless there are radical changes in the Agricultural policy there could be a bust-up.

This was the last time that Europe was discussed by the PT before the General Election, which was held on 9th June 1983. Commentators have discussed what might have happened if Peter Shore (as many originally expected) had led the Labour Party at this moment instead of Michael Foot (who himself had supported Peter Shore, until he changed his mind and stood for the leadership himself). Despite his impeccable credentials as an opponent of membership, Foot's change of mind was unfortunate for those who regarded the loss of national sovereignty as the supreme question facing the country. Shore's priority in Opposition would have been to concentrate public attention on the political implications of Britain's EEC membership, but Foot blurred the message by giving equal time to the case for ridding this country of nuclear weapons – which was far less popular. Whether Shore's policy would have been more successful politically is arguable – perhaps nothing could have counterbalanced the Falklands factor. In any case, the consequence of the Conservative victory was that Britain's EEC membership continued without any electoral interruption, and the general expectations of the PT were fulfilled. Following the election, the European issue turned to the more mundane and secondary issue of whether the Prime Minister should be less "confrontational" or more "constructive" in her general approach.

Unhappily for those who longed for harmony, the first European issue to be confronted in Mrs Thatcher's second term was the size of the UK's budget rebate. By January 1984, Mrs Thatcher was demanding that £450 million should be paid to the UK by the end of March. On the first occasion when the PT's interest in this subject was tested (Ebury Note 362), no response was forthcoming. But when the issue was raised again three months later in April 1984 (Ebury Note 372), fundamental questions were again asked over the EEC's direction following the failure of the summit on 20th March to agree a figure. This was the occasion when Greece was reported as saying "It would be a great relief if Britain left the EEC." *The Economist* speculated in an editorial:

A looser community, minus farm policy, but with a free trade area, plus co-operation on defence and technology? A community minus Britain, Ireland and possibly Denmark? The present Europe is not the only possible one.

Britain's membership of the EEC was yet again in question: but with an additional element, namely that if the issue of Britain's budget rebate could only be settled, the Community would then be free to move towards a new relationship based upon a wider membership, and more majority voting. The PT's view was not supportive of the Prime Minister:

> It was felt that this country is too preoccupied with the C.A.P. and the rebate, and should be thinking about co-operation in Defence, and a closer movement to Europe diplomatically as the U.S. is moving into territory that it is hard for us to follow, such as their action in Grenada and their attitude to Central and South America. At the present time we are being left out of the talks the French and Germans are having with the Russians. (11th April 1984)

Predictably, the British turnout in the elections for the European Parliament on 14th June was, at 32 per cent, the lowest in Europe and widely considered derisory. It was held under the 'first past the post' system in England, Scotland and Wales but not in Northern Ireland where the Single Transferable Vote was employed. The PT's excuse for the low attendance was that "if the European Parliament had more power, the voters in the country might have more interest in it" (4th July 1984). A somewhat unrealistic view, but the unusually large number of PT members who participated in this discussion is demonstrative of how far the PT was detached from a growing Eurosceptic mood.[*]

The PT's reluctance to discuss Britain's membership of the

---

[*] Those attending were: Sir Paul Bryan, Nicholas Baker, Mark Lennox-Boyd, Michael Colvin, William Benyon, John Hannam, Charles Morrison, Sir John Osborn, Richard Ryder, Robert Rhodes James and Jim Spicer.

EEC persisted, until events intervened – and one such event was the EEC summit in Milan in June 1985. It was significant because it endorsed Lord Cockfield's plan for market liberalisation, which many assumed at the time was a victory for Mrs Thatcher in shifting the EEC's attention from political to economic objectives. Few were alive to the political consequences of Lord Cockfield's proposals, although an Ebury Note (No. 406) did raise the question:

> If a common market is to be created, and if national differences are to be reconciled within a European dimension, then more rapid decision-making is essential. And this means more majority voting, and probably more legislative powers for the European Assembly ... many feel that majority voting is essential if all internal obstacles to trade are to be eliminated by 1992, which is the target.

With the mention of '1992', a new chapter in the European debate was opened, although the PT was unexcited by the prospect:

> Members agreed that more power for the Assembly should be far down the line. They were against two tier majority voting ... It was agreed that Sir John Osborn should ask Lord Cockfield to dine with the PT as he is knowledgeable on the subject ... it was noted that we will have to change our Immigration laws relating to Fiancées because of a Common Market ruling. (12th June 1985)

In noticing the implications for UK immigration policy "of a Common Market ruling", the PT was unusually perceptive. Given its general stance on the EEC, the PT might have been expected to support Michael Heseltine when his quarrel over Westland, with its European dimension, came to a head in January 1986. Heseltine resigned from the Cabinet on 9th January, and the PT devoted the whole of its meeting a week later to the issue, which again attracted a significant attendance.* It was Sir James Spicer,† by no stretch of the imagination someone hostile to the EEC, who was most critical of Heseltine, perhaps because of his constituency interest. He pointed out

> ... that the whole of the west country is behind the American deal, and that there was concern over the European consortium as both Augusta and Aerospatiale are in difficulties. The Government's handling was criticised but it was agreed that Mr Brittan should be supported by colleagues in the House that day. It was agreed that Mr Heseltine on the backbenches will be a dangerous threat to the Government. It was hoped that if the Economy goes well this could be forgotten by the time of the Election. (15th January 1986)

Heseltine had regarded Westland as a test case for the Government's commitment to Europe, but the PT failed to back him.

Ironically, at a time when Mr Heseltine was challenging

---

* Those attending were: Sir Paul Bryan, W. Benyon, Esmond Bulmer, Harry Greenway, David Heathcoat-Amory, Ian Gow, Sir Peter Hordern, Richard Ryder, Jim Spicer, Peter Thurnham and Peter Viggers.

† Sir James (Jim) Spicer (1925–2015) was the Member of Parliament for West Dorset between 1974 and 1997. He was an enthusiastic member of the PT. During his career, his appointments included Chairman of the Conservative Group for Europe, a Vice Chairman of the Conservative Party and a member of the European Parliament.

Mrs Thatcher's commitment to Europe, she was about to introduce the measure which he subsequently cited as evidence of her European credentials – namely the European Communities (Amendment) Bill whose purpose was to give legal effect to treaty changes agreed in the Single European Act which had been signed on 17th February and which set the objective of creating a Single Market by 31st December 1992. On 12th May, an Ebury Note (No. 454) expressed surprise that the Bill had received so little attention given its implications both for majority voting, and for the role of the European Parliament (no longer permitted to be termed an 'assembly'). When the PT came round to discussing the note a month later, "reservations were expressed about 'majority voting' and giving up the Veto" (4th June 1986). But the issue again went quiet, and for over two years Europe was hardly referred to at PT meetings.

Not until 25th April 1988 did an Ebury Note (No. 505) return to the subject of the EEC under the heading of '1992 – The Political Implications'. The prospect of a single currency in the context of a Single Market was now widely discussed, with commentators such as Sam Brittan arguing that "if we are to have a unified goods or capital market, EMS realignments will need to become an unnecessary anachronism." Already, disagreements over the exact requirements of a Single Market were apparent. The PT observed that Lord Young, who was Secretary of State for Trade and Industry, believed that a Single Market involved merely the removal of technical barriers, free movement *for professionals* (author's italics), and free trade in financial services and procurement. Lord Cockfield, on the other hand, argued that a Single Market required the removal of all border controls, even though Lord Young felt they were necessary "because of Drugs and

Terrorism". Rumours that Lord Cockfield would not be reappointed as a Commissioner (rumours which turned out to be correct) strengthened the sense that 1992 was not working out entirely as the Government had expected.

Mrs Thatcher made her celebrated speech at Bruges on 20th September 1988, during Parliament's summer recess. A few days earlier, Jacques Delors had delivered as President of the European Commission a speech to the Trades Union Congress which was an important landmark in softening the Labour Party's opposition to the economic objectives of the EEC. Mrs Thatcher's experience in office on the one hand, and Labour's frustrations in Opposition on the other, produced in 1988 a marked contrast with the previous positions of both political parties as they reacted to the ambitions of the Commission's President and his prediction that "in ten years, 80 per cent of economic legislation – and perhaps tax and social legislation – will be directed from the Community."

Fresh from the Tory Conference and following the Bruges Speech, Mrs Thatcher gave an important interview to *The Times* on 26th October 1988, which caught the attention of the PT's Political Committee. She covered a wide area, including her relations with her Chancellor, Nigel Lawson, and her confidence in her own economic adviser, Alan Walters, whom she confirmed would be returning to No. 10 in the New Year. Of greatest interest, however, was her heightening suspicion of developments within Europe (still known, at this stage, as the EEC). She complained of a growing socialist tendency within the EEC, and took credit for "bringing out into the open" its federalist ambitions which went "against the grain of our people". She also dismissed the need for a European Company statute, and was adamantly opposed to a European Central Bank.

The PT was beginning to share some of these concerns, and even went further in sensing from her *Times* interview that she "had gone too far overboard on harmonisation". However, in respect of her interview as a whole, the Political Committee concluded she had "the right feeling as long as she does not overplay it" (26th October 1988). This meeting was chaired by Sir Ian Gow,* in Sir Peter Hordern's absence. It may explain partly the PT's less hostile stance to her general approach, since Sir Ian was an unusually Euro-sceptic (albeit very popular) member of the PT. None of the others at the meeting could be so described.† When the PT finally discussed the Bruges Speech itself on 7th December 1988, Sir Peter Hordern (who had become PT Chairman following the 1987 General Election) summed up somewhat optimistically:

> ... Mrs Thatcher's speech at Bruges, and Mr Heath's speech, both excellent, were in fact fully complementary. It was felt that if we allowed cohesion to develop naturally, as in banking, then the politics will follow on. It was regretted that Britain does not have the same commitment to the EEC as other European countries, and how little interest we take in what goes on in the European Parliament ... It was hoped that the House of Commons would welcome the MEPs before the June elections and wish them 'bon chance'.

---

* Sir Ian Gow (1937–1990) was the Member of Parliament for Eastbourne from 1974 until his assassination by the IRA. He had been PPS to Margaret Thatcher between 1979 and 1983 and was one of her closest confidants.

† Alistair Burt, Nicholas Baker, John Hannam, Michael Marshall, Robert Rhodes James, Lord Rees, Peter Thurnham and Tim Smith.

Mrs Thatcher's interview in *The Times* was a harbinger of events which would eventually lead to her removal. Britain's place in Europe was again set to become toxic for Conservatives, although this time the trigger was over whether or not Britain should become a full member of the European Monetary System (EMS). The debate was confused because some advocates of EMS membership, such as Nigel Lawson, were against a single currency and yet expressed their support for the EMS believing it to be essential for controlling inflation. Jacques Delors, on the other hand, believed Britain's participation in the EMS was a necessary condition of an efficient Single Market, and Lord Cockfield said "The view I have always expressed is that we ought to have a single currency as soon as possible after 1992." If this were not enough, there was the added complication of Alan Walters who, contrary to what is sometimes thought, did not at the time oppose total monetary integration in Europe but regarded EMS as a "half-baked" proposal which was no guarantee of exchange rate stability.

The seriousness of this disagreement was not fully appreciated by the PT when the subject was discussed on 8th March 1989 noting "that as the Prime Minister was against joining the EMS" the Chancellor "did the next best thing" in shadowing the Deutsch Mark but conceding "the PM seems to have been right although her reasons were political" and this will not change "whilst Mrs Thatcher is Prime Minister". Ebury papers attempted, from time to time, to remind the PT of the Single Market's political implications, even to the extent of holding out the prospect of a possible EEC ban on hunting (Ebury Note, No. 354). The PT did not rise to the bait. But the splits within the Government were now too obvious to be ignored, especially when the Social Charter raised new causes of disagreement.* A debate took place in the House of Commons on 'Developments in the European Community' on 18th May 1989. The day before the debate, the PT believed

> … that if we want to avoid a split in the Party Geoffrey Howe should open the Debate tomorrow. We ought to present a case for a low-key E.C. that people want to see. There is a case for a Social Charter which is workable by Tories, and this point should be made by Geoffrey Howe. We do not wish to appear sulky as people hate this, especially the young.

Ten members of the PT were present at this discussion.† The following day, Mrs Thatcher said in the House of Commons during Question Time that "From all the accounts that I have received about the social charter, it is more like a Socialist charter of unnecessary controls and regulations" and she reiterated the Government's opposition to the Delors Report (which argued for a single currency). But in the debate that followed, which was not opened by the Foreign Secretary but by the Minister of State (Lynda Chalker), there were a large number of Conservative interventions that echoed criticisms of the EEC made by the Prime Minister. Instead of putting up a committed critic of the EEC to speak for the Opposition, the Labour Party chose George Robertson to

---

* The Social Charter is defined as guaranteeing "a broad range of human rights with respect to everyday essential needs." Originally adopted in 1961, its revisions were adopted in 1996 which included controversial new rights and amendments.

† Those attending were Sir Peter Hordern, Nicholas Baker, Dudley Fishburn, Nigel Forman, Andrew Hunter, Michael Jack, Lord Kimball, Robert Rhodes James, Peter Thurnham and Tim Yeo.

lead the attack on the Government and exploit Conservative Party divisions, which were now frequently reported in the press. Prominent Conservatives including Edward Heath, Michael Heseltine, Lord Cockfield and Lord Plumb had all recently criticised Mrs Thatcher's approach to Europe both in practice and as outlined in her speech at Bruges.

There was now a significant number of Conservative MPs who questioned whether it had been wise to pass the Single European Act, given the disagreements over the Single Market's practical implications. This, in turn, led to the reappearance of the word 'sovereignty' in the speeches of both supporters and opponents of the EEC. The PT discussed the issue of 'sovereignty' on 24th May, but despite the attendance of John Redwood* at this meeting, nothing new was suggested. According to the minutes, "Most members felt that having signed the Single Act we must accept the consequences" and urged a "pragmatic approach" to joining the EMS.

Elections to the European Parliament took place in the UK on 15th June 1989, where the turnout was again the lowest in Europe. Apart from a strong performance by the Green Party, this was the first election since October 1974 when Labour overtook the Conservatives as the largest Party, winning thirteen more seats. It was unlikely, however, that the result owed much to Europe. An Ebury Note (No. 539) a few days before had reminded the PT that "HMG is going through its roughest patch for many years – renewed disagreement between the PM and the Chancellor, coupled with economic anxieties" and yet, "despite Mr Heath's interventions, it does

---

* John Redwood (b. 1951) has been the Member of Parliament for Wokingham since 1987. He became a member of the PT in 1989, but was not an active member.

not appear as if voters will make their decision on the basis of pro or anti Bruges" and so far as Mrs Thatcher was concerned, "she has probably done enough to alienate full blooded supporters of the EEC without galvanising the anti-federalists."

The PT was relatively relaxed over the outcome of these elections, and if they suspected the forces mobilising against Thatcher's leadership, they showed little sign of it:

> ... there is no evidence that the electorate does not agree with the line the Prime Minister is taking ... the results were reminiscent of 1962/63 with thirteen years of a Tory Government and a new look Labour Party ... anyone under forty accepts the move towards Economic and monetary union, and that the Government's posture must be "Yes – but" rather than our hitherto bunker mentality ... the Greens should be treated with kindness, and we must steal their thunder ... our campaign had been incompetent and we must work hard at getting a positive view towards Europe. It was ridiculous that Labour look more united on Europe that we do ... Europe may not be the most important factor at the next election, but it is still important to get it right ... the PM must be more positive when she goes to Madrid, and the country will not thank her in the future if she has lost opportunities for the UK... (21st June 1989)

Nine PT members attended this meeting,* and the minutes record a mood typical of the Conservative Parliamentary Party at that time. The PT understood why many in the country shared Mrs Thatcher's opposition to the EEC's direction of

---

* Sir Peter Hordern, Lord Brookeborough, Nigel Forman, Harry Greenway, John Hannam, Andrew Hunter, Gillian Shephard, Allan Stewart and Nicholas Soames.

travel which, for the first time, they conceded might end in economic and monetary union. They nevertheless considered Mrs Thatcher too obstructionist in her dealings with Europe, and believed that Britain's influence would be greater if the Prime Minister was more "positive". Although there was no mention of Michael Heseltine, and while many in the PT were still supporters of the PM – some even shared her growing scepticism – Mrs Thatcher could not have looked with any confidence towards the PT for vocal support in her dealings with Europe.

The Madrid Summit took place on 26th and 27th June 1989. In her statement to the House of Commons on 29th June, the Prime Minister said that while "the objective of progressive realisation of economic and monetary union was reaffirmed … no definition of it was agreed in Madrid." She emphasised that "stages 2 and 3 of the Delors report were not endorsed" which, she believed, would lead in practice to "the creation of a federal Europe". She claimed this was also the view of her Chancellor, Nigel Lawson. On the Exchange Rate Mechanism, she reaffirmed Britain's intention to join "but we must first get our inflation down." Neil Kinnock as Leader of the Opposition pressed her on this, but very little objection to her statement was forthcoming from the Conservative benches, who congratulated her on her performance at Madrid. The PT's Chairman (Sir Peter Hordern), however, raised the issue where she was least comfortable:

SIR PETER HORDERN: May I congratulate the Prime Minister most warmly on her firm commitment to join the Exchange Rate Mechanism. Is she aware that one of the conditions that she has set out lies not fully within our control – the abolition of exchange controls? Will she therefore have

a word with Mr Mitterrand and tell him that life in the
Community without exchange controls is very agreeable...
(Hansard c. 1122)

In private, the PT's reaction to Mrs Thatcher's performance
at Madrid, chaired on this occasion by the Heath loyalist Sir
Charles Morrison, was less complimentary:

> ... the Government's perception of what the people want is
> wrong. The people are switched off by Europe bashing. The
> Government are still using the wrong phraseology ... The
> average person thinks that we must get on with our fellow
> Europeans. It was hoped that the PM would get out of the
> ring and leave it to others. (26th June 1989)

Even making allowance for the temporary Chairmanship of
Sir Charles and the unrepresentative sample of PT members
who attended this particular meeting (which included Robert
Rhodes James, Sir James Spicer and Nigel Forman*) the
suggestion that the Prime Minister should stand down was
untypical of the Progress Trust – although with Labour now
polling around 47 per cent to 48 per cent in opinion polls
and the Conservative Party facing, according to John Biffen,†
a return to "two party politics", many in the PT shared the

---

* Nigel Forman (1943–2017) was the Member of Parliament for
Carshalton, Sutton between 1976 and 1997. He was Chairman of the PT
between 1994 and 1997.

† John Biffen (1930–2007) was the Member of Parliament for Oswestry
between 1961 and 1997. He was one of the leading Parliamentarians of his
time, a former Leader of the House of Commons, but interestingly failed
to become a member of the PT when his name was proposed each time in
1965, 1966 and 1967.

conviction that Mrs Thatcher faced election defeat at the hands of a new 'Social Democratic' Labour Party.

The first setback after the Party Conference season was Nigel Lawson's resignation on 26th October 1989 as Chancellor, because of the influence and continuance of Sir Alan Walters as Mrs Thatcher's economic adviser. This was discussed by a very large attendance (seventeen members)* at a PT meeting on 1st November when "only one member present suggested that there should be a new leader before the Election." However,

> ... it was urged that Europe must be put on the Cabinet agenda, as they must get a clear view as we cannot continue being divided at the top on Europe ... the PM could throw the next election away, and that a lot depends on her performance ... It was suggested that as the PM cannot change, other members of the Cabinet should be brought forward to soften the image.

When the first of the leadership challenges actually took place on 5th December, with Sir Anthony Meyer as a 'stalking-horse' candidate securing thirty-three votes, the PT noted that there was "still no consensus on Europe in the Party" but that "in one year's time the Community will look very different" (6th December 1989).

This last thought was not developed, but "in one year's time" another leadership contest took place which did indeed make a difference as it removed Mrs Thatcher from office.

---

* The members were: Sir Peter Hordern, Sir Peter Blaker, Nicholas Baker, Alistair Burt, Michael Colvin, Ian Gow, Nigel Forman, Michael Jack, John Hannam, Sir Charles Morrison, Michael Marshall, Robert Rhodes James, David Sumberg, Sir James Spicer, Nicholas Soames, Lord Rees and Tim Yeo.

Even so, during this final year of her premiership, Europe was seldom discussed by the PT at their meetings, unless raised by a research paper. Ebury Note 551, for example, posed two questions:

- to what extent will the European Commission (and Parliament) insist upon pushing to the fore issues which on their own terms and leaving aside the EC implications, are controversial within Britain? Because when this happens, it inevitably raises the second question
- leaving aside the merits or otherwise, is a British Prime Minister always to be considered anti-European when he, or she, is in a minority on an important policy matter e.g. the social dimension, or the EMS? (9th January 1990)

The PT felt more comfortable discussing the role of Members of the European Parliament, who were now accused of behaving as "unguided missiles". In order to form with them a closer alliance, Lord Bethell* was proposed as the first MEP to become a member of the Progress Trust (an invitation he accepted on 31st January 1990). But while Lord Bethell's views on Europe were hardly in accord with those of the Prime Minister, the PT now felt that Mrs Thatcher's line on the EEC was aligned with Germany's, and that it was France who was "flying in the face of reality". It was the Prime Minister's tone, as opposed to her policy, which worried them.

Mrs Thatcher reiterated the Government's "strong opposition" to economic and monetary union as proposed in the

---

* Lord Nicholas Bethell (1938–2007) was a longstanding member of the European Parliament having been first a member of the European Assembly in 1975 and leaving the Parliament as an elected member in 2003.

Delors Report when she spoke, on 28th June 1990, to the House of Commons on the Dublin Summit which had taken place a few days earlier. In his reply, Neil Kinnock sought to exploit the differences between her and her Chancellor (John Major) and Foreign Secretary (Geoffrey Howe) whom, he claimed, supported a single currency. He argued that Mrs Thatcher was opposing policies at home which she supported in Europe. There was very little criticism of her approach from the Conservative benches, but it was notable that she agreed more effusively with the remarks of Tony Benn and Peter Shore than with those from her own side. Whatever she said in denial, there was obvious disagreement within the Government on the prospects and desirability of a single currency and on the scope for qualified majority voting.

The Dublin Summit provided the PT with its last opportunity to comment on Europe, before the events of the autumn led to Mrs Thatcher's removal. On 27th June 1990,

> ... It was agreed that the Prime Minister's tone was different, but that all her remarks on a common currency show that she is still against it ... there are very few fanatics left in our Party on Europe, and the Prime Minister will be pragmatic when the time comes ... the Labour Party are more divided on Europe than we are ... legally we have a veto, but the time has come for us to decide whether we want to play a major part. The Chancellor's plan is a slow boat to Delors (2), as he wants it to be palatable politically and to balance the pros and cons ... It was suggested that we cannot afford to have a national monetary policy any more, it is too important to be left to individual governments ... It was thought that the Cabinet is happy and that the policy of moving the PM step by step is working.

It is hard to explain how a group of well-informed MPs could so underestimate Mrs Thatcher's opposition to a single currency. Admittedly, it was a small meeting but the group included Robert Rhodes James, Dudley Fishburn,* Nigel Forman and John Hannam† all of whom were influential and well-informed backbenchers. Despite feeling in July that it was time the Prime Minister was "invited to dine in the near future", by October it was grudgingly recognised "that we cannot change the Leader because of the system, otherwise she would have gone by now." This was said at the Political Committee's first meeting after the recess (24th October 1990), which also happened to follow Ian Gow's assassination and the loss of his Eastbourne constituency in the consequent by-election.‡

Six days later, however, Mrs Thatcher gave what the PT described as a "virtuoso performance" in the House of Commons, following the latest meeting of the European Council which had taken place in Rome on 27th and 28th October. On this occasion, she was uncompromising in her assertion that "it is our purpose to retain the power and influence of this House, rather than denude it of many of its

---

* Dudley Fishburn (b. 1946) was the Member of Parliament for Kensington between 1988 and 1997 before returning to the worlds of business and journalism.

† Sir John Hannam (b. 1929) was the Member of Parliament for Exeter between 1970 and 1997.

‡ The assassination of a Tory MP by an IRA terrorist was considered by Labour and Liberals as an insufficient reason not to contest the ensuing by-election in 1990 – in stark contrast with the media and public's reaction to the murder of the Labour MP Jo Cox in 2016, whose seat was not contested by the Conservatives and whose death revealed a startling change in national attitudes and sang-froid since Gow's assassination.

powers." This was the famous occasion when she said:

> ... The President of the Commission, Mr Delors, said at a
> press conference the other day that he wanted the European
> Parliament to be the democratic body of the Community, he
> wanted the Commission to be the Executive and he wanted the
> Council of Ministers to be the Senate. No, no, no. (Hansard,
> 30th October c. 873)

Her critics said this was inconsistent with the legislation she
had already passed. When the PT discussed these exchanges
a day later, the attendance at the meeting was too small to be
considered representative even though the views of Sir Peter
Hordern and Robert Rhodes James were probably typical of
most in the PT at this moment:

> ... there was an uncomfortable feeling amongst members that
> there was a difference between her statement, and her off the
> cuff answers to questions later. Her Boadicea act is old hat
> and the young do not like her tone. Roy Jenkins is right we
> cannot be left behind by the rest of Europe ... It is a mistake
> playing the patriotic card and saying that we will never give up
> sterling, but if we sign up and have a Central Bank we would
> then inevitably be on the road to federation ... The question
> was put as to whether she could win an election 'on going no
> further'. It was thought not because it would be impossible to
> contain in a campaign ... The Cabinet are divided on Europe,
> so it would not help making 'going no further' a campaign
> point. (31st October 1990)

The following day Sir Geoffrey Howe announced his
resignation as Foreign Secretary, although his devastating

resignation speech to the House did not take place until 13th November, which led the following morning to Michael Heseltine announcing his intention to challenge the Prime Minister for the leadership of the Conservative Party. The PT met that same morning with eleven members present.[*] These were their conclusions:

> The Chairman said that a week ago we had hoped that we would not have to go through a leadership election ... the timing is bad with the serious situation in Kuwait. If the Party does not pull itself together next week we have had it. It is not the time to have a leadership election, a leader must emerge. There were hopes that Douglas Hurd would stand ... It was thought that Heseltine would get 159 votes ... one hundred votes against her plus abstentions would be dangerous. If the PM does not get a two thirds majority she must be told to stand down in the interest of the Party. Our duty is to the Party.

Little else could have been expected from the PT, given its history and composition. Most PT members had no great liking of Heseltine, which possibly explains their hope that Douglas Hurd (the nearest on offer to a Conservative of the Macmillan era) would emerge as a candidate. Their predictive powers were not far off the mark. Heseltine secured 152 votes on the first ballot (which took place on 20th November) with sixteen abstentions. The day after, Sir Peter told the PT "that at the moment it looks unlikely that there will be a third candidate for the second round of the Party

* Those attending were Sir Peter Hordern, Sir Nicholas Bonsor, William Benyon, Lord Bethell, Alistair Burt, Sir Paul Bryan, Harry Greenway, Lord Kimball, Robert Rhodes James, Sir James Spicer and Lord Rees.

Leadership contest" and the PT repeated its view that the PM must withdraw:

> The Party must come first and individual loyalties cannot count any more. She can no longer unite the Party, the three basic areas of concern are the Community Charge, Europe and style. A lot of members had voted for Michael Heseltine because he has "shipwrecked the Community charge ... if she stays there will be more resignations, and the prospect of a third round was horrific. A wider choice of candidates was wanted, and it was suggested that the 1922 Committee must go and 'bang on the table'. It was feared that she will not withdraw in spite of advice, that we are heading for a 1906 situation, and we have got to get ourselves out of it.

To this minute, in his own handwriting, Peter Hordern added the words "And we did!" But he was only right up to a point. While "a 1906 situation" was averted temporarily, the scale of the eventual defeat of 1997 was equivalent to the worst the PT had feared.

Immediately following John Major's succession as Prime Minister, many Conservative MPs assumed that he would play his cards in a more 'constructive' fashion than his predecessor, and that this would lead to fewer disagreements between Britain and the rest of the Community. But there was still anxiety over "whether or not the severity of the recession is being unnecessarily compounded by membership of the ERM?" (Ebury Note 582). Now that Mrs Thatcher was gone, the PT considered "that we went into the ERM at the wrong level ... it was vital politically that we get interest rates down" (16th January 1991). There was also concern that the European Community had been dangerously divided and ineffective on the first Gulf War and that this would arrest any movement towards political union.

The proposed Maastricht Treaty dented all such optimism of a new accord within the Conservative Party. The first specific Ebury Note on Maastricht was not sent to PT members until 6th November 1991 (No. 600), and was written in anticipation of the two-day debate in the House of Commons which was due a fortnight later on 20th November. The PT did not discuss the paper until after the debate had taken place when a small meeting of PT members well disposed to John Major's new approach concluded:

> … we should not sign [the Treaty] if they insist on a minimum wage in the Social Chapter, as this would affect our part-time workers. Members were also worried about asylum and immigration being decided by the twelve without individual Parliamentary involvement … if there is unanimity on Defence, and if we get the opt out on a single currency then it will be possible to sign … when Mrs Thatcher charged the PM with arrogance for not agreeing to a referendum on Maastricht, she was harming herself … the PM will come out of Maastricht a hero whatever he does … Lord Bethell reported that the MEPs are going ahead with an alliance with the Christian Democrats. (4th December 1991)

Apart from the short previous reference to the right of fiancées to join their husbands, this was the first time that the PT discussed immigration and asylum in ways which would become familiar during the second referendum debate in 2016. Indeed, when on 11th December the PT considered the results of John Major's negotiations at the Maastricht Council the day before, relief was expressed "that we did not have to give way on immigration". This heightened the PT's hope that with agreement at Maastricht, and the opt-outs secured, the issue of Britain's continuing membership of the EC had again been resolved, with only longstanding opponents of Britain's membership seeking to prolong the argument. An Ebury Note (No. 613) suggested how the European issue might still play a part in the forthcoming General Election which John Major subsequently announced would be held on 9th April 1992 and which led again to the return of a Conservative Government, albeit with a much reduced majority. The note pointed to the paradox "that for some the EC offers a cast-iron guarantee against Socialism; whereas recent experience is that in so many policy areas, the EC seems to be drifting towards a corporatist, high-spending and interventionist administration." But essentially, the PT did not wish to revisit the European question:

> We must remember that the young are pro-Europe and cannot understand what older people are worrying about. It was hoped that our people on both sides keep quiet. It was noted that the Bruges Group is moribund. (26th February 1992)

So it might have remained were it not for the Danish rejection of the Maastricht Treaty in a referendum on 2nd June 1992. This caused the postponement of the Maastricht Bill, as well as the scheduled Parliamentary debate for 3rd June. Surprisingly, the PT was

> ... pleased with the result of the Danish referendum rejecting the Maastricht treaty as it was felt that we had been trying to run before we could walk. It was wondered whether Delors would be able to proceed with his federalist ideas. The danger

would be if the eleven move ahead without the Danes, we must watch out for this and support the Danes ... there will be pressure for a referendum from the Labour Party, and we will get letters pressing for one as well ... important that we concentrate on widening rather than deepening ... the PM is pragmatic over Europe... (3rd June 1992)

Knowingly or not, the PT had identified the problem facing the new Conservative Government. Those Conservatives who were never happy with Maastricht – but who, in advance of a General Election, were prepared to give the new Prime Minister the benefit of the doubt – now believed that Denmark's rejection of the Treaty reopened the issue, and invited the question why Britain should not have its own referendum on Maastricht too. The PT raised this aspect with the Chief Whip, Richard Ryder,* over dinner at the end of June, and his 'rigidity' on this occasion was regretted. The PT's view was:

... We fought the election on Maastricht and we will have to go through with it. But it will have to be changed after the Danish 'No' vote. Colleagues are annoyed by the cumulative effect of silly rules. Subsidiarity must be defined and the PM must firm it up. Individual states should be making the decision as to what subsidiarity covers – not the other way round. (1st July 1992)

Just before the summer recess, an Ebury Note (No. 623) reminded the PT that "summer recesses produce their own

---

* Richard Ryder, later Lord Ryder of Ensum (b. 1948), was the Member of Parliament for Mid Norfolk between 1983 and 1997. He was a member of the PT for a brief period (1984–1989) prior to joining the Government.

surprises". The summer recess of 1992 was no exception, when on 16th September 'Black Wednesday' took place and the United Kingdom was forced to withdraw from the Exchange Rate Mechanism, resulting in the recall of Parliament from its holidays for two days on 24th September. From this point, the debate over the Maastricht Treaty and whether Britain should now join Europe's single currency became critical for the new Government's future. At the Conservative Party Conference following 'Black Wednesday', an Ebury Note (No. 624) commented that, amongst the representatives, "hostility to the ERM was far more obvious than to the Maastricht Treaty ... perhaps this explains why the Prime Minister made no reference to the ERM in his speech." But back at Westminster, preoccupation lay with the Maastricht legislation which, in turn, was linked with John Major's personal authority – especially as he now threatened a General Election if he failed to win support from his Party.

A crucial vote took place on 4th November 1992, with over ninety MPs wishing to speak. Consideration of the European Communities (Amendment) Bill had been put on hold in the light of uncertainty caused by both the French and Danish referendums on the Treaty. The Government now demanded approval for proceeding with the Bill. A few days before, the sense in the PT was that "Maastricht is a goner and that there will be no referendum" but that nevertheless the vote on the Bill had to be treated as an issue of confidence. As always, the calculation was that by making it a vote of confidence, pressure would be maximised on anti-Maastricht Tories to come to heel, but at the risk of uniting the Labour Party in opposition to a Bill which some of them supported.

PT members were encouraged to "speak to their whips today" and it was important "that the PM attends a meeting of the whole party on Thursday [29th October] as this is his best chance of getting support". The day before the debate on 4th November, the PT inevitably returned to the subject of Maastricht. An Ebury Note (No. 626) suggested that "Major's personal authority is now inextricably linked to a Bill whose problems are by no means over, whatever happens tomorrow evening. How many amendments would have to be made to the Bill for HMG to admit that it no longer has the authority to ratify the Maastricht Treaty as it stands?" So many issues of contention had come to the fore following the unexpected, yet narrow, Conservative victory in the election. As the note argued:

> ... the battle-lines on the 'Treaty on European Union' (which is what it should be called) are drawn up between those who believe it modifies so-called 'excesses' of the Single European Act and those who argue that it constitutes a further significant step towards making the EC less of an economic, and more of a political, community. In particular, is HMG's reading of the Treaty at odds with everyone else's?

Amongst the controversial components of the Treaty were European Citizenship (and the implications for immigration) and the European Parliament. But "clearly the greatest argument is over whether the Treaty – despite the UK's opt-out – makes economic union and a single currency only a matter of time":

> Would a country aspiring to be 'at the heart of Europe' opt-out of a single currency, if it ever came to the point? Does Maastricht lead the E.C. in the direction of an a la carte European menu or, as it says in its common provisions 'an ever closer union'

with common commercial, agricultural, and transport policies based on general economic coordination and convergence? If the latter, then those who wish to say 'thus far, no further' ought to oppose ratification. If the former, then Major is entitled to feel peeved that his achievement (*in negotiations*) is not recognised by Tory 'rebels'. (Ebury Note 626)

The PT believed that if the Government could win the vote on 4th November, "the Labour Party will come back in line after tomorrow, even if we only win the vote by one or two." On the substance of the issue, the PT felt that "many have elements of doubt about the Treaty, but the economic arguments for ratification far outweigh the doubts. This debate is about whether we stay in Europe or not." Finally, it was noted "that the Whips are pessimistic." In the event, the Opposition amendment was defeated by six votes; but afterwards, when it came to the Government's own motion, it was carried by just three votes, only one more than the PT had predicted the day before.

The Bill's problems were not over. The Maastricht proceedings occupied the House of Commons right up until the summer recess. As early as February 23rd, the PT believed the Government's position to be precarious "as there are up to fifty colleagues who will not vote with the Government on a procedural vote". This situation persisted throughout the first half of the year, but it was not until a few days before another crucial debate on 22nd July – this time on the Social Chapter provisions of the Bill – that Maastricht returned to the PT's agenda:

The Chairman [Sir Peter Hordern] said that we ought to have a word on Maastricht and try and forecast what will happen on

Thursday [22nd July] and weigh up the consequences. We are now down to the hard core, and their views will not change. Unless a deal is done with the Irish we will lose the vote. If we are defeated then the options will be –

1) Come back in the Autumn with different wording
2) Ratify, including the Social Contract
3) Hold a vote of confidence

It was thought that there is a danger of the Cabinet splitting if we flout the will of Parliament by going ahead and ratifying Maastricht having lost the vote. If it falls then the PM would have to go. The rebels want it to fall on the floor of the House, and do not care what they have done to the Party. We are stuck with Europe and could not leave even if Portillo takes over, so the rebels must think about this. (20th July 1993)

The Government was defeated on the Social Chapter provisions of the Bill (which arose from the new Social Charter), and John Major immediately called for a vote of confidence the following day – which he won. Parliament went into the summer recess almost immediately afterwards (on 27th July), and the PT didn't meet again until 19th October, following the Party Conference season. Its view then was "John Major's survival is going to be proved in the next six months. The Party wants to unite after Maastricht." It was also thought that the growing threat posed by the Liberals should be met by attacking their enthusiasm for a "Federal Europe".

There then took place one of the rare occasions when the Progress Trust featured in the press. The meeting on 19th October had also observed that "The Party craves for direction, and we must be braver, stop giving in all the time, and placating the rebels." The following Sunday (24th October 1993) *The Observer* carried a story by Anthony Bevins, its political editor, stating that "A shadowy group of leading Conservative MPs has decided that five members of the influential backbench Tory 1922 Committee should be ousted from office as punishment for repeated rebellion over the Maastricht legislation." This "shadowy" group was named as the "highly secretive" Progress Trust, and *The Observer* claimed to have been directly in contact with some of its "right-wing members". Both Sir Peter Hordern and Sir Cranley Onslow were named as supporters of the proposal although Sir Cranley had never been a member of the PT and Sir Peter had not attended the meeting in question.* The report was accurate, however, in stating that the PT had discussed elections to the Parliamentary Party's Policy Committees:

> We used to have more clout in achieving middle of the road candidates. What has happened on the Executive has been a disgrace, and the Chairman of the 1922 [Sir Marcus Fox] has been unable to count on every member's loyalty. There will be attempted blood letting in the Autumn elections, and the situation must be looked at. It was suggested that the PT should consider whether it should support certain 'loyalist' candidates for the various committees and it was agreed that this should be raised again at the next meeting.

Significantly, this is one of the rare occasions when the PT minutes were amended by hand to avoid a damaging impression. Much of *The Observer's* article was then devoted to the Progress Trust itself:

---

* Those attending on 19th October were: Matthew Carrington, Michael Colvin, Archie Hamilton, Sir John Hannam, David Lidington, David Martin and Sir James Spicer.

The Progress Trust is thought to have been set up after the Second World War and is one of the few backbench groups never to have been exposed. It contains about 30 members from across the party and nominations for membership can be blackballed. One member said last week: 'We have no shits.'

The article also claimed that the five MPs identified for removal from the 1922 Executive were Sir Rhodes Boyson, Sir George Gardiner, Sir Ivan Lawrence, James Pawsey and John Townend.

The Observer 'leak' was discussed at the PT's next meeting on 26th October. The fact that the article was not altogether inaccurate – the PT had indeed discussed the possibility of supporting 'loyalist candidates' – suggested that the leak originated from someone who had attended the meeting on 19th October but it did not follow that anyone present had spoken to *The Observer* directly. Moreover, *The Observer* would seldom have been the PT's paper of choice. With Sir Peter Hordern back in the chair, the PT agreed "that it was not much good looking for the culprit". The ensuing discussion confirmed, however, that in many respects the PT remained loyal to the principles which supported its creation in the first place:

… the joy of the PT is that it does not leak, and that a note should be sent round to members to remind them of the fact.[*]

---

[*] The only other occasion when the proceedings of a PT meeting were leaked to the press arose from a discussion on Ebury Note 486, 25.10.87 entitled 'The Press and the Royal Family'. Without mentioning the PT specifically, *The Sunday Times* on 8th November 1987 reported that "A group of senior Conservative MPs (all experienced and well-connected veteran backbenchers) met privately last week to express their dismay at the danger

It was suggested that the '92 Group had used the leak in *The Observer* for their own ends, so that they appeared as victims. It was agreed that it was not a good idea to have a "slate" for the Committee elections, but if anyone has an interest in any particular Committee tell the Chairman and he will let members know, but that no notes should be sent round. The PT should vote for supporters of the Government, and the '22 Executive must reflect the general mood of the Party, and not just one group ... if certain members of the '22 Executive were not re-elected there would be no more leaks ... the '22 Executive has an important role when it reports to the PM.

In the end, the only casualty of these elections, which took place on 25th November, was Sir George Gardiner in what *The Times* reported as "a limited strike". He was voted off the Executive of the 1922 Committee, and replaced by David Evans, the Member of Parliament for Welywn and Hatfield, a former Parliamentary Private Secretary to John Redwood, whose views might well have been regarded as even more 'right-wing' than Sir George Gardiner's.

The next European challenge arose in the summer of 1994 when the European Parliament faced new elections. The PT was pessimistic, noting on 15th February "that there is a frightening scenario for our chances in the European elections, as our candidates have gone native and do not care

---

of the royal family becoming involved in continuing controversy over their public roles and private lifestyles." There was some truth in this account, and on 11th November Sir Peter Hordern stated that it was of such concern that he intended to speak to every member who had attended (i.e. Sir Nicholas Bonsor, Virginia Bottomley, Alick Buchanan-Smith, Alistair Burt, Michael Colvin, Harry Greenway, John Hannam, Robert Rhodes James, Peter Rees and David Sumberg).

what happens here." This was a reference to the tendency of Conservative MEPs to accept any European Commission proposal, good or bad, so long as it demonstrated their commitment to 'Europe'. On 2nd March, the PT drew comfort from Sir Peter Hordern's involvement in writing the Conservative Manifesto alongside Bill Cash and Hugh Dykes as "it would be a disaster if we travel down the Dykes path." Some in the PT were now moving towards a more sceptical position.

Another problem, however, was raised in advance of the elections when the debate over EC enlargement became embroiled with the dilution of the UK's voting rights in an expanded Europe. Once again, a UK Government which proclaimed its desire to be at the heart of Europe was in danger of finding itself in a minority of one. The PT discussed this new development on 16th March 1994:

> ... this is a crisis that should never have happened. It was felt we should compromise and accept 27 (as the requisite blocking number) with large countries having safeguards, as it is more important that the four new countries enter on 1st January 1995. Only one member present thought that the fight for 23 was more important.

On 30th March, the accession negotiations concluded successfully with Austria, Finland, Sweden and Norway joining the European Community (although Norway subsequently decided, by referendum, not to do so). The Euro elections resulted in Labour winning the highest share of the vote (42.6 per cent) with the Conservatives coming second (26.8 per cent). The Liberal Democrats won 16.1 per cent but this represented the largest increase from the previous elections – a growth in their share of 10.2 per cent. The PT's verdict was:

> ... the Tories had stayed away ... people did not share the PM's belief in a multi-track Europe, but without his statement we would have been down to single figures ... we now have a problem with the pro-Europeans rather than the hard right ... they should be asked not to rock the boat. (15th June 1994)

A further crisis facing the Conservative Party and Europe arose in the autumn concerning the European Communities (Finance) Bill. The Conservative Party Conference in October had been deeply divided over Europe, and the PT noted that "fringe meetings on Europe (notably the one addressed by Jimmy Goldsmith) evoked a passion (and an attendance) that many had assumed had disappeared from British politics a long time ago" (Ebury Note 681). Shortly after Parliament's return, the Government introduced the Bill to increase the UK's contributions to the EC budget. The Prime Minister let it be known that even an amendment to the Bill, let alone its defeat, could be regarded as a resignation issue. The PT expected the Government to win, although "even if we do the matter will rumble on" (23rd November). When it came to the vote, eight Conservative MPs abstained in what had been declared a confidence vote, and as a result they had the Tory Whip withdrawn.* No member of the PT was

---

* The Conservative MPs who had the Whip withdrawn were: Nicholas Budgen, Michael Carttiss, Christopher Gill, Teresa Gorman, Tony Marlow, Richard Shepherd, Sir Teddy Taylor and John Wilkinson; Richard Body joined them voluntarily so there were nine Conservative MPs in total without the Whip.

amongst the rebels, although both Sir Nicholas Bonsor[*] and Andrew Hunter[†] had either voted against the Government or abstained on previous votes related to Maastricht. These were the only members of the PT to have done so. The PT's view on the Whip's withdrawal was pragmatic, arguing it had to be withdrawn "because we would not have won any amendments on the European Finance Bill" and because votes of confidence would have been necessary "all through to Bill". Equally significantly, at the same meeting:

> There was a discussion as to whether we will have to have a referendum on Europe. We do not want to appear as being pushed into one, but there are circumstances where it would be necessary: 1) If there is a big loss of sovereignty 2) If Delors gets in 3) If there is a loss of veto. (30th November 1994)

The PT attached importance to the fate of the 'rebel' MPs since "if we are not careful we will be having a Socialist Government"; therefore, "the rebels must be brought back quickly, however embarrassing." Not all agreed. Sir Peter Hordern who had recently resigned as PT Chairman – he was succeeded by Nigel Forman – "thought the rebels beyond redemption, and we might as well have an election". The general view, however, was that "as there is no more European stuff to vote on ... we will be able to count on the rebels." The meeting added "there is the 'carrot' of a referendum if there are significant developments" even though "we hate

---

* Sir Nicholas Bonsor (b. 1942) was the Member of Parliament for Nantwich between 1979 and 1983 and then Upminster between 1983 and 1997.

† Andrew Hunter (b. 1943) was the Member of Parliament for Basingstoke between 1983 and 2005.

referenda." But "as there was a slight difference of opinion between Sir Peter Hordern and Sir James Spicer on how to deal with the rebels Sir Peter and Sir James should have a drink with the Chief Whip [Alistair Goodlad] and discuss the matter" (7th December 1994). The Whip was eventually restored to the rebel MPs on 25th April 1995.

Although this marked an end to the immediate legislative threats, the European Union was now heading in a direction regarded as inimical by many in the Tory Party (the PT now referred to the European *Union* in its minutes). The PT's concern was that, despite ratifying Maastricht and increasing its contributions towards the European budget, the UK remained marginalised while the rest of the EU "cannot understand our continual questioning". The political necessity of a referendum also became a frequent topic, however much the PT disliked the idea. Most important of all, the PT now conceded that the EU was heading towards a single currency "and that only the UK and Denmark are out of step". At one meeting, Nigel Forman, Sir Kenneth Carlisle[*] and Mark Lennox-Boyd[†] – all of whom were well disposed to Britain's membership of the EU – suggested that "We can say if it comes to a single currency there will be a referendum" but "it is not a single currency that is the threat, but the consequences of the decision" including the implications for political union (14th December 1994).

Repeatedly the Europe question resurfaced, even amongst MPs who had no wish to debate or reopen the question. The latest phase was over whether Britain would be compelled

---

[*] Sir Kenneth Carlisle (b. 1941) was the Member of Parliament for Lincoln between 1979 and 1997.

[†] Sir Mark Lennox-Boyd (b. 1943) was the Member of Parliament for Morecombe and Lonsdale (then Lunsdale) between 1979 and 1997.

to join the single currency, and if so whether it should do so willingly or grudgingly. This was taken up by the first Ebury Note of 1995:

> No major new legislation is expected. But both the Prime Minister and the Foreign Secretary are staking much on their assertion that the federalist tendency has been halted; that the issue of a single currency is a long way away; and that enlargement will support the British approach ... The Portillo worry – namely, that whatever politicians and electorates say, the inexorable trend towards a single currency and (eventually) fiscal union is irresistible – is what alarms many Conservatives. (No. 688)

The PT was more optimistic. A meeting of ten PT members on 11th January 1995 felt "We can only see a change for the better with the departure of Mitterrand and Delors" and that "the rebels are breaking up."* But as always, their biggest concern was that "we will find ourselves run by them in spite of ourselves. Without allies in Europe we will be destroyed." The PT's sense was that the Prime Minister should remain disingenuously non-committal on the single currency, keeping all options open, but that "if we could win the Election it would not be difficult for the PM to say 'we will now go in'" (1st February 1995). By the time the single currency was again discussed on 22nd February 1995, PT members "held differing views", which was unsurprising since two members present on this occasion were the arch-sceptic Sir Archie

---

* Those attending were: Nigel Forman (in the chair), Lord Brookeborough, Matthew Carrington, Michael Colvin, Alan Howarth, Lord Kimball, Mark Lennox-Boyd, David Martin, Sir James Spicer and Ray Whitney.

Hamilton* and the Euro-enthusiast Quentin Davies† (who subsequently joined the Labour Party). They noted that the Governor of the Bank of England, Eddie George, was "agnostic on the subject", and that he should be invited by the PT to discuss the issue.

By the middle of the year, discussions on the single currency centred upon divisions within the Cabinet and the Prime Minister's attempt to remain uncommitted. In the words of the PT "He will not agree to anything, and is pragmatic." Also, "if members of the Cabinet do not like it, then they must go" (14th June 1995). Another PT meeting – attended by eight members – took place a week later when "it was hoped that there will be no contest for the leadership" but on the substantive issue of the single currency, the PT shared the general uncertainty over the Prime Minister's real views although "it is an issue now, and we must try and deliver something together."‡

The PM forced the leadership issue a few weeks later (22nd July) by both resigning his leadership of the Tory Party and standing for re-election. Most in the PT were supportive of

---

* Sir Archie Hamilton, later Lord Hamilton of Epsom, (b. 1941) was the Member of Parliament for Epsom & Ewell between 1978 and 2001. He was Chairman of the 1922 Committee between 1997 and 2001 as well as being a PPS to Margaret Thatcher.

† Quentin Davies, later Lord Davies of Stamford, (b. 1944) was the Member of Parliament for Grantham & Stamford between 1987 and 2010. He defected to Labour in 2007 and was subsequently rewarded by Gordon Brown – whom he had regularly attacked prior to his 'conversion' – with a ministerial job and then a seat in the House of Lords.

‡ Those attending on 21st June 1995 were: Nigel Forman (in the chair), Sir Kenneth Carlisle, Sir John Hannam, Sir Peter Hordern, Lord Kimball, Mark Lennox-Boyd, David Martin and Sir James Spicer.

his decision although "it was impossible to guess the result, as there are so many unhappy people in the Parliamentary Party" (28ᵗʰ June 1995). In the event, John Major defeated John Redwood by a convincing majority on 4ᵗʰ July. Even so, eighty-nine Tory MPs supported Redwood.

After the leadership election, there was a lull in discussing European issues as the PT concentrated upon other issues which they hoped would recover political support for a deeply unpopular Government. The use of a referendum as a device for resolving the single currency issue was raised by an Ebury paper in March 1996:

> Euro-enthusiasts cannot have it both ways. They are willing to transfer powers to European institutions which, many admit, reduce the authority of national parliaments. But in dismissing the referendum as a continental aberration and in denying the British electorate a means of expression which their European neighbours enjoy, they invoke the authority and supremacy of Parliament as a justification. Some would perceive an inconsistency here. (No. 723)

The PT dismissed the idea of a referendum on Maastricht (as demanded by Sir James Goldsmith) but conceded that it could be legitimate on whether or not to join a single currency – except that this could not become a possibility until the next decade. Thus, again it was thought that there was no need to force the issue especially as "a referendum would not mollify the Euro-sceptics, their goal is to take us out" (13ᵗʰ March 1996). A month later, the EU's worldwide ban on UK beef exports provided a fresh excuse to revisit practical issues of sovereignty and how this would be exploited by Sir James Goldsmith's Referendum Party. Five senior members of the

PT* discussed this new development on 1st May 1996 in their last substantive discussion on the EU before the General Election and before, along with the Conservative Party as a whole, the PT was decimated by electoral defeat:

> ... we always seem to lose the argument in Europe, although we have used both the Thatcher and the Major approach ... one of the difficulties in our dealings with the EU is that we have a different style of politics. We aspire to a clear position, backed by mandate, but because of PR they have a system of 'fudge and mudge' in order to get co-operation from minorities ... Goldsmith could act as a catalyst in the Party. Very few people want to come out of the EU, but it was agreed that the media only present those who hold extreme views ... The PT has an important role, and can show that its membership comes from all sides of the Party ... we must not panic over Goldsmith. He calculates that we will lose the Election, and would like to be the cause ... non Euro-sceptics must come together to show where the Party can unite – we must be seen as a broad church. (1st May 1996)

In the final months of 1996, all thoughts turned to the forthcoming General Election and the role which Europe would play. By this time, the issue was discussed exclusively in terms of Party management. For example, on 20th November 1996 "it was wondered how we keep Kenneth Clarke from going into orbit if the PM changes policy next year." On 15th January 1997, the PT believed "there is now a growing wish for the PM to come out and say that we are not going to join a common currency in the next Parliament ... there would

---

* They were: Nigel Forman, Sir Mark Lennox-Boyd, Sir Peter Lloyd, Sir Peter Hordern and Sir James Spicer.

be great electoral benefit in saying this." But by then it was too late. It was a Labour Chancellor of the Exchequer who, in his statement on economic and monetary union of 27th October 1997, set out the new Government's five economic tests for joining a single currency – tests which, as is now known, Gordon Brown never intended to meet.

Throughout this whole period the PT's hope had been that, as a co-operative and positive member, Britain could help shift the EU in a direction favourable to British interests. As with many others in the Conservative Party, however, the PT had difficulty in reconciling this position with the EU's ultimate destination. By the time the European issue was debated by the PT for the last time, on 21st May 2003, there were only two MPs present, Henry Bellingham* (the new PT Chairman) and Virginia Bottomley. Their view was that "the Conservative Party has been good about not going on about Europe during the past year, but Conservatives will have to decide what side they are on." Thirteen years later, this opportunity finally came.

---

* Sir Henry Bellingham (b. 1955) has represented North West Norfolk since 1983, although his period as an MP was interrupted in 1997 by the intervention of a UKIP Candidate which lost him the seat until he regained it in 2001.

8

THE PROGRESS TRUST AND 'THATCHERISM'

"The Chairman thought it was possible to sympathise with the dissident members of the Cabinet…"
(18th March 1981)

"If high spending was the route to growth and popularity, the government should be in clover."
(The Economist *June 1985*)

As the last chapter discussed, Mrs Thatcher's Euroscepticism never met with the PT's full approval. But the PT's general attitude towards Thatcherism is better judged on the home front – and especially in the economic and industrial areas where her reforms were radically different from any post-war Government.

It has already been suggested that Enoch Powell's arguments unintentionally prepared the way for Mrs Thatcher's leadership of the Conservative Party. In Opposition, Mrs Thatcher was distrusted by many free market enthusiasts, partly because of her failure to resign from Mr Heath's Government, but mostly because when speaking on economics she appeared to lack the intellectual weight and conviction which both Powell and Keith Joseph displayed. Many doubted her radical instincts, and certainly her determination to see them through. Most in the Conservative Parliamentary Party, including the PT, gave her support somewhat grudgingly, only because they wanted her to win an election – not because they wanted a new direction. But at least this meant that the PT was spared the disappointment prompted by her 1979 manifesto, which free marketers judged as depressingly less radical than the 'Better Tomorrow' promised by Mr Heath in 1970. Only by becoming Prime Minister, with a workable majority of 43, would the country discover whether Mrs Thatcher had the determination to offer a clean break from post-war Conservative Governments – and whether her Party grandees would permit this. The PT was distinctly uneasy from the start. But it too had to define its new role, and align this with its resources, now that a Conservative Government was back in office.

Following the General Election, the PT's Political Committee was reduced to nine members. At the first post-election meeting of the PT Council on 23rd May 1979 Lord Strathclyde announced his resignation as Chairman – to be succeeded by Sir Paul Bryan – and noted that of past PT members Sir John Gilmour,* Jasper More and Rear Admiral Morgan Giles† had retired from the House of Commons; while Peter Blaker, Robert Boscawen,‡ John Cope,§ Patrick Mayhew,¶ Paul Channon and Geoffrey

---

* Sir John Gilmour (1912–2007) was the Member of Parliament for East Fife between 1961 and 1979.

† Rear Admiral Morgan Giles (1914–2013) was the Member of Parliament for Winchester between 1964 and 1979.

‡ Robert Boscawen (1923–2013) was the Member of Parliament for Wells between 1970 and 1983 and then Somerton & Frome between 1983 and 1992.

§ John Cope, later Lord Cope of Berkeley (b. 1937), was the Member of Parliament for South Gloucestershire between 1974 and 1983 and Northavon between 1983 and 1997.

¶ Sir Patrick Mayhew, later Lord Mayhew of Twysden (1929–2016), was

Pattie* had all received posts in the new Government. Nevertheless, no new members were elected until the autumn.

The PT's wage bill was now running at around £4,000 per annum – equivalent to some £14,000 today. The British United Industrialists remained the main source of funds. The PT held on deposit at around this time some £9,000, today's capital equivalent of over £20,000. The Trust continued to look for new sources of finance. By 1984, the PT Council estimated that they required around £7,000 p.a. to meet their running costs, which included the salary of Bridget Lakin, the fees received by the PT's researchers, and the payment to a lobby correspondent for his weekly notes. In 1986, it was even suggested that members of the PT should contribute a portion of their Parliamentary research allowance to the PT – which some did, producing an additional income of £2,000 as a result. By the time that Mrs Thatcher ceased to be Prime Minister, the PT's Political Committee comprised over thirty members, and the BUI was contributing some £8,000 p.a. – "but if the BUI stops giving us money, we would have to shut up shop" (November 1990). This was a possibility, because of a dispute running at the time between the BUI and the Treasurer of the Conservative Party[†] over where their donations were best deployed; the BUI felt that their interests were better appreciated by the PT, but the PT was embarrassed if their industrial support was at the expense

the Member of Parliament for Tonbridge Wells between 1974 and 1997. He was elected to the PT in 1976 but was not an active member.

* Geoffrey Pattie (b. 1936) was the Member of Parliament for Chertsey & Walton between 1974 and 1997.

† The Conservative Party Treasurer at this time was Max Aitken, 3rd Lord Beaverbrook.

of the Conservative Party as a whole.

During Mrs Thatcher's and John Major's premierships, the PT was more or less financially secure and able to procure the services of outside researchers. By May 1986, Sir Paul Bryan reported to the Council that "the quality of meetings and membership is excellent but numbers attending the dinners were disappointing". Possibly this was because, as noted in November 1988, "the food is now so bad in the House." Whatever the reasons, Sir Peter Hordern was still able to inform the Council on 6th November 1991 that "we have a good relationship with the Chief Whip. These contacts are where the PT can show 'clout'."

The Political Committee continued to decide how and where this clout was best applied. One obvious area was the economy. On 12th June 1979, the PT described Geoffrey Howe's first Budget the day before as "a courageous Budget from a cautious man". But six months later, "members were conscious of the delayed success of the Government's economic policy and the prospect that the raising of the Minimum Lending Rate [MLR] will inhibit investment for even longer" (14th November 1979). Further doubts surrounding Mrs Thatcher's first steps to pursue a different economic course were expressed a few days later:

> ... abolishing exchange controls was not helping the Government in their task as people can borrow abroad ... the tight control on the money supply could not succeed alone. It must go hand in hand with cuts in public spending and reasonable pay settlements. At the moment the pay settlements are still too high and the cuts insufficient. (28th November 1979)

The PT's early lack of enthusiasm for Mrs Thatcher's economic approach is apparent in a number of references in the minutes of this period. Reading them one after the other may exaggerate the PT's lack of 'Thatcherite' faith, but is indicative of a general coldness towards her:

20.2.80: In response to a hawkish Ebury Note (No. 257) on 'denationalisation', the PT concluded "that there was a case for selling off the peripherals, but in the main it was better to try and improve the efficiency of the Nationalised Industries and avoid Government interference."

5.11.80: "it would be most dangerous to have any contact with George Gardiner's '92 Group,* which could lead to a row in the 1922 ... It was hoped that the Government would not deflate further during this winter, but that it was important to get Inflation down to 2 per cent and not to be content with 8–10 per cent.

3.12.80: In agreement with a critical Ebury Paper (No. 278) on 'The Monetary Muddle', the PT "thought that it had been a mistake to set targets as the market is so sophisticated."

4.3.81: In reply to a 'bullish' Ebury paper (No. 287) on the economy, "Fears were expressed that with a neutral Budget unemployment would reach three million by the winter."

11.3.81: "A less severe Budget had been hoped for, and it was felt that the 20 pence on petrol had been the most emotive proposal."

18.3.81: "The Chairman [Michael Hamilton] thought it was

---

* This was a group chaired by Sir George Gardiner, the Conservative MP for Reigate, and was portrayed as a very influential group of 'right-wing' Tory backbenchers. It was viewed with suspicion and dislike by many traditional Conservatives. (See also previous chapter concerning Sir George's place on the 1922 Committee.)

possible to sympathise with the dissident members of the Cabinet."

25.3.81: "... the image of the Party and Mrs Thatcher is appalling ... a suitable person should be found to help Mr Pym in a better presentation."

Consistent with such sentiments was the PT's opposition to specific policies associated with Mrs Thatcher's brand of Conservatism – such as doing away with sub-post offices, which the PT took up with the Chief Whip (11.2.80); opposition to student loans (2.4.80); and criticism of the Government's handing of the miners dispute described as "a debacle" and "the whole affair had been badly handled"* (25.2.81). However, as noted above, all changed with the Falklands crisis. The war may not have made Mrs Thatcher's economic policies any more palatable, but it did increase the PT's respect for her as Prime Minister.

One area where PT members might have been expected to support the robust views of Mrs Thatcher was defence, and especially the renewal of the nuclear deterrent. Yet, when an Ebury Note (No. 317) suggested contentiously during the Falklands crisis that "whatever the outcome ... it is bound to revive the argument that we might be wiser to strengthen our conventional forces rather than replace Polaris with new Trident missiles," the PT was unexpectedly receptive. This

* Mrs Thatcher had, on 10th February 1981, rejected the Opposition's demand that she should intervene in the miners' dispute over pit closures, but on 18th February the Government announced the withdrawal of the plan to close 23 pits and promised more state aid. What is now known is that Mrs Thatcher concluded that coal stocks at power stations were inadequate to resist a miners strike. At the time, this was described as 'game, set and match' to the miners, a sentiment with which the PT concurred.

note had presented the case 'for' and 'against' Trident objectively, but the PT was mindful that "Trident might become obsolete five or six years after delivery" (21st April 1982); over a year later, the PT doubted "whether we should be able to afford Trident, and that warnings should be given now otherwise the Party may look silly in fifteen years' time" (11th July 1983). This view was repeated the following year:

> ... It looks as though Trident is going to be far too expensive, and that although it will be difficult for the Government to change direction, it would be better to stop now before too much is spent ... we should be much more flexible about weapons ... Trident will make disarmament talks more difficult ... everything should be done to stop the escalation of the arms race, and to work towards a nuclear freeze. (9th May 1984)

This view was repeated on 17th July 1985, when the life of Trident was predicted to come to an end around 2025 and the PT again urged its immediate cancellation "as the foundations for Trident will soon have gone too far for the Government to change round". In the following year, "it was noted that a lot of PT members are against Trident owing to its appalling capability" (19th February 1986). This is the last reference to Trident in the PT's minutes; if those present at the time were reassembled, they would have some cause for satisfaction in their foresight.

The long-awaited crisis involving the coal industry, following 1981's preliminary skirmish, began in 1984. When a year before, in March 1983, the miners had voted against a national strike – and against the unanimous recommendation of their union's executive – two members of the PT (Sir

Paul Bryan and John Hannam, who was an expert on energy policy) "agreed that it was a great victory ... but that it would be a great mistake to think that the result had given the PM a mandate to put in MacGregor, and that the miners are still a force to be reckoned with." Unofficial and localised strikes in the mining industry had already started in the early months of 1984, and on 12th March Arthur Scargill – the leader of the National Union of Mineworkers (NUM) – declared the union's backing for those regional strikes taking place in Yorkshire and Scotland and which he hoped would now be supported by strike action throughout the entire workforce. Crucially, however, he did not put authorisation for this strike to a ballot.

In the early months of the strike, the PT failed to display the resilience which Mrs Thatcher might have expected from such a quarter. On 16th May 1984, the PT feared "that the country was critical that the Government were allowing the miners strike to drag on" even though "it was thought difficult to get Scargill off the hook." The PT's bias was normally towards compromise over confrontation, but for those determined to 'defeat' Arthur Scargill this attitude smacked more of appeasement than compromise. To add insult to injury, the PT voiced support at the same meeting for maintaining NEDDY (The National Economic Development Office), a body regarded as anathema by opponents of corporatism and state planning.

As the strike rose in intensity and bitterness so did the PT's misgivings, although now their concern was more directed at the Coal Board's management. On 20th June, "it was feared that the political situation is going against us"; on 31st October, "members were not happy with Mr MacGregor's handling of the strike" and feared now that the Government was being undermined by the Coal Board's offers to the mineworkers. As the strike continued into the New Year, "it was thought that the coal strike was dragging on to our detriment at the moment" (13th February 1985). However, although the strike did not end formally until 3rd March, the last Ebury Note on the subject (No. 393) speculated on 28th January that "the coal strike will be over by the time this note is discussed, or very soon afterwards." The PT appreciated how fortunate Mrs Thatcher had been in Mr Scargill's refusal to accept the Coal Board's offer in October when the outcome might well have been interpreted as a defeat for the Government. It was left to Peter Hordern to adopt a 'Thatcherite' stance in suggesting that:

> … later on the Government should de-nationalise electricity so that they deal directly with the Coal Industry and remove politics from their negotiations. It was even thought that there are people in the UK who would be prepared to take on the profitable parts of the coal industry – but not yet. It was thought that the mines will never do well whilst nationalised. (6th February 1985)

Once the miners' strike ended, Mrs Thatcher's premiership could claim two major victories – one abroad and one at home – both of which tightened her grip on the Conservative Party. After the miners' dispute, there were fewer critical references from the PT to Mrs Thatcher's leadership on the home front. A well-attended PT meeting on 26th June 1985* expressed some scepticism "about the value of tax cuts" in political

---

* Those attending were: Sir Paul Bryan, Kenneth Carlisle, Lord Dundee, Harry Greenway, Charles Morrison, Sir John Osborn, Richard Ryder, Robert Rhodes James, Peter Thurnham and Peter Viggers.

terms and noted that "the main complaints now are about Education and the Health Service." An Ebury Note (No. 408) warned on 17th June that "this is the critical moment of the Government's life ... should the Conservatives enter the next election boasting that public expenditure has *not* been cut? Or should they cut taxes further? The most dangerous course is to *claim* to have cut spending, and *not* to cut taxes. Then we get the worst of both worlds." *The Economist* supported this analysis at the time, reminding its readers that "If high spending was the route to growth and popularity, the government should be in clover." The PT agreed "that as the Government's spending has not fallen we are being hurt by our own propaganda ... too many groups feel that they are disliked and that the Government is taking on too many fights" (26th June 1985). The PT's only consolation was "that we are not so unpopular as in 1981".

Any governing Party is prone to mid-term blues, and many Conservatives thought that a defeat at the next General Election – which could be held no later than June 1988 – was distinctly possible. On the other hand, the PT noted on 12th February 1986 "that the PM is very buoyant at the moment, and it was thought that it would be a good thing if she is seen about the country". The PT's assessment following poor results in a by-election in Fulham and the local government elections in May[*] was

    ... the Prime Minister is an asset as long as she is not cut off

---

[*] Labour captured Fulham in the by-election which took place on 10th April 1986, but the Conservatives won it back in the 1987 General Election. In the local elections held on 8th May, the Conservatives lost 975 seats, Labour gained only 13 seats, but the Liberal–SDP Alliance gained 338 seats.

from the Cabinet … It was regretted that Robin Butler* is no longer with her as he was a 'political animal' and bridged the gap. However, it was noted that there are signs that Mrs Thatcher is bridge-building and receptive… (21st May 1986)

The PT's instincts, however, were still at variance with much of Thatcherism. For example, rumours circulated in March 1986 that Dr Rhodes Boyson might be chosen to succeed Sir Keith Joseph as Secretary of State for Education. In fact, Joseph was succeeded by Kenneth Baker† on 21st May 1986, who soon became a popular appointment with all sections of the Party. But the PT's opposition to Dr Boyson – and to the introduction of education vouchers which he favoured at the time – was significant because his views on education were more radical, and some assumed closer to the policy which Mrs Thatcher ideally would have pursued if Party management were not a factor. It provided further indication of where the PT stood on the political spectrum – as did its enthusiasm for the Anglo-Irish Agreement (an enthusiasm certainly not shared by Mrs Thatcher herself); its concerns over the City of London's "lack of social conscience" (5th November 1986); its opposition to a radical restructuring of the rates (29th October 1986); and surprisingly, given its record, its lack of support for the criticisms levelled by

---

* Sir Robin Butler (b. 1938), later Lord Butler of Brockwell, ended his career as Cabinet Secretary and Head of the Civil Service. Previously, he was Principal Private Secretary to Margaret Thatcher. In the House of Lords he has been a passionate opponent of Brexit.

† Kenneth Baker, later Lord Baker of Dorking (b. 1934), was the Member of Parliament for both Acton and St Marylebone 1968–1974, and finally Mole Valley until 1979. He was elected to the PT in 1969, but was not an active member and soon achieved his first job in Government in 1972.

Norman Tebbit against the BBC for lack of balance (5th November 1986). Taken together, Mrs Thatcher would have been excused for treating the PT with caution, even though there was never a suggestion that it was disloyal.

On 11th June 1987, Mrs Thatcher won her third election in a row, and once again her critics were silenced. At the first meeting following the election, the PT's Political Committee was down to seventeen and the decision was taken to recruit new members[*] (1st July 1987). One of the main challenges facing the new Government was their manifesto commitment "to abolish the unfair domestic rating system" and to replace it "with a fairer community charge". An Ebury Note (No. 481) asked, on 29th June 1987, "If the abolition of the rates is an inescapable commitment, how can the Community Charge be made to look preferable? That is now the real issue." The discussion on the note concluded

> ... everyone has some qualification but no one is absolutely against it [i.e. the Community Charge] ... the actual winners will be a very small group. It was hoped it would be brought in quickly rather than becoming a 'long running sore'. Only 23 per cent will be raised by the Poll Tax so local government will still have to raise money ... taking out Education had been ruled out but ... we ought to pay teachers from the centre. (8th July 1987)

---

[*] Between July and November, the PT was joined by Henry Bellingham, Nicholas Bonsor, Alick Buchanan-Smith, Alistair Burt, Michael Marshall, Philip Oppenheim, Tom Sackville, Tim Smith and David Sumberg. The MPs retiring included Sir Paul Bryan (Chairman of the Political Group but remaining on the Council), Lord Cranborne, Michael Hirst and Sir John Osborn.

For almost three years the PT did not return to this subject in any detail even though it anticipated, on 21st October 1987, that "the Community Charge will cause the Government the most trouble in this Session." On 17th February 1988, Sir Peter Hordern commented that, personally, "he felt happier defending the Uniform Business Rate than the Poll Tax as at least some of the depressed areas would gain." As so often, Sir Peter's instincts were correct, and it is significant that he – a loyal Conservative – now referred to the Community Charge as a 'poll tax', despite the Government's disapproval of the term.

But it was not until 1989 that the dangers really hit home. By the summer recess "The Poll Tax was thought to be our biggest problem as it has been a muddled operation ... the Government must be seen to be generous over the safety net" (19th July 1989); this fear was confirmed at the first meeting after the summer recess when it was reported that "Loyal activists in the Party are now becoming critical of the Prime Minister ... the Poll Tax was impossible to sell to the elec-torate and we are in a hideous muddle over it" (25th October 1989). Even so, it was not until the following year that the political problems were discussed in detail. One explanation for this omission was suggested by an Ebury Note (No. 557):

> Everyone understood, even before the legislation was enacted, that the so-called poll tax would be unpopular with those who didn't pay rates ... but it was felt that there would be winners and losers; that many households would be better off than under the existing system if only because the new tax was to be spread over a much wider population ... all that is really killing the poll tax is that it is set at too high a level.

The PT finally discussed the Poll Tax as a separate topic at their meeting on 28th February 1990, with this Ebury Note before them. Their conclusions were that "the principle is sound" but that local councils, even Tory councils, "have set a high figure to see what happens". They also supported teachers being paid from the centre as another means of reducing the charge but Sir Peter Hordern pointed out "that she [Mrs Thatcher] had been against the idea for twenty years". However, there was still a sense that eventually the policy could be made to work – "it was hoped that the combined wisdom of John Major and Christopher Patten will help the situation."

Two months later, on the eve of the local government elections, the PT "noted that the electorate now accept that each individual should pay something towards local government" and Alistair Burt,* a younger, 'progressive' PT member, reported "he is getting a better reception now because the rebates are coming through" (25th April 1990). The results of the local elections (held on 3rd May 1990) were every bit as bad as the PT had expected – the Conservatives lost 222 seats, and Labour gained 284 bringing their number of councillors to 8,920, Labour's highest total since 1981. Nobody was certain, however, whether this was because of the Government's general performance, the rows over Europe and Nigel Lawson's resignation – or whether they were much worse because of the Community Charge. The Tories had performed better than predicted by the opinion polls, and the results in Wandsworth suggested that voters still supported councils with tight control over their spending. The

---

* Alistair Burt (b. 1955) was the Member of Parliament for Bury North between 1983 and 1997 and has been the Member of Parliament for North East Bedfordshire since 2001.

PT hoped that "an alarming increase in Labour voters" might be assuaged by new legislation which would "attend to the anomalies, such as non-working married women and empty houses" (9th May 1990).

This was the last time that the PT discussed the Community Charge under Mrs Thatcher's premiership. By the time it was raised again at the end of November by an Ebury Note (No. 580), Mr Major had succeeded Mrs Thatcher as Prime Minister and Michael Heseltine was charged with reforming the measure fundamentally. When the PT discussed the options on 5th December 1990, the emphasis was placed on 'the ability to pay', given that the main complaints from constituents had been its 'unfairness'. The PT believed that "half the problems would have vanished if we had had individual assessment."

One reason why the PT was, at the start, more relaxed over the Community Charge than events merited was because of widespread disagreement within the Conservative Party over the desired nature of Mrs Thatcher's third term. When Parliament reassembled after the post-election Party Conferences in October 1987, an Ebury Note (No. 484) reminded PT members of Lord Hailsham's dictum: "A political party is never in greater danger than when it has been overwhelmingly successful." At exactly the same time a year later, the corresponding post-recess Ebury Note (No. 513) commented that "all discussion of the Prime Minister's retirement has ceased. She is said to be at the peak of her powers. She has dominated the political agenda throughout the recess ... The opposition parties show no sign of recovery, having had pretty dismal conferences. Can this really last?"

The answer was that it couldn't. By December, with inflation rising, questions again surfaced over the Government's handing of the economy, and in particular its reliance upon high interest rates to dampen down the economy. There was also a sense in some quarters that the Government was attempting too much. Committed Thatcherites regarded the third term as a unique opportunity to introduce even more radical reforms; but there were plenty of others who were content just 'to consolidate'. The PT asked its researcher for "ideas as to how best keep Parliament busy and to maintain the Government's momentum, without running into needless political dangers." In answering this question, an Ebury Note entitled 'Busy, Reforming and Popular' (No. 526) suggested that "Most so-called popular measures call for higher public expenditure. So-called unpopular measures often turn out to be popular in the end. The Tory Party is still not united on whether the objective should be minimal rates of taxation, or increased state expenditure now that the financing of that expenditure is no longer a problem." The PT's answer to its own question was as follows:

> It was hoped that in 1990 and 1991 we would stop being unpleasant to everyone and produce some popular Bills, as most of the reforming legislation has been presented ... we are losing the intellectuals, the teachers, and we must not under-estimate the loss of farmers ... we are in a period of mid-term blues, but the money in peoples' pockets at the time of the election is the most important thing. The only real problem is that the electorate will think that the Tory Party is stale and that it is time for a change. (1st March 1989)

The combination of an economy in difficulties, the unpop-ularity of the Community Charge, disagreements within Government over the EMS and, above all, Europe led to Mrs

Thatcher's dismissal – although in retrospect there are strong grounds for saying that it would have been much better if this dismissal had been at the hands of the electorate, rather than of the Conservative Parliamentary Party. Most members of the PT were not, in the end, sorry to see her go. On 28th November 1990, following Mrs Thatcher's resignation, "it was thought that John Major will be terrific and that it will be a new Government, and the Labour Party is not happy." There was no such effusive praise for Mrs Thatcher when she removed Mr Heath.

This, however, is not surprising. The PT's instinct for survival meant that it could never embrace Thatcherite policies with the enthusiasm of her most committed supporters. When in trouble, Mrs Thatcher could rely generally upon the PT's loyalty; but only a few PT members were active in defending her policies intellectually or with enthusiasm. The PT was too broad a church for enthusiasts of any persuasion.

9

THE FINAL YEARS

"The old left-wing ideas are dead, and middle class values are now pretty universal." (PT, 2ⁿᵈ February 1999)

"The Conservatives should never say 'never' about the Euro – it is not Conservative practice."
(PT, 18ᵗʰ May, 1999)

The final years of the Progress Trust coincided with what was the bleakest period of the Conservative Party's post-war history.* At least when the Conservative Party suffered its electoral defeat in 1945 the ensuing period in Opposition was destined to be relatively brief, and accompanied by an intellectual revival in Tory thinking. The comparable defeat in 1997 had no such compensations. By the time a Conservative Prime Minister again occupied No. 10 Downing Street thirteen years later, albeit in coalition with the Liberal Democrats, the divisions over Europe were still unresolved and the PT had ceased to exist. The last ever meeting of the PT's Political Committee took place on 14ᵗʰ December 2005. With morning sittings, the growth of Select Committees and depleted numbers, there were not enough MPs to provide a weekly quorum at PT meetings. In addition, the funds had dried up.

The death pains, however, were not felt immediately. Both the Conservative Party and the PT were slow in adjusting

---

* Perhaps one should add the qualification "to date". Nobody knows how the Conservative Party will emerge from the current divisions over Brexit.

to an unprecedented period of Opposition, following their worst defeat since 1906. Eight MPs and two peers* attended the first PT Political Committee after the election, when it was unanimously agreed that Michael Colvin should succeed Nigel Forman as Chairman, following the loss of his seat.† They agreed "that the Progress Trust was a combination of principle and pragmatism" and that "we have to accept the magnitude of our defeat." They also stated "We have left the country in good order, and not much will be undone" (21st May 1997).

Understandably, but still regrettably, John Major created the unfortunate precedent – followed ever since – of resigning his leadership of the Conservative Party immediately following the election defeat, rather than allowing time for the Party to lick its wounds and consider who best should take over. There were five candidates in the first ballot for the leadership which took place on 10th June – Kenneth Clarke, William Hague, John Redwood, Peter Lilley and Michael Howard. A week before, on 4th June, the PT discussed the leadership contest and considered "that the idea mooted in the constituencies that Ken Clarke should be the leader now, and then make way for William Hague was not on, as things do not work out that way." Otherwise, those attending the weekly meeting kept their leadership preferences to themselves, and

---

* Those attending were Lord Kimball (in the chair), Virginia Bottomley, Lord Brookeborough, Michael Colvin, Edward Garnier, Sir Archibald Hamilton, Peter Temple-Morris, Peter Viggers and Sir Ray Whitney.

† Michael Colvin (1932–2000) was the Member of Parliament for Bristol North West between 1979 and 1983, and then Romsey from 1983 until his death in 2000 when he, and his wife Nicola, died in a fire at their house (Tangley House, near Andover) on the morning of February 24th.

William Hague's election as Leader on 19th June 1997 passed without comment.

The PT's first priority was to recruit new members and donors. At a meeting of the PT Council, it was reported that the Grosvenor Estate had given £7,000, and that a further £2,000 was expected from Sir Barrie Stephens, Chairman of Siebe. The Council acknowledged on 19th January 1999, however, "that it is getting difficult to find people to support us, as they give directly to Central Office". Neither the Landowners nor the BUI was still supporting the Progress Trust.

By the start of 1999, fourteen new members had been recruited, including surprisingly (given his rebellious past) Iain Duncan Smith.[*] While they attended occasional PT dinners, very few became regular participants of the weekly political meetings, which had now been moved from Wednesday to Tuesday lunchtimes in order not to clash with the new time and format of Prime Minister's Questions. Attendances at meetings in 1999 occasionally exceeded ten MPs but more often averaged around four to five.

The most sensitive political issue again facing both main political parties was economic and monetary union and whether Britain should sign up to a single European currency. Conservatives considered this one of the few areas where the

---

[*] Iain Duncan Smith (b. 1954) has been the Member of Parliament for Chingford and Wood Green since 1992. He was the second member of the PT to become Leader of the Conservative Party. Other new members following the election included Crispin Blunt, Geoffrey Clifton-Brown, James Gray, Damian Green, Andrew Lansley, Peter Luff, Sir Nicholas Lyell, David Maclean, David Pryor, Nicholas St Aubyn, Keith Simpson, Andrew Tyrie and Sir George Young. Both Theresa May and Philip Hammond were on a reserve list for joining.

new Labour Government was vulnerable, although they themselves remained divided. The active members of the PT at this moment were Michael Colvin, Virginia Bottomley, Sir Peter Lloyd* and Lord Cope – none of them was sympathetic to their new Leader's principled opposition both to a single currency and the Amsterdam Treaty:

> ... it was agreed that William Hague's speech on EMU had been a mistake, and that he should not have been so definite about not joining for ten years. It was suggested that he had been pushed into making a statement on *The Today Programme* ... we must be pragmatic and ... see how it works before going in ... We must also push for enlargement of the Union as Eastern Europe will be against a Federation. (11th November 1997)

Gordon Brown had already announced the Government's decision to remain detached from economic and monetary Union, but had added that "on the question of principle ... if, in the end, the single currency is successful and the economic case is clear and unambiguous, the Government believes that Britain should be part of it" (27th October 1997). Gordon Brown's scepticism surrounding a single currency was not then as fully appreciated as was Tony Blair's enthusiasm for joining. For this reason, William Hague's decision to oppose a single currency on principle – a stance which met with opposition from Ken Clarke and his supporters – was a decisive moment in the Conservative Party's history.

The weekly Political Committee meeting continued to discuss issues and policies chosen by the weekly Ebury Notes,

---

* Sir Peter Lloyd (b. 1937) was the Member of Parliament for Fareham between 1979 and 2001.

dictated either by the actions of the new Labour Government or by some policy disagreement within the Conservative Party. A few extracts from the minutes suggest the breadth of topics raised and the opinions related to them:

10.2.98: Blair may have made a mistake in supporting Clinton over Iraq if it all ends in failure ... the froth and glitz of the Government was deplored, and it was hoped that William Hague will not travel down the same path ... we alienate our supporters by apologising too much about what we did when in Government.

3.3.98: The proposed lowering of the drink/driving limit will mean the destruction of social life in the country, and pub life will die.

19.1.99: The Government are cracking, and making policy errors, but it is going to take a long time before we will gain any benefit ... our front bench should be snappier.

26.1.99: Criticism of Lord Wakeham's acceptance of the Chairmanship of the Royal Commission on House of Lords reform: "any Tory taking Blair's offer of a job delays the return of a Tory Government."

2.2.99: Conservatives should be worried about Blair's plans to occupy the middle ground with the Liberal Democrats by means of PR. If successful this could put the Conservative Party in permanent opposition ... The old left-wing ideas are dead, and middle class values are now pretty universal.

23.3.99: We must drop the slogan 'In Europe but not run by Europe'.

20.4.99: There are no British interests involved in Kosovo, and we would have washed our hands of it if the trouble had occurred in Africa. Internationalism is emerging.

18.5.99: The Conservatives should never say 'never' about the

Euro – it is not Conservative practice.

29.6.99: The new bus lanes are causing chaos.

28.3.00: Capitalist companies like BP are becoming unpopular as their leaders are becoming too powerful.

16.5.00: It looks as though Hague was liberal when he came in, but now it looks as though he is being opportunist.

One of the most surprising meetings of this period took place on 4th July 2000, when those attending included Quentin Davies, David Prior,[*] Sir George Young[†] and Sir Ray Whitney[‡] none of whom was associated with a Euro-sceptical view. Nevertheless, according to the minutes, this meeting agreed "that there should be no extension of Qualified Majority Voting and that we must have the veto". The meeting also felt that "coming out of the EU ten years ago seemed preposterous, but it does not seem absurd now." At least, the PT's political instincts had not vanished entirely, although some of the topics in the above list suggest that certain members of the PT were losing the plot.

Sir Peter Lloyd had taken over the Chairmanship from Michael Colvin, following his death in a fire on 24th February 2000. He, in turn, was succeeded by Peter Viggers[§] following the General Election of 7th June 2001. Despite a

---

* David Prior, later Lord Prior of Brampton (b. 1954), was the Member of Parliament for North Norfolk between 1997 and 2001.

† Sir George Young, later Lord Young of Cookham (b. 1941), was the Member of Parliament for Ealing Acton between 1974 and 1983 and North West Hampshire between 1997 and 2015.

‡ Sir Ray Whitney (1930–2012) was the Member of Parliament for Wycombe between 1978 and 2001.

§ Sir Peter Viggers (b. 1938) was the Member of Parliament for Gosport between 1974 and 2010.

feeling on 27th March that "our chances have improved," the Conservative Party faced once more the task of choosing a new Leader in the immediate aftermath of a second major electoral defeat. This time the franchise had been extended to members of the Conservative Party outside Parliament. Again, however, the PT refrained from discussing the new leadership candidates at their meetings. Iain Duncan Smith was elected the new Leader in September 2001, but this was not referred to at the first meeting on 23rd October following the Party Conferences. This was probably because attention was focused on the aftermath of the Twin Towers attack at the World Trade Center in New York on 11th September. As an Ebury Note emphasised (No. 854), "the Conservative Party's new Leader has emphasised the 'loyalty' of Her Majesty's Opposition and the Conservative Party's support for the action [i.e. of bombing Afghanistan]." But the note also asked these questions:

> Should the Conservatives become more belligerent (for example, in encouraging attacks upon Iraq)? Or keep its options open in case the US strategy runs into serious difficulties? And in particular, to what extent can the war be allowed to become an excuse of illiberal measures at home?

The PT understood "that the position could become difficult if the Labour Party starts showing cracks, and we end up supporting Blair whilst his own backbench are withdrawing their support". By this time, however, the PT's Political Committee was regularly attracting fewer than five members at each meeting, and the discussions were increasingly academic since the PT had no influence upon the Government, and very little on the Opposition. The PT dinners continued to be well supported, but the new Parliamentary timetable was by now taking its toll on any discussion of policy.

The PT's difficulties were not unique. On 6th November, the Chief Whip (David Maclean,* a former PT member) attended a meeting of the Political Committee and said that "he was keen to use the Progress Trust as a sounding board." When Peter Viggers expressed concern over poor attendance, David Maclean "said that it is symptomatic of the Party, members are not attending the Chamber, or policy groups". On 29th January 2002, David Cameron† attended his first and only meeting of the Political Committee, although he attended PT dinners on occasions. On 12th February, it was thought that "IDS is making a good start, and is not being opportunistic. He is not taking the easy catches."

It was also at this meeting that Quentin Davies, on the subject of health policy, suggested "that compulsory insurance should be introduced as in France. Pay first and then get reimbursed." His defection to the Labour Party in June 2007, and his new-born enthusiasm for Gordon Brown, was hard to reconcile with the views he habitually expressed as a member of the PT. He had been associated with the economically liberal wing of the Conservative Party, and was highly antagonistic towards the Labour Government's economic policy. Following the Conservative Party's third election defeat on 5th May 2005, he was especially critical at a PT meeting on 12th July of Michael Howard's failure to

---

* David Maclean, later Lord Blencathra (b. 1953), was the Member of Parliament for Penrith and the Border between 1983 and 2010.

† David Cameron (b. 1966) was the Member of Parliament for Witney between 2001 and 2016. He and Sir Alec Douglas-Home are the only members of the PT to have become Prime Minister. He was elected to the PT in 2002.

fight an aggressive campaign against Gordon Brown's economic legacy. And yet, two years later, on the eve of Gordon Brown's accession to the premiership, Quentin Davies was televised sitting next to him in a publicity stunt organised by Gordon Brown and the Labour Party. Such is politics. He, and Alan Howarth,* were the only members of the PT who 'crossed the floor' to Labour.

Iain Duncan Smith was deposed as Leader of the Conservative Party on 23rd October 2003. His vulnerability had been commented upon at the start of the year:

> IDS must raise his game. He has had a good start to the year and is moving forward. We must support him. He knows that he has got to deliver, so we must not undermine him. A quiet man will not survive beyond May. (15th January 2003)

The view a few months earlier had been even more pessimistic:

> Conservatives are a rabble and unless something happens Iain Duncan Smith will crumble. What can the Tory Party coalesce around? If we are not careful we are in melt down. We must get a grip on ourselves. There is no glue in the Party ... We need a good Party Chairman, but who would want the job? Theresa May is influenced by Central Office." (6th November 2002)

By this time Henry Bellingham was the new, and final, Chairman of the Progress Trust. He had taken over from Peter Viggers five months before, and shortly in advance

---

* Alan Howarth (b. 1944), later Lord Howarth of Newport, represented Stratford-on-Avon as a Conservative between 1983 and 1987, and subsequently Newport East as a Labour MP between 1997 and 2005.

of Iain Duncan Smith's "inept handling of David Davis' sacking in the summer" as Conservative Party Chairman (6th November 2002). This had triggered new dissension within the Conservative Party.

By the time Iain Duncan Smith had been replaced by Michael Howard, the PT was no longer meeting regularly and hardly anyone attended when it did. It struggled on until December 2005, but the intervals between meetings became longer and longer. At the last meeting of the PT Council on 7th May 2003 it was recorded that

> The Progress Trist is a voice of sanity and can liaise between the Commons and Lords. The Party now has an agenda, and can become a credible Opposition. The Ebury Notes continue to be important, and we must market them.

At the last meeting of the Political Committee on 14th December 2005:

> It was agreed that Richard's next note should be on 'Police State Stuff'.

There was no next meeting, and no further Ebury Notes. From March 1971 to December 2005, nearly 870 notes had been sent to PT members on a weekly basis while Parliament was sitting. They still serve as a reminder of the chronology and topicality of the political issues which dominated political discussion throughout this period.

As had been hoped at the last meeting of the PT Council, Michael Howard did much to transform the Conservative Party into a "credible Opposition" but it took a further seven years, and the replacement of Michael Howard by David

Cameron, for Conservatives to return to Government in coalition with the Liberal Democrats. By then, the Progress Trust was history.

10

In Retrospect

"... a poor player that struts and frets his hour upon the stage, and then is heard no more."
(William Shakespeare, Macbeth *Act V, Sc. 5)*

It is a reflection on today's House of Commons that if anything like the Progress Trust existed now it would be considered an anachronism. The idea of a self-perpetuating group of (mostly) well-heeled MPs meeting each week in premises away from Parliament, free from media scrutiny, and with a confidential 'hot-line' to the Chief Whip, is inconceivable. Of course, Members of Parliament will always form alliances and associate closely with like-minded colleagues, and to that extent the PT was not unusual. But such alliances normally represent a faction, or exist to promote a particular policy or philosophy. The idea of a permanent, well-resourced Parliamentary group without any doctrinal purpose exercising permanent, albeit modest and selective, influence behind the scenes and through a private network of contacts is a different concept and incongruous with today's political climate.

That is the case against. A contrary view could be expressed, but there isn't much point in doing so. Today's Parliamentary timetable, the volume of legislation and the importance of Select Committees has rendered impossible such an approach to politics, even if it were desirable. In addition, the expectations of constituents have changed. Past members of the PT spent most of their time in Westminster. They would have expected to deal with local constituency issues only as a matter of last resort, and certainly not as welfare officers on 24-hour call. Those who didn't live permanently in their constituencies visited them regularly in order to hold surgeries, attend Party meetings and important local events. But they regarded their main duty as protecting their constituents' interests on the floor of the House of Commons between the hours of 2.30pm and whenever the House finally rose later that evening or even early morning the following day.

This political approach was neither dilatory nor amateurish. Throughout every phase of the Progress Trust's existence, its members played the political game professionally. Some were experts in Parliamentary procedure. Others had deep knowledge of particular subjects. Others were assiduous simply in their Parliamentary attendance. And, as has already been emphasised, the representation of PT members on other Conservative Parliamentary Committees – especially the 1922 Committee – was impressively large.

This is why the PT's existence is of significance to anyone with an interest in the history of the Conservative Party. Although a glance through the list of PT members will reveal many MPs who occupied high offices of state, they are of less importance to this history than names which are unfamiliar or forgotten. After all, if someone is controversial or has occupied senior posts in Government, his views will already be known. But what has been under examination here is how lesser-known backbench MPs "strutted and fretted" their hour upon the political stage until they were "heard no more". Their names may be forgotten, but they were listened to in their time: and because in some respects the realities of politics remain constant, their opinions expressed in the privacy of a small group of associates may still sometimes be relevant today, or at least help explain why events turned out as they did.

In this context, the benefit of hindsight – or lack of it – is of particular interest. The Progress Trust comprised people who were well informed, and whose extensive personal contacts should have provided them with a privileged vantage point from which to observe events. Their political judgement could reasonably be expected to be of a higher calibre than the average pundit. And yet, in the middle of any crisis – whether it be Suez, the Falklands, or Conservative divisions over Europe – the PT often seemed to be struggling to know what to advise. Indeed, on occasions it appears to have had no better insight than the rest of us.

At other times it was well informed and took the initiative. The problem, however, is that because its advice and criticisms were proffered privately, man-to-man, over a drink, and 'off-the-record', it is almost impossible to measure their effectiveness. On the one occasion when the PT's actions were under scrutiny and credited with playing a decisive role, it arguably got it wrong. Post-war politics might have been so different had Butler succeeded either Eden or Macmillan – especially in 1963, when both Iain Macleod and Enoch Powell would have remained in the Government, with less temptation to make trouble and with every opportunity to deploy their considerable talents. Or if the PT had lent more support to Mrs Thatcher in the early years, the split between 'dry' and 'wet' might have been less debilitating. Given the PT's commitment to free enterprise, it should have welcomed more effusively the opportunity provided by Mrs Thatcher to reverse the ratchet of socialism. The PT's support would have had more influence on its 'wet' friends in the Cabinet than any amount of pressure from more Thatcherite groups.

This, however, is to misunderstand its function which primarily was to minimise risks. Pressure from PT members might sometimes have slowed things down, or caused Ministers to think twice, but they were not in business to promote a fundamental shift of policy. This is not a criticism. To delay something even desirable can be an invaluable service in politics if it gives a greater chance of acceptance and eventual success. Exercising this sort of caution was something for which the PT was well suited. But any Tory with a libertarian or anarchic streak would have found few allies in the Progress Trust. I know, because this was the line which many of my Ebury Research Notes mischievously proposed. They were read and discussed with kind attention, but I knew they were often outside the PT's comfort zone. To have expected the PT's support for a radical policy of reform was to invite disappointment. The instincts of most PT members were more towards consolidation than upheaval. They were in no doubt that a Conservative Government was in the national interest, and that socialism was a creed to be resisted at all costs. Many of them had opinions on certain subjects, such as capital punishment, which justified the label 'right-wing'. But provided a Conservative Government was competent and was moving the country in a Conservative direction, the PT was reasonably content and was never going to make trouble.

Many of the issues which occupied the Trust in 1943 and throughout its existence are still with us today. They may reappear in different forms and under different names, but MPs continue to grapple with problems which have perplexed previous generations of politicians. Indeed, if one looks back over the major questions facing the PT during its existence, it is tempting to ask whether any of them has been resolved satisfactorily. Living standards have improved, but the weakness of the British economy remains. The National Health system is in crisis. There is still disagreement over Britain's role in the world. The legacy of Empire and the fudge of Commonwealth still beset any attempt to control immigration wisely and humanely. Our relationship with the European continent is as problematic as ever and could still destroy the Conservative Party – Enoch Powell was certainly right about that. Despite brief moments since 1945 when a Government and Prime Minister seemed in command of events, the general sense is one of disappointment as everything gets more difficult.

If so, who is to blame? If a country gets the politicians it deserves, then the blame rests as much with the electorate as the politicians whom they elect. And yet, a House of Commons comprising entirely of rebels and free-thinkers would make Government impossible. The traditional political parties may be losing favour, and the young alienated from the political process, but the idea that our Parliamentary system of Government could be sustained without Party loyalists is still inconceivable. The Progress Trust never made that mistake. Its mistrust of Suez, Maastricht, or Powellite rebels made sense if all that mattered was a Conservative Government's continuance.

It would be pleasant to think that the PT left an important political legacy, but that would be to claim too much. Maybe, the most to hope for is that the Progress Trust serves as a reminder of the decency of politics when played by the rules, with respect for one's opponents, and with a hefty dose of patriotism. Whatever else the PT may have got wrong, in this it remains a beacon to us all.

Appendix I

The Progress Trust
Past Chairmen Of Council
Sir Alexander Erskine-Hill 1943–1945
Sir Thomas Galbraith (later Lord Strathclyde) 1955–1982
Sir Paul Bryan 1982–1987
Sir Peter Hordern 1987–1994
Mr Nigel Forman 1994–1997
Mr Michael Colvin 1997–2000
Sir Peter Lloyd 2000–2001
Sir Peter Viggers 2001–2002
Sir Henry Bellingham 2002–2005

Past Chairmen of Political Committee
Sir Alexander Erskine-Hill 1943–1945
Sir Thomas Galbraith 1945–1951
Sir Guy Lloyd 1951–1959
Major John Morrison (later Lord Margadale) 1959–1964
Sir Spencer Summers 1965–1970
Sir Tufton Beamish 1970–1973
Mr John (Jack) Temple 1973–1974
Sir Michael Hamilton 1974–1982
Sir Paul Bryan 1982–1987
Sir Peter Hordern 1987–1994
Mr Nigel Forman 1994–1997
Mr Michael Colvin 1997–2000
Sir Peter Lloyd 2000–2001
Sir Peter Viggers 2001–2002
Sir Henry Bellingham 2002–2005

Members of Progress Trust who also Chaired the 1922 Committee
Sir Alexander Erskine-Hill 1940–1944
Major John Morrison 1955–1964

Sir William Anstruther-Gray 1964–1966
Sir Harry Legge-Bourke 1970–1972
Mr Edward du Cann 1972–1984
Sir Archie Hamilton 1997–2001

List of Members of the Progress Trust
1943–1945 (* = Founding Member & Member of PT Council)
Mr A. G. Erskine-Hill* (Founding Chairman)
Hon. Lionel Berry
Sir Bernard Bourdillon
Commander Rupert A. Brabner*
Mr Henry Brooke*
Captain E. C. Cobb*
Mr J. Dermot Campbell
Squadron Leader Patrick W. Donner*
Mr J. A. L. Duncan
Lord Dunglass
Commander T. D. Galbraith* (Chairman)
Hon. J. F. Gretton
Dr A. B. Howitt
Wing Commander A. W. H. James
Major E. Guy Lloyd*
Mr R. E. Manningham-Buller*
Colonel Harold Mitchell*
Mr J. G. Morrison
Sir Joseph Nall
Major B. Neven-Spence
Mr Kenneth W. M. Pickthorn*
Mr R. Donald Scott
Mr W. McN. Snadden
Sir. Archibald Southby
Mr H. G. Strauss
Major H. G. Studholme
Mr G. Spencer Summers*
Lord Teviot
Sir Douglas Thomson, Bart.*

Mr Henry (Harry) U. Willink*
Mr G. I. Woodham-Smith*

1945–1951
12 members of the PT lost their seats in the 1945 election but were allowed to continue as members of the PT if it was their intention to seek re-election.
Commander T. D. Galbraith, MP (Chairman of Council & Political Committee)
Major E. G. (Guy) Lloyd, MP (Vice Chairman of Political Committee)
Sir Alexander Erskine-Hill (Chairman of Council, died 1947)
Major Tufton V. H. Beamish, MP
Sir Peter Bennett, MP
Lt. Col. E. N. C. Birch, MP
Sir Bernard Bourdillon
Major J. A. Boyd-Carpenter, MP
Commander Rupert Brabner
Mr J. Dermot Campbell
Captain E. C. Cobb
Lt. Col. U. Corbett, MP
Squadron Leader Patrick W. Donner, MP
Lord de L'Isle and Dudley
Captain J. A. L. Duncan, MP (re-elected in 1950)
Lord Dunglass (re-elected in 1950)
Mr F. J. Erroll, MP
Lord Gretton
Lord Hawke
Viscount Hinchingbrooke, MP
Squadron-Leader Christopher Hollis, MP
Lord John Hope, MP
Wing Commander Sir Archibald James
Major E. A. H. Legge-Bourke, MP
Mr A. T. Lennox-Boyd, MP
Mr J. Selwyn B. Lloyd, MP
Brigadier A. R. W. Low

Brigadier H. R. Mackeson, MP
Mr R. E. Manningham-Buller, MP
Colonel Sir Harold Mitchell
Major J. G. Morrison, MP
Rt. Hon. W. S. Morrison
Major C. E. Mott-Radclyffe, MP
Major Sir Basil Neven-Spence, MP
Commander Allan H. P. Noble, MP
Mr Kenneth W. M. Pickthorn, MP
Brigadier Ralph Rayner, MP
Rt. Hon. J. S. C. Reid, MP
Mr R. Donald Scott, MP (re-elected in 1950)
Mr John Senter
Mr W. McN. Snadden
Comdr. Sir Archibald Southby, MP
Major H. G. Studholme
Mr Henry G. Strauss, MP
Mr G. Spencer Summers, MP (re-elected in 1950)
Lord Teviot (Vice Chairman of Council)
Lord Teynham
Sir Douglas Thomson
Lord Tweedsmuir
Mr W. M. F. Vane, MP
Mr Henry (Harry) U. Willink
Mr Gerald Wills, MP
Mr G. I. Woodham-Smith

1951–1955
With a Conservative Government returned to office, those members of the PT appointed to Government posts were required by the rules to resign their membership of the Trust.

[All PT members are now assumed either to be members of the House of Lords or House of Commons.]

Commander T. D. Galbraith (Chairman of Council)
Major Sir Guy Lloyd (Chairman of Political Committee)
Major J. G. Morrison (Vice Chairman of Political Committee)
Major W. J. Anstruther-Gray
Rt. Hon. Ralph Assheton
Mr Anthony Barber
Lord Bennett
Sir Peter Bennett (appointed Parliamentary Secretary, Ministry of Labour)
Mr Nigel Birch (appointed Under-Secretary of State for Air)
Mr J. A. Boyd-Carpenter (Appointed Financial Secretary to the Treasury)
Sir Edward Boyle, Bt.
Viscount Cranborne
Colonel A. D. Dodds-Parker
Lord de L'Isle and Dudley (Appointed Secretary of State for Air)
Captain J. A. L. Duncan
Lord Dunglass (appointed Minister of State for Scotland)
Mr F. J. Erroll
Colonel Alan Gomme-Duncan
Lord Hawke
Viscount Hinchingbrooke
Mr C. J. Holland-Martin
Lord John Hope
Mr H. B. H. Hylton-Foster
Viscount Lambton
Major E. A. H. Legge-Bourke
Mr A. T. Lennox-Boyd (appointed Minister of State, Colonial Office)
Mr J. Selwyn B. Lloyd (appointed Minister of State, Foreign Office)
Major C. E. Mott-Radclyffe
Brigadier Sir Harry Mackeson, Bt. (Member of Council)
The Rt. Hon. J. S. Maclay
Sir R. E. Manningham-Buller (appointed Solicitor General)
Commander S. L. C. Maydon
Rt. Hon. M. McCorquodale

Commander Allan H. P. Noble (appointed Financial Secretary to the Admiralty)
Hon. W. D. Ormsby-Gore (appointed PPS)
Mr Kenneth W. M. Pickthorn (appointed Parliamentary Secretary, Ministry of Education)
Mr J. Ramsden
Brigadier Ralph Rayner (Member of Council)
Mr John Senter (Member of Council)
Mr Henry G. Strauss (Appointed Parliamentary Secretary, Board of Trade)
Mr G. Spencer Summers
Lord Teviot (Vice Chairman of Council)
Lord Teynham
Lord Tweedsmuir
Mr W. M. F. Vane (appointed PPS)
Captain the Rt. Hon. C. Waterhouse
Mr Gerald Wills
Hon. Richard Wood (appointed PPS)

1955–1959
Lord Strathclyde (Chairman of Council)
Lord Teviot (Vice Chairman of Council)
Major Sir Guy Lloyd (Chairman of Political Committee)
Major John G. Morrison (Vice Chairman of Political Committee)
Major Sir William J. Anstruther-Gray
Mr Humphrey Atkins
Colonel Tufton Beamish
Lord Bennett
Mr Edward du Cann
Lord Clitheroe
Lord Denham
Major The Rt. Hon. Sir Thomas Dugdale, Bt.
Captain Sir James Duncan, Bt.
Colonel R. Glyn
Colonel Sir Alan Gomme-Duncan
Mr Alan Green

Mr John E. B. Hill
Viscount Hinchingbrooke (resigned Tory Whip over Suez, and left PT)
Mr Christopher J. Holland-Martin
Mr Marcus Kimball
Mr A. J. Leavey
Major E. A. H. Legge-Bourke
Lord McCorquodale
Brigadier Sir Harry Mackeson (Member of Council)
The Rt. Hon. J. S. Maclay
Mr Angus E. U. Maude (resigned Tory Whip over Suez, and left PT)
Lt. Commander S. L. C. Maydon
Major Sir Charles Mott-Radclyffe
Mr James Ramsden
Brigadier Ralph Rayner (Member of Council)
Mr John Senter (Member of Council)
Sir Spencer Summers
Lord Teviot (Vice Chairman of Council)
Lord Teynham
Mr W. M. F. Vane
Mr J. K. Vaughan-Morgan
Captain The Rt. Hon. C. Waterhouse
Mr Paul Williams (resigned Tory Whip over Suez, and left PT)

1959–1964
Lord Strathclyde (Chairman of Council)
Major John Morrison (Chairman of Political Committee)
Sir Spencer Summers (Vice Chairman of Political Committee)
Mr Robert Allan
Major Sir William J. Anstruther-Gray
Mr Humphrey Atkins
Sir Tufton Beamish
Sir David Campbell
Mr Gordon Campbell
Mr Edward du Cann
Lord Clitheroe

Lord Colville of Culross
Lord Crathorne
Lord Denham
Sir James Duncan, Bt.
Sir John Eden
Sir John Gilmour
Sir Richard Glyn
Mr Alan Green
Lord Robert Grosvenor
Mr Michael Hamilton
Mr Stephen Hastings
Mr Christopher J. Holland-Martin
Mr Richard Hornby
Mr David James
Mr A. Kershaw
Mr Marcus Kimball
Mr J. A. Leavey
Major E. A. H. Legge-Bourke
Lord McCorquodale
Brigadier Sir Harry Mackeson (Member of Council)
Lt. Commander S. L. C. Maydon
Mr Jasper More
Sir Charles Mott-Radclyffe
Mr John Peyton
Mr James Ramsden
Mr Peter Rawlinson
Brigadier Ralph Rayner (Member of Council)
Mr Willam Roots
Sir John Senter (Member of Council)
Mr John Temple
Lord Teviot (Vice Chairman of Council)
Lord Teynham
Mr David Webster

1964–1966
Lord Strathclyde (Chairman of Council)

Major John Morrison (Chairman of Political Committee until December 1964)
Sir Spencer Summers (Chairman of Political Committee)
Sir Tufton Beamish (Vice Chairman of Political Committee)
Mr Robert Allan
Mr Humphrey Atkins
Mr Paul Channon
Mr Robin Chichester-Clark
Lord Colville
Sir John Eden
Sir John Gilmour
Sir Richard Glyn
Mr Michael Hamilton
Mr Stephen Hastings
Mr Peter Hordern
Mr A. Kershaw
Mr Marcus Kimball
Lord Margadale (Member of Council)
Mr Charles Morrison
Sir Charles Mott-Radclyffe
Mr John Osborn
Mr James Prior
Mr Peter Rawlinson
Mr Willam Roots
Sir John Senter (Member of Council)
Mr John Temple
Lord Teynham (Member of Council)
Mr David Webster
Mr George Younger

1966–1970
Lord Strathclyde (Chairman of Council)
Sir Spencer Summers (Chairman of Political Committee)
Sir Tufton Beamish (Vice Chairman of Political Committee)
Mr Michael Alison
Mr Kenneth Baker

Mr Peter Blaker
Mr Thomas Boardman
Mr Paul Bryan
Mr Paul Channon
Mr Robin Chichester-Clark
Lord Colville
Mr David Gibson-Watt
Rear Admiral Morgan Giles
Sir John Gilmour
Sir Richard Glyn
Mr Michael Hamilton
Mr Stephen Hastings
Mr Peter Hordern
Lord Kilmany (Member of Council)
Mr Marcus Kimball
Mr David Lane
Lord Margadale (Member of Council)
Mr Charles Morrison
Sir Charles Mott-Radclyffe
Mr John Osborn
Mr John Peyton
Mr Willam Roots
Mr Selwyn-Lloyd
Mr John Temple
Lord Teynham (Member of Council)

1970–1974
Lord Strathclyde (Chairman of Council)
Sir Tufton Beamish (Chairman of Political Committee until 1973)
Mr John (Jack) Temple (Vice Chairman of Political Committee, Chairman from 1973)
Mr William Benyon
Mr Peter Blaker
Mr Robert Boscawen
Sir Paul Bryan
Mr Adam Butler

Mr David Crouch
Rear Admiral Morgan Giles
Sir John Gilmour
Major Gen. d'Avigdor-Goldsmid
Mr Michael Hamilton
Mr John Hannam
Mr Stephen Hastings
Mr Robert Hicks
Mr John Hill
Mr Peter Hordern
Lord Kilmany (Member of Council)
Mr Marcus Kimball
Mr David Lane
Mr Richard Luce
Lord Mansfield
Lord Margadale (Member of Council)
Mr Jasper More
Mr Charles Morrison
Mr John Osborn
Mr Cecil Parkinson
Mr James Ramsden
Mr Peter Rees
Lord Sandys
Lord Selsdon
Mr Marcus Worsley

1974–1979
Lord Strathclyde (Chairman of Council)
Mr Michael Hamilton (Chairman of Political Committee)
Mr William Benyon
Mr Peter Blaker
Mr Robert Boscawen
Sir Paul Bryan
Mr Paul Channon
Mr John Cope
Lord James Douglas-Hamilton

Rear Admiral Morgan Giles
Sir John Gilmour
Sir Victor Goodhew
Mr Stephen Hastings
Mr Robert Hicks
Mr Peter Hordern
Lord Kilmany (Member of Council)
Mr Marcus Kimball
Lord Margadale (Member of Council)
Mr Patrick Mayhew
Mr Jasper More
Mr Charles Morrison
Mr John Osborn
Mr Geoffrey Pattie
Mr John Peyton
Mr Robert Rhodes James
Mr Jim Spicer

1979–1983
Sir Paul Bryan (Chairman of Council & Chairman of Political Committee from 1982)
Mr Michael Hamilton (Chairman of Political Committee until 1982)
Mr Wiliam Benyon (Vice Chairman from 1982)
Mr Peter Hordern (Vice Chairman from 1982)
Mr Nicholas Baker
Mr Esmond Bulmer
Mr Kenneth Carlisle
Mr Michael Colvin
Lord Cranborne
Lord James Douglas-Hamilton
Mr Victor Goodhew
Mr Harry Greenway
Mr John Hannam
Mr Stephen Hastings
Mr Robert Hicks

Lord Kilmany (Member of Council)
Sir Marcus Kimball
Mr Ian Lang
Mr Mark Lennox-Boyd
Mr Richard Luce
Lord Margadale (Member of Council)
Mr Charles Morrison
Mr John Osborn
Mr John Patten
Mr Reg. Prentice
Mr Robert Rhodes James
Mr Jim Spicer
Mr Malcolm Thornton
Mr Peter Viggers

1983–1987
Sir Paul Bryan (Chairman of Council & Chairman of Political Committee)
Mr Wiliam Benyon (Vice Chairman)
Sir Peter Hordern (Vice Chairman)
Mr Nicholas Baker
Sir Peter Blaker
Mrs Virginia Bottomley
Mr Alick Buchanan-Smith
Mr Esmond Bulmer
Mr Alistair Burt
Mr Kenneth Carlisle
Mr Michael Colvin
Lord Cranborne
Lord James Douglas-Hamilton
Lord Dundee
Mr Roger Freeman
Mr Ian Gow
Mr Harry Greenway
Mr John Hannam
Mr David Heathcoat-Amory

Mr Robert Hicks
Mr Michael Hirst
Lord Kilmany (Member of Council)
Lord Kimball
Mr Mark Lennox-Boyd
Lord Margadale (Member of Council)
Mr Michael Marshall
Mr Charles Morrison
Sir John Osborn
Mr Robert Rhodes James
Mr Mark Robinson
Richard Ryder
Mr Tom Sackville
Mr Tim Smith
Mr Jim Spicer
Mr David Sumberg
Mr Malcolm Thornton
Mr Peter Thurnham
Mr Peter Viggers

1987–1992
Sir Peter Hordern (Chairman of Council & Political Committee)
Mr Wiliam Benyon (Vice Chairman of Political Committee)
Mr James Arbuthnot
Mr Nicholas Baker
Mr Henry Bellingham
Lord Bethell
Sir Peter Blaker
Sir Nicholas Bonsor
Mrs Virginia Bottomley
Lord Brookeborough
Mr Alick Buchanan-Smith
Mr Esmond Bulmer
Mr Alistair Burt
Mr Matthew Carrington
Mr Michael Colvin

Mr Dudley Fishburn
Mr Nigel Forman
Mr Ian Gow
Mr Harry Greenway
Mr John Hannam
Mr David Heathcoat-Amory
Mr Andrew Hunter
Mr Michael Jack
Lord Kilmany (Member of Council)
Lord Kimball
Lord Margadale (Member of Council)
Mr Michael Marshall
Mr Andrew Mitchell
Sir Charles Morrison
Hon. Phillip Oppenheim
Mr William Powell
Mr John Redwood
Lord Rees
Mr Robert Rhodes James
Mr Tom Sackville
Mrs Gillian Shephard
Mr Tim Smith
Mr Nicholas Soames
Sir James Spicer
Mr J. Allan Stewart
Mr David Sumberg
Mr Peter Thurnham
Mr Tim Yeo

1992–1997
Sir Peter Hordern (Chairman of Council & Political Committee until 1994)
Mr Nigel Forman (Chairman of Political Committee from 1994)
Mr Michael Alison
Mr Michael Ancram
Mr Nicholas Baker

269

Mr Henry Bellingham
Lord Bethell
Sir Nicholas Bonsor
Lord Brookeborough
Mr Esmond Bulmer
Sir Kenneth Carlisle
Mr Matthew Carrington
Mrs Chaplin
Mr Geoffrey Clifton-Brown
Mr Michael Colvin
Sir John Cope
Mr Quentin Davies
Mr David Faber
Mr Dudley Fishburn
Mr Edward Garnier
Mr Harry Greenway
Sir Archie Hamilton
Sir John Hannam
Mr John Horam
Mr Alan Howarth
Lord Kilmany (Member of Council)
Lord Kimball
Mr Mark Lennox-Boyd
Mr David Lidington
Sir Peter Lloyd
Mr Michael Marshall
Mr David Martin
Mr Stephen Milligan
Hon. Philip Oppenheim
Mr William Powell
Lord Rees
Mr Mark Robinson
Dame Angela Rumbold
Sir Giles Shaw
Sir James Spicer
Mr Richard Spring

Mr David Sumberg
Mr Ian Taylor
Mr Peter Temple-Morris
Mr Peter Thurnham
Mr Peter Viggers
Mr Charles Wardle
Mr Ray Whitney
Mr John Whittingdale
Mr Tim Yeo

1997–2001
Mr Michael Colvin (Chairman of Council & Political Committee until 2000)
Sir Peter Lloyd (Chairman of Council & Political Committee from 2000)
Mr Michael Ancram
Mr James Arbuthnot
Lord Bethell
Mr Crispin Blunt
Mrs Virginia Bottomley
Lord Brookeborough
Mr Geoffrey Clifton-Brown
Lord Cope
Mr David Curry
Mr Quentin Davies
Mr Iain Duncan Smith
Edward Garnier
Mr James Gray
Mr Damian Green
Sir Archie Hamilton
Lord Inglewood
Mr Michael Jack
Lord Kimball
Mr Andrew Lansley
Mr David Lidington
Sir Peter Lloyd

Mr Peter Luff
Sir Nicholas Lyell
Mr David Maclean
Mr Francis Maude
Mr James Paice
Mr David Prior
Mr Nicholas St Aubyn
Mr Keith Simpson
Mr Nicholas Soames
Mr Richard Spring
Mr Gary Streeter
Mr Peter Temple-Morris
Mr Andrew Tyrie
Mr Peter Viggers
Mr Nigel Waterson
Sir Ray Whitney
Mr John Whittingdale
Mr David Willets
Mr Tim Yeo
Sir George Young

2001–2005
Mr Peter Viggers (Chairman, Council & Political Committee until 2002)
Mr Henry Bellingham (Chairman, Council & Political Committee from 2002)
Mr Greg Barker
Mr Crispin Blunt
Mrs Virginia Bottomley
Lord Brookeborough
Mr Alistair Burt
Mr David Cameron
Mr Geoffrey Clifton-Brown
Lord Cope
Mr Quentin Davies
Mr James Gray

Mr Christopher Grayling
Mr Michael Jack
Lord Kimball
Mr David Lidington
Mr Peter Luff
Mr David MacLean
Lord Marlesford
Mr Stephen O'Brien
The Earl Peel
Lord Selsdon
Mr Nicholas Soames

Appendix II

(Brendon Sewill notes)

140.	Conditions for Parliamentary Support	26.4.75
141.	Proportional Representation	4.5.75
142.	How egalitarian is Britain?	11.5.75
143.	Public Expenditure	31.5.75
144.	Facing a strike	7.6.75
145.	Economic recovery in Italy	15.6.75
146.	Cash Limits for Public Expenditure	22.6.75
147.	Northern Ireland	29.6.75
148.	Public Finance for Political Parties?	7.7.75
149.	An effective Second Chamber?	13.7.75
150.	Old Moore's Almanack	20.7.75
151.	Economic developments during the Recess	5.10.75
152.	Highest Tax on lowest paid	12.10.75
153.	Convoluted Devolution	19.10.75
154.	Local Government Finance	26.10.75
155.	Some points for discussion (on current situation)	1.11.75
156.	Opposition Tactics	16.11.75
157.	Public Expenditure	25.11.75
158.	A better constitution?	7.12.75
159.	Educational Vouchers	7.12.75
160.	Northern Ireland: Repartition	18.1.76
161.	Capitalism	25.1.76
162.	The Party Organisation	1.2.76
163.	Direct elections to European Parliament	8.2.76
164.	Expenditure & Taxation	15.2.76
165.	Nationalisation of Financial Institutions	22.2.76
166.	Landowning as a business?	29.2.76
167.	Budget Forecast I	7.3.76
168.	Budget Forecast II	14.3.76
169.	The New Prime Minister (written before 1st ballot)	21.3.76
170.	Who is to run the nationalized industries?	28.3.76
171.	Is Solzhenitsyn right?	25.4.76
172.	Some pension propositions	2.5.76
173.	The political situation in Scotland	9.5.76
174.	(Conservative) Leadership Election Machinery	16.5.76

420.	New-Year Banana Skins	6.1.86
421.	-	
422.	Ulster	19.1.86
423.	Oil Prices	27.1.86
424.	America, Trident and Defence	10.2.86
425.	The Tory Party and the Bar	17.2.86
426.	Education	24.3.86
427.	Sunday Trading	3.3.86
428.	The Budget	10.3.86
429.	The Arts	17.3.86
430.	Education	7.4.86
431.	Institutional Care	14.4.86
432.	Ulster	28.4.86
433.	Chernobyl and Sizewell	2.5.86

[an error in numbering took place at this juncture: what should have been note 434 was numbered 454, probably through misreading a '3' for a '5'. At this stage, the notes were still handwritten and sent to a typist agency to be typed up before distribution]

454.	Single European Act	12.5.86
454(a).	The Election – what next?	21.5.86
455.	Profit Related Pay	2.6.86
456.	South Africa Sanctions	9.6.86
457.	Student Loans	23.6.86
458.	Women Priests – constitutional considerations	30.6.86
459.	-	
460.	Post Conference Assessment	13.10.86
461.	The Big Bang	27.10.86
462.	Rates	10.11.86
463.	Aids	17.11.86
464.	South Africa – disinvestment	24.11.86
465.	The USA – an election issue?	1.11.86
466.	Education	5.1.87
467.	Cut Taxes?	12.1.87
468.	The Farming Lobby	19.1.87
469.	The SDP/Liberal Alliance	27.1.87
470.	The Sizewell Inquiry	2.2.87

New Century

APPENDIX III

Observations on the BBC made by the Progress Trust at meetings of the Council, Business and Political Committees

15th April 1943: Mr Kenneth Pickthorn expressed concern over the BBC and following dissatisfaction with a speech by the Minister of Information (Mr Brendan Bracken) in the House of Commons during a debate on the <u>British Broadcasting Corporation (Propaganda),</u> he said he would be seeking assurance that the way in which the BBC had 'pre-boosted' and allowed no criticism of the Beveridge Report would not be permitted with future Reports; he also wanted scripts of BBC broadcasts to Europe and elsewhere to be made available to Members. Mr Pickthorn said during this remarkable wartime debate: "How do you lose a war? You lose a war when there are enough people on your side, or who ought to be on your side, who think the war is futile." (Hansard, 8th April 1943 c. 854)

22nd June 1944: "It was suggested that if members had criticisms to offer on the Political broadcasts of the BBC they should write direct to Mr George Barnes at the BBC." (*Mr Barnes was the controller of the Third Programme, now known as Radio 3.*)

8th March 1945: "Members were asked to consider what line should be taken when the revision of the BBC charter comes up for consideration." (*The Charter was due to expire on 31st December 1946.*)

5th May 1948: The Political Committee discussed the "Communist Manifesto series of broadcasts on the BBC Overseas Service. It was agreed that nothing further should be done at the moment."

11th July 1951: BBC's treatment of the Beveridge Report was again raised.

5th March 1952: "It was generally agreed that the BBC monopoly should be broken, but this view-point was not unanimous."

17th March 1954: "Major Morrison raised a question arising out of Members of Parliament visiting other Members' Constituencies to take part in Quiz Programmes arranged by the BBC and it was agreed that the matter should be pursued in the appropriate quarter." (*Because it broke the convention that MPs should be notified of any visit by another MP to their constituency.*)

11th April 1956: Mr Fells was asked to prepare a memorandum covering "BBC Broadcasts in the Middle East."

25th April 1956: "Referring to BBC Broadcasts in the Middle East, it was intimated that there would be a meeting on Thursday when the matters under review would be discussed. It was agreed to await further information before deciding what action, if any, might be taken."

30th July 1958: "Sir Guy Lloyd asked Mr Fells to tell the Committee how the BBC appointed two members of Parliament – one Labour and one Conservative – to attend the Party Conferences, and it was regretted that the BBC did not seek the advice of the Party Headquarters in their choice." (*Around this period the BBC presented a nightly programme Live from the Conference when a Labour and Conservative MP would attend each other's Party Conference and discuss the events of the day. On occasions these two MPs were Enoch Powell and Tony Benn.*)

22nd July 1959: "Sir Guy Lloyd said that the BBC are running a programme quoting accusations of people against the Police of ill treatment – none of which have been proved. It was suggested that the cutting should be sent to Mr Butler in case he had not seen it."

6th July 1960: "There was agreement in principle that it would be a good thing to break the monopoly of the BBC, but it was agreed to let the matter lie for the present."

23rd November 1960: "It was agreed that Major Morrison and Colonel Tufton Beamish should write a letter to Mr Carlton Greene (*Director General, BBC*) complaining about the BBC's tendency to ask <u>Conservative</u> Members of Parliament to appear on political programmes at the last minute."

2nd May 1962: Major Morrison, Chairman of the PT and of the 1922 Committee, dined with the BBC on this date, and in preparation the PT raised the following points for discussion:

(i) The BBC do not always give a fair hearing to European interests in Africa".

(ii) On the Continent, programmes are graded with the equivalent of an (X), (A) or (U) certificate and this grading appears in one corner of the screen during the film. As there have been so many criticisms of violence in programmes here, wouldn't this be a good system for the BBC to adopt?

(iii) Mr Gibson-Watt said that he and Sir David Campbell were members of the Advisory Council to the BBC, and that the BBC were very worried about the American influence in programmes, not the Westerns but the American attitude to marriage and certain aspects of their way of life.

27th February 1963: "It was important to break the BBC monopoly and to press for a second Commercial channel."

6th March 1963: "It was agreed that it was a gross error on the BBC's part to interview M. Bidault" (*a prominent French politician opposed to President de Gaulle's policy on Algeria and who the year before had been accused of conspiring against the state and who was stripped of his Parliamentary immunity*).

12th February 1964: "Mr Stephen Hastings referred to direct propaganda for the trade unions in a BBC broadcast. It was agreed that it would be a mistake to raise this in the House but that it would be better to attack the BBC direct."

12th June 1968: "It was felt that the BBC had a left wing bias on subjects that were not strictly party issues – such as hanging and corporal punishment. It was also felt that they should be more responsible over sensational reporting of events."

25th November 1970: "Mr Boardman said that a very biased anti-apartheid film was appearing on BBC Television that evening, and it was suggested that Lord Renwick should be approached to put out a film on Commercial Television showing the other side. Members did feel that South Africa and Rhodesia made it very hard for their friends to support them as they make no effort to improve secondary education for Africans."

26th July 1972: The PT circulated amongst its members a letter from the BBC's Director of Programmes, External Broadcasting (Mr D. M. Hodson) dated 17th July to Richard Luce in which the BBC stated "We could do more broadcasting in more languages if we were given the money, though not overnight as broadcasting requires technical facilities which take a considerable time to set up." Mr Luce feared that the BBC was failing to reach "major communities."

9th April 1975: "It was agreed that it would be very serious if the BBC gave equal coverage to the anti-marketeers which appears to be their plan."

22nd February 1984: "It was agreed that it had been a mistake for the Party Chairman (Mr John Gummer) to complain about the Panorama broadcast on the right wing element in the Tory Party as the BBC never apologises." This meeting concluded that standards were high in BBC's sound broadcasting and that a licence fee was justified. However, there was opposition to BBC's involvement in *Breakfast TV* and local radio. "It was very difficult to charge the BBC with bias as the Government of the day must expect to 'get stick' … it was a fact of life that most modern playwrights are left wing."

5th November 1986: "Members were critical about the way Mr Tebbit has presented his case to the BBC on bias, and it was hoped that he will not go down the same road as Mr Wilson and not become paranoid about the BBC."

16th March 1988: "Members were pleased with Mrs Thatcher's thinking on the NHS but regretted her dislike of the BBC. It was felt that the BBC are trying to put their house in order, and that they should be supported."

23rd January 1991: "Apart from one programme about setting fire to the oil wells which was not balanced, it was agreed that the coverage of the war had been unbiased, but it was thought it had been excessive." The meeting also praised the World Service, but feared the political bias of many BBC journalists. The Licence Fee was described as similar to "The Poll Tax shot through with anomalies" and that a new funding basis was required "administered by something like the University Grants System."

The BBC was also the subject of Ebury Research Notes 54, 366, 390, 583, 622, 726, 733, 814 & 850.

Index

This index includes for the most part names as they were recorded at the time in PT minutes and papers.

122-5, 140, 144, 162, 302
Ferry, Sir Richard 11
First World War 18n
Fishburn, Dudley 195
Finances and PT
  British United Industrialists
  (BUI) 49, 71, 73, 123, 221,
  239
  Estates Business Group 73,
  Grosvenor Estates 69, 239
Foot, Michael 47, 167, 174,
  178-9
Forman, Nigel 191, 195, 211,
  212, 238
Fox, Sir Marcus 206
Freedman, Max 77n

Gaitskell, Hugh 144
Galbraith, Commander T. D.
  (Lord Strathclyde) 9-13, 37,
  43, 54-5, 59, 61, 68, 70-71,
  112, 120-21, 127, 220
Gardiner, Sir George 207, 208,
  223
Garnier, Edward 238n
Gaulle, Charles de 163, 303
George, Eddie 214
George VI 84-5
Gibson-Watt, Mr 303
Gilbert, W. S. 117
Giles, Rear Admiral Morgan
  135n, 220
Gill, Christopher 210n
Gilmour, Ian 81
Gilmour, Sir John 220
Glyn, Sir Richard 100
Goldsmith, Sir James 210, 215-

16
Gomme-Duncan, Colonel Sir
  Alan 72, 76n, 142
Goodhart, Philip 78n, 99-100
Goodhew, Victor 88n
Goodlad, Alistair 212
Gorman, Teresa 210n
Gow, Sir Ian 185, 195
Gray, James 239n
Green, Alan 76n, 99
Green, Damian 239n
Green Party 188, 189
Greene, Carlton 302
Greenway, Harry 177n, 182n,
  189n, 197n, 208n, 227n
Griffiths, Peter 144
Gummer, John 304

Hague, William 238-9, 240,
  241, 242
Hailsham, Lord 25, 111, 233
Hall, John 103
Hamilton, Sir Archie 213-14
Hamilton, Michael 135, 169,
  172, 175, 223-4
Hammond, Philip 239n
Handley Page, Sir Frederick 72
Hannam, Sir John 195, 226
Harris, Robin 24, 25
Hastings, Stephen 87, 88n, 134,
  303
Harvey, Sir Arthur Vere 149
Hawke, Lord 72
Healey, Denis 172-3
Heath, Edward xiv, 87n, 99-
  101, 121-2, 129-31, 134-35,
  147, 150-51, 152n, 170, 171,